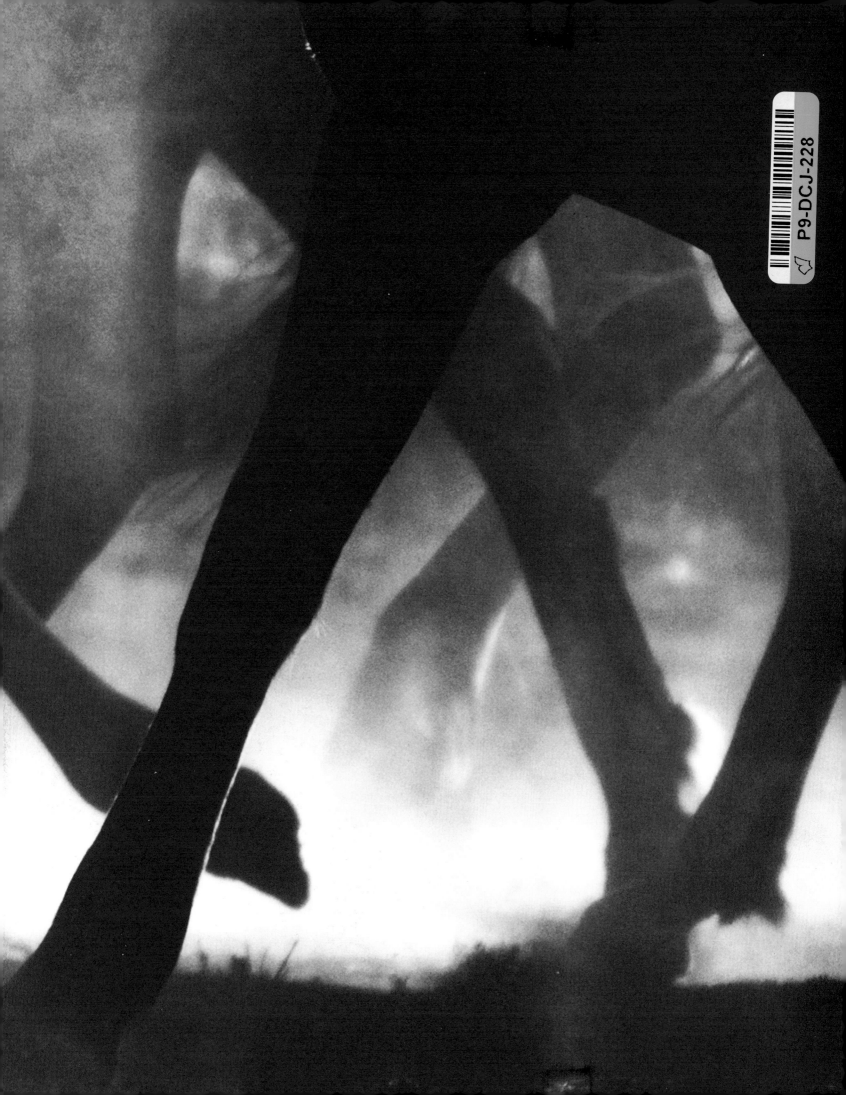

THE
MAJESTY
OF THE
HORSE

An *illustrated* history

THE
MAJESTY
OF THE
HORSE

An *illustrated* history

Tamsin Pickeral

Photography by Astrid Harrisson

Foreword by Pat Parelli

A Quintessence Book

This edition for the United States and Canada published in 2011
by Barron's Educational Series, Inc.

ISBN: 978-0-7641-6416-3

Library of Congress Control No. 2011928582

All inquiries should be addressed to:
Barron's Educational Series, Inc.
250 Wireless Boulevard
Hauppauge, New York 11788
www.barronseduc.com

This book was designed and produced by
Quintessence Editions Ltd.
226 City Road, London, EC1V 2TT

Editor	Philip Contos
Designer	Dean Martin
Additional Design	Alison Hau, Tom Howey
Editorial Director	Jane Laing
Publisher	Mark Fletcher

Color reproduction by KHL Chromagraphics, Singapore
Printed in China by 1010 Printing International Ltd.

9 8 7 6 5 4 3

CONTENTS

FOREWORD *By Pat Parelli*   16

INTRODUCTION   17

1 | NOBLE BEGINNINGS   18

2 | MARTIAL GRACE   72

3 | SUBLIME POWER   116

4 | NEW WORLD SPLENDOR   154

5 | ENERGETIC GRANDEUR   202

6 | OUTSTANDING AGILITY   246

INDEX   282

CREDITS   286

ACKNOWLEDGMENTS   288

FOREWORD *By Pat Parelli*

I simply cannot imagine a life without horses.

For more than thirty years, my wife, Linda, and I have dedicated our lives to helping the world become a better place for horses and the people who love them. We teach all over the world, helping others to realize a richer relationship with their horses, and have had the privilege of connecting in person with many of the breeds featured in this book. In fact, we have some seventeen different breeds in our own barns—so we are most obviously avid about the stunning diversity of horses around the world!

Every day, we encourage people to see each horse as an individual, to take their unique Horsenality (equine personality) into account, and Astrid has done that in spades, showing us the grandeur and beauty of some of the finest representatives of their breeds.

Astrid's images and Tamsin's words together have produced one of the most stunning works we've ever seen. It not only captures the beauty and magnificence that consumes us horse lovers, it provides a rich background on the history and evolution of the breed, and its relationship to society. There is no question that we will be recommending this book to our students all over the world—it should be on every horse lover's coffee table.

Congratulations on this magnificent work, and thank you for including us. We salute you for helping to make a better world for these glorious horses.

Pat Parelli
Natural Horseman

INTRODUCTION

The horse is an extraordinary creature, an enigma in an age in which so much has been unraveled. It embodies majesty, beauty, and spirituality, and though shaped by humans for thousands of years, it has retained an intrinsic wildness that remains untouched by domestication. The horse's spirit, remote and beyond human comprehension, is both magical and humbling.

Horses roamed the earth long before humans did and have witnessed their end countless times on battlefields across the centuries. Of all animals, the horse has had the most profound influence on human history and development, and one that cannot be underestimated. Their influence on human cultures and their key role in wars, transportation, and agriculture lasted long into the twentieth century. Today, they no longer power societies but instead fuel our dreams through pleasure riding and equestrian sports.

Horses have performed at every level of society. They have worked the fields in step with farmers and have been the gifts of kings. They have been tools of political diplomacy and weapons of martial ferocity. Despite their natural instinct to flee danger, horses have fearlessly carried warriors into battle for centuries. Kingdoms have been won, and lost, from the back of a horse. The allure of their beauty, agility, and athletic prowess has made them status symbols and vehicles of power. Monarchs and leaders have aligned themselves with this noble animal, committing their painted and sculpted images to the annals of history as reminders of their own omnipotence.

The horse is man's great sporting ally as no other animal is. Horses have raced with pounding hearts, leaped obstacles with courage, covered interminable miles with tenacity, and performed dancing steps with grace. They have fought, galloped, endured, and given their all. The horse has become an extension of the human ego, perhaps the greatest testament to the power of this extraordinary animal over the fragility of man's desires. It is teacher and student, bending to human will, but imparting the greatest lessons in understanding and respect to those who listen.

The Majesty of the Horse follows the changing journey of horses and humans, tracing their spread and development around the world and examining in detail some of the most important and influential breeds. It is a tribute to the magnificence of horses across the globe.

1 | NOBLE BEGINNINGS

There is no other animal that has contributed on such a grand scale to the rise and spread of human culture as the horse. It was not the first animal to be domesticated—this is commonly believed to have been the dog around fourteen thousand years ago—but it has certainly been the most significant to humankind. Pragmatically, the horse has been a decisive and pivotal creature in early human development, but it is also touched by a certain sense of magic, shifting energy, and esoteric spirit that is unmatched in other domestic animals. In all its many shapes and sizes, the horse is a majestic being, a combination of fire and spirit, kindness and intelligence, speed and dexterity. Even when it is tamed and trained, there always remains a tiny spark of something wild.

The ancestor to the horse evolved approximately sixty million years ago in North America and spread down into South America and into Asia via prehistoric land bridges, then across to Europe and down into Africa. Sometime around the end of the last ice age (c. 10,000 years ago), the Bering Strait, a theorized land bridge joining Alaska to Russia, disappeared beneath the sea as waters rose with ice melt, and around one thousand years later horses became extinct in the Americas. It is generally held that horses were domesticated in Eurasia, considered the fountainhead of horse breeds, around six thousand years ago. It was here, and primarily in Kazakhstan and Mongolia, that horse breeding and horse cultures developed, with nomadic peoples spreading across the vast interior and taking their horses with them.

One theory to explain the development of different types of horse cites four primitive glacial and post-glacial horses as the ancestors to today's horses. These are the Asiatic Wild Horse (*Equus ferus przewalskii*, or *Equus caballus przewalskii*), which is the world's only truly wild horse still in existence; the Tarpan (*Equus ferus ferus*), which became officially extinct in the early twentieth century, but has been reconstituted using its close descendant the Hucul

and Konik; the heavy Forest Horse (*Equus caballus silvaticus*), now extinct but the probable ancestor to the large, heavy, cold blood draft breeds of Europe; and the Tundra Horse, also extinct and not of great influence on modern horse breeds.

In the twentieth century, three experts on equine prehistory, led by J. G. Speed of Edinburgh, postulated a theory citing a further subgroup of four horse types that could account for all modern horse breeds. Speed suggested that, prior to horse domestication, four types of horse/pony had evolved: the first being Pony Type 1. This small pony (up to 12 hands high) lived in northwest Europe and was primarily descended from the Tarpan. Pony Type 1, also referred to as the Celtic pony, was tough, hardy, and weather resistant; its modern equivalents are the Exmoor Pony and the Icelandic Horse. The second postulated horse type is Pony Type 2, a larger version of Type 1 (up to 14.2 hands high) that lived in the frigid climate of northern Eurasia. This dun-colored, coarse-headed pony resembled the Asiatic Wild Horse, and its modern equivalent can be seen in the Highland Pony, the Norwegian Fjord, and the Noriker. Horse Type 3, one of the most significant of the four, was a desert horse with the desert characteristics that are seen in all modern equivalents. Type 3 was fine-boned and fine-skinned, lean and angular with no excess fat, and extremely resistant to the heat. It lived primarily in Central Asia and accounts for the desert horse breeds such as the ancient Turkmenian and the modern Akhal Teke. Finally, Horse Type 4 was small in stature and light in build, with a delicately chiseled, straight or concave profile and a high-set tail. This horse lived in western Asia and descended most probably from the Tarpan. Its modern equivalent is the Caspian and possibly even the Arabian. Speed's theory is an oversimplification of horse evolution, but it gives the non-scientist a loose framework with which to consider this complicated subject. Of further confusion is the term "breed," which is generally used to refer to

types of horse that have been selectively bred by man and exhibit distinct characteristics. For purposes here, and to address ancient types of horse with naturally occurring similarities, the word "breed" is applied to both man-made and naturally occurring types with common traits.

There are two primary factors that contribute toward the development of different breeds of horse, and these are geography or environment, and human interference. The earliest horse breeds evolved to meet and thrive within their climatic and geographic habitat, such as the weather-resistant Exmoor pony and the mountain-dwelling Hucul. Following domestication, humans began to take these horses and impose a system of breeding in order to fix certain characteristics to suit their purposes. Sophisticated horse management dates back around three thousand years, and it was practiced by the pastoral nomads of the Eurasian steppes, such as the Cimmerians and the Scythians. Astonishing discoveries in the caves of Pazyryk, Siberia, provide evidence of the Scythian methods. Here, preserved through climatic conditions, numerous horses were found buried. The well-preserved horses exhibited clear types, for riding and draft, and, suggestive of breeding policies, they had also been castrated and fed on grains.

Remnants of horse equipment such as saddle cloths, bridles, ornate headdresses for the horses, bits, and whips were also found and shed further light on this extraordinary and highly advanced equestrian culture.

Long before the Scythians, and around five thousand years ago, the nomadic people of the Central Asian steppes had centered their cultures around the horse. Horses were kept in large herds and would have provided a constant source of meat and milk. They were ridden, used for pulling loads, and probably also packed. Horse skin was utilized, sinew made into thread, and bones used as various tools. Importance and wealth were measured according to an individual's horses. Horses were also entertainment: they were raced, and fast and furious games played.

These ancient Eurasian horse cultures spread, taking their horses and languages with them. In around 3,000 B.C.E., the Indo-European Hittites battled their way into what is now Turkey. The Hittites are credited with producing the first manual on horse training and management, written by Kikkuli c. 1360 B.C.E. In ancient Mesopotamia (Iraq), two important horse cultures existed, the Sumerians in the south whose empire ruled during the third millennium B.C.E., and in the north the Assyrians who held power from c. 2,000 to 612 B.C.E. Assyrian reliefs on the palace walls at Nineveh and Nimrod reveal a culture of expert horsemen who raced chariots, traveled, battled, and hunted from horseback, being able to shoot arrows at a gallop with no saddle. This skill was perfected many years later by the Parthians, who waged battles across the Persian (Iranian) borders. The Parthians were able to shoot arrows behind them (the parting shot) while at a flat gallop on their finely built desert horses, which bore much in common with the ancient Turkmenian, the Iomud, and the Akhal Teke.

Persia (Iran) was an important early center of horse breeding, and Persian horses were much sought after during the time of the Persian Empire (550–330 B.C.E.). In particular, there was the legendary Nisean horse, one of the superhorses of prehistory that was widely prized for use in the military. The Nisean could have developed from crossbreeding between the Tarpan, the Asiatic Wild Horse, Horse Type 4, and Horse Type 3. They were taller and faster than their contemporaries and contributed greatly toward Persian military dominance; it is possible that they were the ancestor of the Akhal Teke and Iomud through the ancient Turkmenian. It was also in Persia that the tiny Caspian horse evolved, a horse breed that is still in existence today. These diminutive animals were widely used in chariot racing and famed for their bravery and speed.

The use of horses in battle to win new territories and expand borders was one of the major factors in early horse breeding systems, because the dominance of land was a priority. Warring nomads such as the Scythians and Parthians, and much later Genghis Khan (c. 1162–1227), waged their wars from the backs of their horses, and consequently needed stock that was quick, agile, brave, and easy to mount. Other ancient cultures, however, adopted different methods. The early Greeks, for example, commonly rode to battle in chariots pulled by small chariot horses, but fought on foot. By around 550 B.C.E., the Greeks incorporated mounted archers into their military strategy, and began to breed larger, heavier horses to carry their soldiers and to pull heavier carts of equipment. Although Greece is not a country whose environment favors horse breeding, the Greeks were highly organized and educated in their endeavors. Most horse breeding took place in Thessaly in northern Greece, where the grass was better quality, and Thessalonian horses became very popular. They were bred for different activities, from riding to draft to packing, and it is believed that the versatile Noriker horse first developed here before being taken by the Romans over the Alps into Austria during their conquests.

With the spread of their empire across Europe, the Romans had one of the most far-reaching early influences over the development of horse breeds. They were not expert horse people, but they were like the Greeks: supremely organized and systematic in their approach to their horses. They bred a wide range of horses for specific purposes and established breeding centers across Europe. As they marched through the continent, they took their horses with them and those of the people they conquered, which led to a wide distribution of different types of horse across Europe. They were greatly impressed by the native British breeds and improved on these, particularly the Welsh ponies. It was during sustained Roman occupation of Britain (c. 43–410 C.E.) that the heavier Welsh Cob is thought to have been developed, and it was also at this time that the magnificent Friesian horse was introduced to British stock, when it was brought over with Friesian laborers to work on the construction of Hadrian's Wall (c. 122). The Romans came across good horse stock when they conquered southern Italy, and even more so in their conquests of Spain and Numidia, an ancient Berber kingdom in North Africa. Spanish or Iberian horses and those of North Africa have had one of the most significant influences on modern breeds. The Roman Empire relied on its horses for long distance transportation of soldiers and supplies and for the delivery of important messages. Their horses had to be tough, fast, and strong; they developed horses of heavier weight and size, the predecessors to the modern draft horse, and horses of incredible speed, which were used in chariot and ridden races.

Across Central Asia, nomadic cultures improved on their horses, too, although they remained small in stature and unprepossessing to look at. Appearance was not a primary objective: these people needed horses to sustain their way of life, and, as such, the horses were bred as tough, fast, and able to subsist on small rations in a harsh environment. Warring tribes plagued the borders of China, which led both to the building of the fortification walls (The Great Wall) along the northern border and to the Chinese implementing their own systematic horse breeding program. The Chinese made enormous advances in horse harnessing, including developing the breast strap harnessing system for use in driving horses and the single horse hitch with lateral shafts. They were the first to drive in tandem and to develop the stirrup. The actual ancient likeness of Chinese horses can be seen in the tomb of Qin Shi Huang (259–210 B.C.E.). Within the tomb, around six hundred life-sized terracotta horses with carriages and soldiers were discovered. The horses bear much in common with Mongolian stock, although are marginally taller, and appear to be well fed and strongly built.

In the middle of the second century B.C.E., there was a concerted (and bloody) effort to improve Chinese horses under the rule of the Emperor Wu Ti (141–87 B.C.E.). He embarked on several missions to "obtain" large numbers of the much sought-after "Heavenly Horses" of Ferghana. These horses are believed to have been the ancient Turkmenian horse and were quality desert animals with a great turn of speed. Improving the quality of the Chinese horse was necessary both to aid military endeavors and for transport, as well as for entertainment purposes. Breeding exercises reached a peak during the Tang dynasty (618–907). By this time, the Chinese silk trade was well established, and horses were frequently traded for Chinese silk and tea, which saw the introduction of "foreign" horses

into the Chinese horse industry. The founders of the Tang dynasty had intermarried with nomadic tribespeople who had become integrated into society. With the horse of central importance to the nomads, this value was in turn transferred onto the Tang, and it became the most horse-oriented period of Chinese history.

Horses from Ferghana and other Central Asian states were used on the mostly Mongolian-derived stock of the Chinese to improve the quality and size of the horses. It was also during this period that polo was introduced to China, possibly by traveling dignitaries from Persia. Horses became not only a means to an end for battle and transport, but suddenly they were also prized for their looks, elegance, speed, and ability to play polo. Surviving pottery models of Tang dynasty horses reveal a horse of great beauty, quite heavy through its frame, but light in the leg, and with a well-set and carried head and neck. Their tack was elaborate, and the horses were often decorated with ornate breast straps and cruppers in a manner not dissimilar to that seen in European horse equipment of the Middle Ages.

While the Tang dynasty flourished in China, farther west the Moorish invasions were sweeping across Europe. The threat of domination by the Islamic Empire led to a rapid turn around in floundering European cavalry tactics and, as a consequence, to the development of an entirely new warhorse, discussed in Chapter Two.

NOBLE BEGINNINGS

ASIATIC WILD HORSE

PREHISTORIC — MONGOLIA — RARE

HEIGHT
Up to 14 h.h.
APPEARANCE
A small, stocky horse of primitive appearance with a large, coarse head. Stocky, muscular neck, with a distinctive short, upright mane. Shoulders are straight, withers are flat, and chest is deep. Short, *sloping croup and short legs with strong, dense bone. Hooves are narrow and oval, but very tough.*
COLOR
Dun, often yellow, sometimes with dark markings such as a dorsal stripe and stripes on legs.
APTITUDE
Undomesticated

SOUTHWEST OF MONGOLIA'S CAPITAL, Ulaanbaatar, in the foothills of the southern Khenti mountain range, stretches the magnificent Hustai National Park. Here, amid the sublime steppe landscape of rugged hills, open river valleys, and dense forest, roams the Asiatic Wild Horse, Przewalski's Horse, or the Taki as it is known to the local people. The herds of these small, primitive horses that live within the sanctity of the park represent a phenomenal international achievement in the reintroduction of these animals to their original wild habitat. Despite their unprepossessing looks, these horses are among the most important and are certainly the oldest living breed of horse that still exists in its original form. They also provide a link between modern horse breeds and the earliest horses that roamed the prehistoric landscape.

The breed hails from the vast steppes of Central Asia and in prehistoric times made its way into Europe, where its likeness was frequently recorded in cave paintings. From extraordinary images such as those at the Chauvet Cave in the Ardèche region in France, which date back approximately 30,000 years, we have a clear vision of just how little the breed's appearance has changed in the intervening millennia.

The Taki is small, rarely more than 13 hands high, and typically has a coarse and heavy head. The coat is dun with dark legs (which can often exhibit zebra-type stripes), a dark mane and tail, and a pale underbelly. Unlike other horse breeds, the mane grows upright to a length of approximately 8 inches (20 cm), and the tail is more

similar to that of a donkey, with short hairs on the upper part and long hairs at the bottom. Most significantly, these horses have sixty-six chromosomes as opposed to the sixty-four of the domestic horse. These differences from domestic horse breeds, combined with the intractable nature of the Taki, which is almost impossible to tame on any level, have led to some doubts that it is a direct ancestor to modern breeds. However, despite the difference in chromosomes, the Taki is able to reproduce with the domestic horse, and the resulting progeny are fertile, although they have only sixty-five chromosomes. When further crossed to a domestic horse, the progeny return to a sixty-four chromosome count. Given the extent and predominance of the Taki from prehistory and throughout the development of the horse, it seems likely that they have contributed at a founding level to some of the more primitive Eurasian horses such as the widespread Mongolian and the horses of Tibet.

Given the extent of its history, it is not surprising that there are many conflicting accounts of the Taki, whose past remains somewhat enigmatic. During pre- and ancient history, these horses were widespread through Central Asia and Europe, but as human cultures flourished and spread, the stout little horses found their natural environment shrinking. Because of their dominant wild nature, it is unlikely that they were favored for capture and domestication, though it is possible that foals might have been domesticated if caught at a young enough age. Far more significant was their value as a consumable, and as a consequence they were widely hunted, forcing them to retreat into increasingly remote areas.

It is unclear when the Taki first disappeared from central Europe, but the first documented mention of it was in the fifteenth century when it was described by Bavarian nobleman Johann Schiltberger (1381–c. 1440) in his unpublished memoirs. Schiltberger had been captured by the Turks in the Battle of Nicopolis in 1396 and passed to the great warlord Timur (1336–1405). After Timur's death, Schiltberger was given to Chekre, a Tatar prince whom he accompanied on a number of missions across Central Asia. It was while he was with the prince in the Tien Shan mountains that he wrote about the Taki horses, providing the first known reference to them in literature.

The next mention of the horses occurs some three centuries later by John Bell (1691–1780), a Scottish adventurer and doctor. Bell was part of an embassy to China through Siberia and the Tatar deserts, and then attended Peter the Great (1672–1725) on his expedition to Derbend and the Caspian Gates; he recounted his experiences in 1763, providing a striking account of the Taki seen in southwestern Siberia: "There is, besides, a number of wild horses, of a chesnut color; which cannot be tamed, though they are catched when foals. These horses differ nothing from the common kind in shape, but are the most watchful creatures alive."

It was, however, Nikolai Przewalski (1839–88), explorer and colonel of the Russian Imperial Army, who is most commonly cited as rediscovering the breed when he observed them on the edge of the Gobi Desert, picking their way through the Tachin Schah mountains in 1879. Przewalski was given a Taki skin by the local Kyrgyz people, and he in turn gave the skin to the zoologist J. S. Poliakov, who was the first to give the breed its scientific description and named it *Equus ferus przewalski*. As news of the existence of this wild breed spread, it became a sought-after specimen for collectors, which later proved to be of great significance for the breed's survival.

In 1882, four Przewalski horses were captured by Russian naturalists in eastern Dzungaria close to the Gobi Desert, and in the following few years more horses were caught, including thirty-two for the Duke of Bedford. In 1902, the first pair of Przewalski horses were shipped to New York for the New York Zoological Society. The capture of these Przewalski horses and their subsequent arrival in zoos and private parks in Europe occurred at an opportune moment; the horses had been on the brink of extinction, and all living Przewalskis today are descended from approximately thirteen of those caught. The last Przewalski living in its natural habitat was seen in 1968 in western Mongolia—the small, prehistoric horses had been hunted into extinction in the wild.

Though Przewalski horses still existed in captivity, they were hard to breed in this environment, and by the 1970s the numbers of horses in captivity were dangerously low, prompting a move to reintroduce the Przewalski to its natural environment and return the horse to its roots. Several release programs were implemented, including one by the Przewalski Horse Reintroduction Project of China, who released a group into the Kalamely Mountains in the Xinjiang region of China in 1985.

Another process to save the Przewalski horse was begun in the late 1970s, with the formation of the Foundation for the Preservation and Protection of the Przewalski Horse (FPPPH) by Jan and Inge Bouman in Rotterdam, who organized a careful breeding plan of horses from different captive populations and developed a computerized studbook. Over time, the FPPPH established a number of semi-reserves in the Netherlands and Germany where the horses could be kept in large areas in semi-wild conditions while still being carefully monitored. In 1990, after several years of searching, deliberation, and international diplomacy, the Hustain Nuruu area of Mongolia was agreed upon as the right place for the Przewalski reintroduction project, and two years later, the FPPPH and a dedicated breeding program from Askania Nova, Ukraine, combined to release two groups of Przewalski horses back into the wild. The area was designated a national park in 1997. Thankfully the reintroduction of the important Przewalski has been successful, and in 2008 the breed was reclassified from being "extinct in the wild" to "critically endangered," a significant achievement.

Although the Przewalski horse has suffered a tumultuous history and survives in small numbers, its relative the Mongolian horse thrives across the steppes of Central Asia and has played a key role in the development of many horse breeds through Asia and Europe. This small, tough horse may lack beauty and refinement, but it makes up for this with its striking constitution and the enormous influence it has had on other horse breeds by passing along its tremendous stamina and hardiness. Like the Przewalski, the Mongolian is primitive in appearance, often with a heavy, coarse head, and is notably stocky. The horses, which play a central role in nomadic life on the steppes, are bred and kept in large herds and are perhaps the ultimate of versatile breeds, used for draft purposes, riding, racing, meat, milking, and sports.

NOBLE BEGINNINGS

NOBLE BEGINNINGS

TARPAN

PREHISTORIC – POLAND, RUSSIA – EXTINCT IN TRUE FORM

HEIGHT
Up to 13.2 h.h.
APPEARANCE
A heavy head with a convex profile and long ears that angle slightly to the outside. Short neck, deep chest, flat withers, and a long back with a sloping croup. Shoulders are *well conformed and sloping, and legs are long, fine, and notably strong.*
COLOR
A primitive dun or grullo, with a dorsal stripe, black lower legs, and often zebra markings.
APTITUDE
Riding, light draft

THE PREHISTORIC CAVE PAINTINGS in Lascaux, France, depict, with astonishing detail, two very different types of horse. One type strongly reflects the characteristics of the Asiatic Wild Horse (Przewalski); the other type, seen in a striking procession of three fine-limbed, elegant horses, bears much in common with another of history's important breeds, the Tarpan.

The Tarpan (Russian for "wild horse") occupies a central role in the development of horse breeds and is widely considered to be a closer relative to the modern horse than the Przewalski. Despite their physical differences, the two breeds have occasionally been confused, primarily because both wild horses roamed across a slightly similar area. The Tarpan spread across western Russia and throughout Eastern Europe and formed the basis for the chariot-driving stock of ancient cultures, from the Greeks to the Egyptians, Assyrians, Scythians, and Hittites. The prepotency of its influence can be seen particularly in the light horse breeds of Eastern Europe and Eurasia, whereas the Przewalski's influence spread through Central Asia, down into China, and east to Japan. In particular, the Tarpan can be connected to the magnificent but diminutive Caspian horse, though perhaps of greater significance is the link believed to exist at a founding level between the Tarpan and the desert breeds of Central Asia, and possibly even the Arabian. In Europe, the Tarpan's influence can clearly be seen in the Portuguese Sorraia— which in turn formed the basis for the majestic Iberian breeds—and in the Romanian Hucul and Polish Konik.

The Konik is the closest descendant of the Tarpan, to which it bears a strong physical resemblance. In fact, it is largely to the Konik that the modern-day Tarpan owes its existence. Like the Przewalski, the Tarpan in its pure form was hunted to extinction—the last wild Tarpan was accidentally killed in 1879 during a capture attempt, and the last Tarpan in captivity died in a Russian zoo in 1909. Several attempts have been made to breed a reconstituted Tarpan, including one by the Polish government, which established breeding herds from stock that most closely resembled the Tarpan. These herds were primarily made up of Konik ponies, and in 1936 Polish professor Tadeusz Vetulani used these Koniks to establish a program to try to re-create the Tarpan. Around the same time, Berlin Zoo director Lutz Heck and Heinz Heck of the Munich Zoo also began a breeding regimen using Konik, Icelandic, and Gotland mares with a Przewalski stallion. Eventually a fixed type of Tarpan physicality was established, with the horses referred to as Heck horses. A Heck stallion and two mares were imported to the United States in the 1950s, where they now have a dedicated following. A further horse of Tarpan characteristics, the Hegardt, was developed in the United States by Harry Hegardt (and previously Gordon Stroebel) based on crossing Mustangs with Tarpan-like ponies, also probably of Konik descent.

Despite the Tarpan's importance, it was not actually recorded and described until around 1768, when German naturalist Samuel Gottlieb Gmelin (1744–74) captured four of the wild horses in Russia. He provided a detailed account of its appearance, which was further recorded in a drawing of a Tarpan colt in 1841. In 1912, Helmut Otto Antonius, director of the Scholbrunn Zoological Gardens in Vienna and one of the first scientists to recognize the importance of the Tarpan in the development of modern domestic horse breeds, named the Tarpan *Equus caballus gmelini* in recognition of Gmelin's description; now the breed's correct scientific name is accepted as *Equus ferus ferus*.

HUCUL

ANCIENT – POLAND, ROMANIA, CZECH REPUBLIC, SLOVAK REPUBLIC – COMMON

HEIGHT
Up to 14 h.h.
APPEARANCE
Robust in build with a rectangular body frame; short, strong, clean limbs; and an attractive head with large, kind eyes. Strong back, with a well-formed,
muscular croup. Heavy through the neck and front end, with a broad, deep chest.
COLOR
Chestnut, bay, black, or grullo, often with a dorsal stripe and zebra markings on the legs.
APTITUDE
Riding, light draft

STRETCHING IN A STEADY ARC across central and eastern Europe are the Carpathian Mountains, Europe's largest mountain range and home of the highly prized Hucul, or Carpathian Pony. It was here among the rugged peaks and diving valleys that the Hucul, a direct descendant of the wild Tarpan, developed. It is also a meeting point of several countries, as the borders of Romania, the Czech Republic, Poland, Hungary, Ukraine, Serbia, and Slovakia come together, and many of these countries either claim the origin of the Hucul or raise and breed the hardy pony. The breed's name derives from the Hutsuls, a Ukrainian culture of highlanders who rely heavily on their horses and whose history goes back many centuries. Despite being their namesake, however, the Hucul pony existed long before and was bred by the mountain tribes of Dacians, for whom the tough and enduring ponies were essential in everyday life, for transport, packing goods, and in warfare. Though they were and are ridden, the Hucul was most widely used in a draft capacity early in its history and was able to negotiate the forbidding, mountainous terrain where other horses failed. Bas-reliefs of Hucul-like ponies—showing little difference in physicality from their present form—appear on Roman monuments depicting battles between the Romans and Dacians. Even when the Dacians fell to the Romans in the battle of Sarmizegetusa in 106 C.E. they continued to breed their indomitable Hucul ponies.

Once the breed was established, the inhospitable and inaccessible mountain habitat of the Hucul contributed to maintaining its purity. The Hucul, which is noted for its quality, is thought to have developed directly from the Tarpan (it is described in early accounts as the "mountain Tarpan"), as well as through breeding with Oriental horses, Mongolian stock introduced to the area by nomadic tribes from Central Asia, and quite possibly even the Asiatic Wild Horse. Other than these relatively infrequent outside influences, the Hucul remained largely untouched until several attempts to improve the breed were made in the late nineteenth century through the introduction of other blood. Despite this, the innate Hucul characteristics—its extreme and virtually unequaled hardiness, its strength in relation to its size, and a certain air of quality not always seen in native mountain breeds—have perpetuated.

The Hucul is particularly prized in Poland and Romania, and it was in Romania that the first specialized stud farm was established at Rădăuți in 1856, the primary aim of which was to produce Huculs for use in the Austro-Hungarian army. After some years, the stud activities floundered, but they were reactivated in 1876, and the program expanded to establish Pietrosul, Hroby, Ghoral, Gurgul, and Oushor bloodlines, with Ghoral being one of the most important and prodigious.

In 1922, thirty-three Huculs were sent to Czechoslovakia, where a new line of Gurgul horses was established, with the breeding still focused on producing horses for use in the military. The breed suffered enormous losses during both world wars, and after World War II, in light of increasing mechanization, Hucul numbers dwindled rapidly. In the 1950s, the State Forest Directorate at Murán Plain National Park in Slovakia made efforts to increase breed numbers, and then in 1972 the Czech Republic's Association for Protection of Nature and Landscape founded the Hucul Club to implement a more effective preservation program. The initiative has been a great success, and Poland, Romania, Ukraine, Hungary, and Austria have all joined in, while the Hucul continues to be bred in Russia.

AKHAL TEKE

ANCIENT – TURKMENISTAN – RARE

HEIGHT	eye, and a narrow face. The mane
14.2–16 h.h.	and tail hair is thin and sparse
APPEARANCE	and the coat very fine and silky.
Long through the body, narrow,	**COLOR**
and slight; fine boned with a	Great range, from metallic dun
sloping croup. The neck is long	to black, bay, cream, or gray.
and slender, and set and carried	**APTITUDE**
high. Distinctive head with a dry	Riding, racing, endurance racing,
"desert" quality, slightly hooded	showing, dressage, jumping

THE AKHAL TEKE IS ONE OF THE OLDEST, most important, and purest of all living horse breeds, and yet it remains little known to the larger public. The significance of this breed, not only to the development of other light horse breeds from the Arabian to the Thoroughbred but also in historic and cultural terms, is monumental.

The breed is a descendant of the now extinct ancient Turkmenian, which was in effect the superhorse of pre- and ancient history. These horses evolved in the huge region of Turkestan, which stretches across Central Asia from the Gobi Desert in the east to the Caspian Sea in the west, and from Siberia in the north to Iran, Afghanistan, and Pakistan in the south. This area is considered the fountainhead of horse breeds, and one of the earliest areas where horse domestication occurred. These agile horses were subjected to both selective and indiscriminate breeding by different tribes, but the overriding qualities of speed, size, and endurance were at their foundation, and these are the qualities that have remained. They were also quite different from, and superior to, the small, stocky horses of the steppes, as typified by the Mongolian horse.

These tall, quick Turkmenian horses bear a close physical similarity to the postulated Horse Type 3 from which they most probably evolved. The Turkmenians' speed and toughness made them highly sought after in the ancient world, since they provided an enormous advantage to the warring nomads of this vast steppe landscape. Through the fluid nature of early nomadic cultures, these horses were distributed across a vast area, and word of their excellence soon spread. They are known to have

formed an important part of the horse culture of the Scythians, ancient warring nomads who originated in Persia (Iran), and are recorded as being used for racing from around 1000 B.C.E. Five hundred years later the same horses defined by their body type and attributes were widely used by the Bactrian horsemen in King Darius of Persia's cavalry. The Parthians from northeastern Iran, famous for their horsemanship and battling alike, rode Turkmenian horses as they waged wars across the steppe territory from the seventh century B.C.E., and in Greece Alexander the Great's father, Philip II of Macedon (382–336 B.C.E.) had acquired large numbers of Turkmenian horses from Ferghana, an area in eastern Uzbekistan that was a famous horse-breeding center in the ancient world. Alexander used these horses in his army, and it is widely thought that his own famous horse, Bucephalus, who is often described as a Thessalonian, was in fact a Turkmenian. Alexander went on to obtain his own huge herd of horses from the Persians that when crossbred to native European stock produced larger, stronger, and quicker animals. These crossbred horses were later in widespread use by the Roman cavalry, which in turn spread the Turkmenian blood across Europe.

The horses from Ferghana were held with special reverence in the ancient world. They were reputed to be the fastest horses of the time and often had a golden, metallic sheen in their coat, such that they were frequently referred to as the "Heavenly Horses" or "Golden Horses." In fact, the coat color so prized in the ancient world is still a predominant feature of the Akhal Teke. These Golden Horses further exhibited "blood sweating" (the appearance of sweating small droplets of blood), which added to their magical allure. Many theories have surrounded the blood-sweating condition, but the most plausible explanation has been put forward by Louise Firouz (who died in 2008), a leading Caspian and Akhal Teke expert, who suggested that it is caused by a parasite that lives in the Gorgan and Ferghana rivers. At a certain time in the

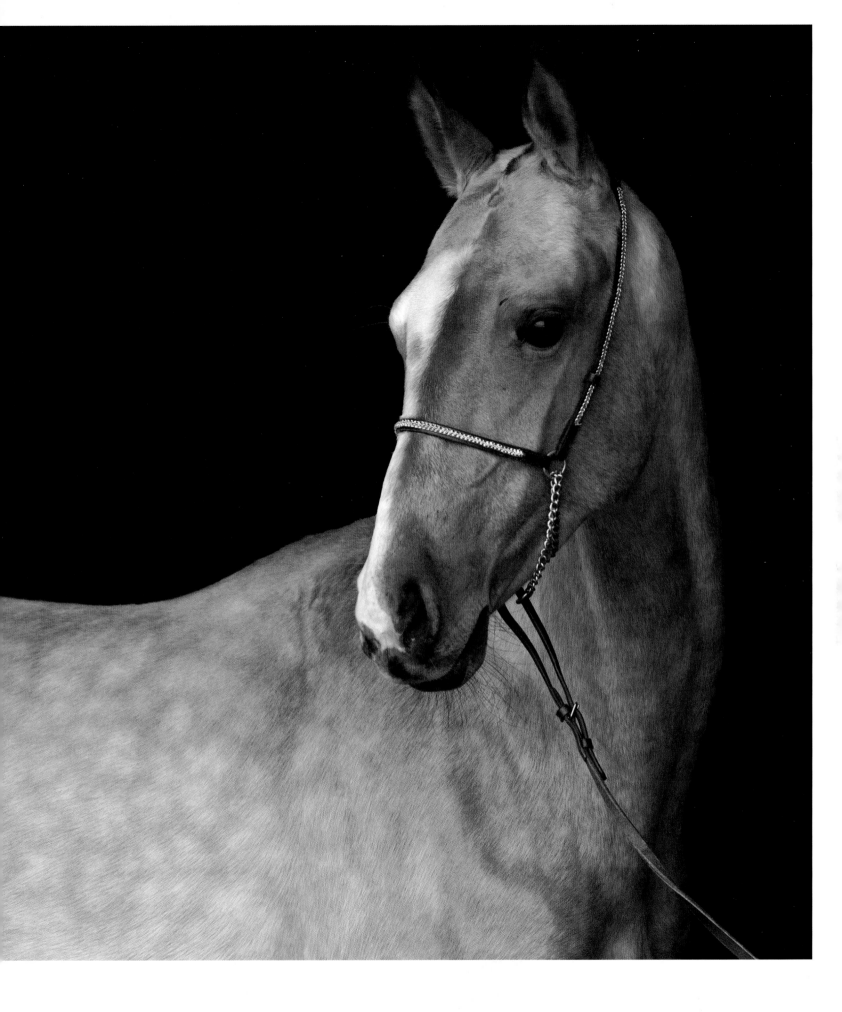

NOBLE BEGINNINGS

life cycle of the parasite, it hatches out through the skin of the infected animal, causing small spots of bleeding.

Given the extent and distribution of the ancient Turkmenian it is not impossible for this breed to have greatly contributed to the development of the Arabian, particularly the Muniqi (or Munaghi) Arabian, a racing strain. In view of the very great antiquity of the Turkmenian it is likely that this horse was one of the earliest hot-blooded horses, along with the Caspian, that evolved within the same geography. With the spread of this horse through Turkestan and down into Saudi Arabia and across to Africa it is a small step to consider it influencing the development of the Arabian and also the North African Barb, which in turn was fundamental to the development of the Iberian breeds. The Turkmenian was also influential in the development of the English Thoroughbred through the Thoroughbred foundation sire, the Byerley Turk, who is thought to have been a "Turk," and through the large number of Turkmenian horses imported to England during the seventeenth and eighteenth centuries, when the Thoroughbred was evolving. The Turk, or Turkoman, breed is one of the modern descendants of the ancient Turkmenian horse, which also gave rise to the Akhal Teke and Iomud. Confusingly, the terms *Turkoman* and *Turkmenian* are often interchanged, with horses bred in Turkmenistan referred to as Turkmenian and those bred in Iran referred to as Turkoman. There is, however, little difference between them.

The Akhal Teke, directly descended from the ancient Turkmenian, and in a sense the modern reincarnation of this breed, has with little exception been bred pure. In the twentieth century there was the introduction of some Thoroughbred blood to the Akhal Teke, to try to increase the size of the breed, but this was a largely unsuccessful experiment. The Akhal Teke (meaning literally "pure" or "oasis" from the Teke tribe) has been bred by the Turkmene people systematically and stringently, living in the difficult desert climate in the oases of Turkmenistan. Ashkhabad, the capital of Turkmenistan, has been a center of breeding for the Akhal Teke and its ancestors since 1000 B.C.E. and is still a major breeding center, although the horses are also bred in Kazakhstan, Dagestan, Russia, and in the northern Caucasus, as well as in small pockets of the United States, the United Kingdom, and parts of Europe. Traditionally, only the fastest progeny were bred so that the qualities of speed and endurance are ultimately fixed within the breed.

The horses are quite unique in appearance, particularly when compared with the European warmblood. The Akhal Teke should be a "meatless" animal: there should be no excess fat, and the horse's muscle mass should be long and unpronounced. To condition the horses, the nomadic tribesmen would wrap them in thick felt blankets to sweat them out during the day, and work them in the mornings and evenings. The young stock would be started at just under two years old even though the breed does not mature until around five.

The Akhal Teke's endurance is legendary; no breeds can match it in terms of speed and stamina. Like its relative the Iomud, the Akhal Teke is also able to exist on minimal water and food. Although most famous as an endurance breed, the Akhal Teke is extremely athletic and has a natural aptitude for jumping. The horses have also excelled in dressage, as demonstrated by Akhal Teke stallion Absent's gold medal win in 1960 in Rome—they are one of the most talented and least recognized of breeds.

The Akhal Teke has tragically suffered a huge reduction in numbers, but efforts to stabilize and increase the breed since 1980 have been relatively successful, although it can still be considered rare.

Rarer still is the Iomud, a breed that is a close relative of the Akhal Teke but little known outside Turkmenistan, its country of origin. The Iomud has much in common with the Akhal Teke: it is a desert-bred horse with tremendous endurance and stamina, though it lacks the Akhal Teke's quality and is not as fine or elegant. The Iomud has a heavier frame with a thicker, shorter neck and an attractive head. Its coat is fine and most often gray or chestnut, and the mane and tail hairs are sparse. Though not as fast as the Akhal Teke, the Iomud is famed for its quick recovery rate after endurance racing.

The Iomud's extreme qualities are a product of both early breeding and the arid desert and semi-desert regions in which the horses are raised. As a result of these harsh conditions, Iomuds are extremely tough and able to exist on minimal rations of water. Early in the breed's development, there would have been crossbreeding with other hardy breeds from the Central Asian steppes, such as the Mongolian and Kazakh, and it is likely that this influence continued throughout its history. There has also been some Arabian influence, and since the 1920s some Akhal Teke blood has been introduced to help preserve and improve the breed. Today, however, numbers are extremely low.

CASPIAN

PREHISTORIC — IRAN — RARE

HEIGHT
10–12 h.h.
APPEARANCE
A small, fine head with an Arabian-like look; the occipital bone gives a slightly hooded look. Nostrils are wide but low on the nose and the ears tiny. A very sloped shoulder and very defined withers, with markedly slender though dense bone in their legs. Extraordinarily tough, oval-shaped hooves.
COLOR
Bay, chestnut, gray, or black.
APTITUDE
Riding, light draft, showing, dressage, jumping

THE TINY, BEAUTIFUL CASPIAN is totally unique among horse breeds, and one of the oldest and most important breeds still in existence. All breeds of light horse are thought to descend from the Caspian and its ancestors, and as such it provides a tangible link between early *Equus* and the modern horse.

These exquisite creatures lived undiscovered in northern Iran for centuries, subsisting among the rocky mountains and dense forests and leading a largely undisturbed life until they were "rediscovered" in 1965 by the American Louise Firouz, who had established a small riding school in Iran. It was on a trip to the southern shores of the Caspian Sea, looking for suitable ponies to use in her school, that she came across three magnificent but tiny horses. Despite their diminutive size, they were decidedly horses and not ponies, exhibiting horse-like conformation and character; today the Caspian is still recognized as a small horse, not a pony. Firouz realized the importance of these animals, which bore a striking resemblance to those seen on the Seal of Darius (c. 500 B.C.E.) and other ancient artifacts, and instigated a five-year study of the horses in their environment. Through dedicated searches and study it was estimated that approximately fifty of these horses were living all along the south coast of the Caspian Sea. Because the area in which they were found was so large, it was also conjectured that they could not be totally purebred, but had retained the strong genetic base of their predecessors.

Extensive study and research has been undertaken into the history of the Caspian, and skeletal examination has revealed that the horses have certain unique characteristics among modern breeds, and that they also bear a significant resemblance to the postulated Horse Type 4, theorized by leading experts on equine prehistory F. Ebhart, J. G. Speed, E. Skorkowski, and R. d'Andrade. Further, many artifacts, such as the Seal of Darius, which depicts the Persian king in a chariot pulled by two minute but magnificent horses, and artifacts of the Oxus Treasure (fifth to fourth century B.C.E.) testify to the existence of a very small, fine and beautiful breed of horse in use during prehistory. Tracing this link reveals that it is possible that the Caspian and its ancestors were also the ancestors to the Arabian horse and the breeds of fine, desert horses that ranged across Eurasia from prehistory to the present. The frequency with which they are mentioned or appear in pre- and ancient history is not insignificant and attests to the great value placed on them. Despite their small size they were widely used for chariot racing and were as prized for their speed and endurance as they were for their appearance.

Unlike other breeds of horse the Caspian reaches its full adult height very rapidly, often within the first six months of life, and then gradually fills out and matures. They reach sexual maturity at under two years old, and most significantly mares tend not to ovulate after foaling for up to a year, which makes continuous breeding programs difficult. Louise Firouz established a stud for breeding the Caspian in Iran, but in 1976 her herd was attacked by wolves. To ensure the safety and continuance of the breed, which was extremely rare at that stage, some of her herd were flown to a stud in Shropshire, England, where they were successfully settled. Today the Caspian horse is a greatly refined model of its prehistoric ancestor, but retains the essential elements that make it such an extraordinary animal. They are wonderful athletes and make fantastic show ponies, but of more importance is their immense historic significance and their impact on the development of modern light horse breeds.

KAZAKH

ANCIENT – KAZAKHSTAN – COMMON

HEIGHT
Up to 14.2 h.h.
APPEARANCE
Although there are several different types of Kazakh horses and they vary greatly in appearance, they tend to be small with tremendous stamina

and hardiness. Muscular through the frame with very hard, sound limbs and feet.
COLOR
Mostly bay, chestnut, dun, or gray.
APTITUDE
Riding, pack, light draft

KAZAKHSTAN IS BORDERED by the Caspian Sea in the west, the Altai Mountains in the east, the Tian Shan Mountains in the south, and the Ural Mountains in the north. Huge herds of Kazakh horses roam in this vast, unforgiving landscape that matches striking beauty with a ferocious climate, a place where many other breeds would quickly perish.

The Kazakh is extraordinarily tough and hardy, resistant to extreme climatic conditions and able to survive and even thrive on the sparsest of diets. It is such a product of its environment that during hard times maturing horses will stop growing; then, as food becomes more plentiful, they will undergo a growth spurt. The horses have strongly developed jawbones designed to cope with tough grasses and foliage, and those horses that live in the desert areas also grow thick hair along the upper lip designed to remove sand from grasses before they are eaten. Like many of the other ancient breeds, the Kazakh has a double-layered, water- and cold-resistant coat.

The Kazakh horse was central to the lives of the nomadic Kazakh people throughout history, and even in modern times the horses continue to be of the utmost importance. The lives of the nomadic Kazakh people revolved around their horses, which provided them with transportation, meat, milk, and entertainment, and far back in history formed part of their religion. Powerful spiritual beliefs were, and in some cases still are, attached to horses. Horse bones—and the skull in particular—are thought to embody supernatural forces and should be treated with respect.

Occasionally, horse skulls mounted on sticks are included in ceremonies, and in exceptional circumstances a gray or white mare (the most prized colors) might be sacrificed—for example, to secure the protection of a family. Horses are also thought to have an omnipotent protective spirit called *Kambar-ata*.

Even today horses play an enormous role in the nomads' culture. Distances are measured in terms of how far a horse can run during a race; a colt's run is approximately 6 to 9 miles (10–15 km), and a stallion's run would be between 19 and 25 miles (30–40 km). Days are divided according to the routine of milking mares, which are milked around five times a day at intervals of an hour and a half. Fermented horse milk, called *koumiss*, is a delicacy and is believed to have curative properties for more than forty illnesses. Horses still also form an important part of many traditional ceremonies surrounding births, weddings, deaths, and festivals.

The Kazakh horse has evolved into a number of significantly different types. The Berik, the heaviest and stoutest, is a workhorse, and the Zhurdak is used as a general riding animal. The Zhuirik is a finer, faster type and is the most highly prized; it is used for racing, a hugely popular pastime. The Adaev is a good riding horse with a high milk yield, and the more massive Jabe is widely used for its meat, an important aspect of the Kazakh diet, and also its milk yield. Despite the significant variation among Kazakh horses, in general, they are slightly unprepossessing in appearance, though this is compensated for by their enormous stamina and hardiness.

The Kazakh shares much in common with the Bashkir, which evolved in the southern foothills of the Urals, and the Buryat of Siberia, which along with the Mongolian horse were fundamental in expanding the ancient geographic boundaries of their associated cultures and saw the spread of humans across Eurasia into Russia and throughout Europe.

EXMOOR

PREHISTORIC — UNITED KINGDOM — ENDANGERED

HEIGHT
Up to 12.3 h.h.
APPEARANCE
Large head with small, intelligent ears and large, hooded eyes. Good, balanced conformation, which allows for particularly good and smooth paces. Distinctive tail that often exhibits a bushy top.

COLOR
Always bay, brown, or dun with black points, often a dorsal stripe, and mealy colored hair around the nose, eyes, under the belly, and on the inside of the flanks.
APTITUDE
Riding, light draft, jumping, dressage, competitive horse sports

IN THE SOUTHWEST CORNER OF ENGLAND bordering thirty miles of breathtaking coastline and stretching inland to incorporate forest, hills, moorland, and valleys is Exmoor National Park, home to Britain's oldest indigenous pony, the Exmoor. This vast park, once a Royal Forest and hunting ground, is still largely undeveloped and provides great areas of relative wilderness and isolation, both factors of immense significance in the development of the Exmoor pony, and in its continuance. Despite this, the numbers of these extraordinary little ponies suffered greatly through the twentieth century, and the breed has been listed as endangered by the Rare Breeds Survival Trust in the United Kingdom since 1974.

Like the Tarpan and the Asiatic Wild Horse, the Exmoor is considered to be one of the earliest pony types to have emerged, making it one of the very few breeds that still exist virtually unchanged to the present day, and consequently of enormous scientific interest. Study of Exmoor skeletons and fossil remains indicates that the ponies originated in North America and were widespread between the latitudes of 45 and 50° north approximately one million years ago. It is conjectured that the Exmoor's ancestor may have evolved most significantly in Alaska, possibly trapped there for many years by ice barriers, and that this extremely hostile climate contributed toward the development of its unique insulating coat, as well as its ability to withstand extreme cold and survive on minimal rations. At some point, while land bridges between continents still existed, the ponies migrated to the British Isles, which then became cut off

toward the end of the Pleistocene era (c. 12,000 years ago) when sea levels rose after the end of the last ice age. During this long period of virtual isolation, the Exmoor's characteristics and adaptability to its terrain and climate became fixed. Even when horses began to be imported from mainland Europe, they did not have a lasting effect on the diminutive Exmoor, and attempts to "improve" the Exmoor by the introduction of foreign blood have only weakened the breed's innate hardiness.

The Exmoor is unique among pony and horse breeds in the configuration of its jawbone, which exhibits the partial development of a seventh molar, also seen in the North American fossils. The ponies exhibit further "primitive" characteristics that reflect the antiquity of their roots, most specifically in the structure and coloring of their coats, in their "ice" tails, which have short, thick, bristly hair at the top and longer hairs at the bottom, and in the heavy ridge of bone over their eye socket, which lends them a hooded look. It is the structure of their coats, however, that is so unusual and such a product of their original environment. The hair grows in two layers, with a short undercoat of woolly-type hair covered by a coat of longer, greasy hairs that are extremely water repellent. It is not unusual for them to have a number of whorls of hair at sensitive areas on the body to help direct water away. Such is the insulating level of these unique coats that snow can remain frozen on the surface of the coat while the pony remains warm and dry underneath.

In order to preserve and honor this ancient breed, the Exmoor Pony Society was formed in 1921 at the Lion Inn, Dulverton, and continues today to encourage and promote the pony and its breeding. The breed flourished in the early twentieth century and between the two world wars, but suffered enormous losses during World War II, partly due to trigger-happy troops, the loss of their owners, and the lure of their meat for food. In 1963, the first studbook was established, and a concerted effort has been made to reestablish this most important breed.

ICELANDIC HORSE
ANCIENT – ICELAND – COMMON

HEIGHT	*hind leg set relatively low to*
13.3–14 h.h. (average)	*the ground.*
APPEARANCE	**COLOR**
Large head with an intelligent	*Wide range of colors, including*
aspect and a muscular neck.	*bay, chestnut, gray, palomino,*
Rectangular body shape with	*skewbald, and piebald.*
short but exceptionally strong,	**APTITUDE**
sound limbs. Shoulders are long	*Riding, showing, competitive*
and sloping and the hocks of the	*horse sports*

ACCORDING TO THE MEDIEVAL Icelandic manuscript Landnámabók (the Book of Settlement), the first person to settle the rocky, volcanic island of Iceland was Norwegian chieftain Ingólfur Arnarson, who landed around 874 C.E. at a place on the southwestern peninsula now known as Reykjavík, the country's capital. Ingólfur was followed by other Norse chieftains of Scottish, Norwegian, and Irish descent who sailed to the island in their small, open boats, carrying with them their families and the best of their livestock. Thus arrived the first horses on the inhospitable land of smoking volcanoes and steaming geysers, and since that time these horses have remained almost completely genetically unaltered, making the Icelandic horse one of the purest and most unique of breeds.

The original equines to arrive were, like their owners, of Scottish, Irish, and Norwegian origin. They were then shaped by their extreme environment and lifestyle to develop the characteristics of the modern-day Icelandic. There is no documented evidence of when the import of foreign horses to Iceland stopped; however, ancient accounts do indicate that the island was fully settled (all territory claimed) within about sixty years. This would suggest that immigration had greatly slowed, if not stopped, by the tenth century, which would mean the import of horses brought with settlers had also stopped. In the late thirteenth century, Iceland came under the rule of Norwegian kings, and following this were centuries of little foreign contact and almost total isolation on the island. The Icelandic horse is the only horse breed to live on

Iceland and is virtually disease free. Because of the lack of exposure to disease, these horses have no resistance to common equine infections, and when infections do arrive on the island, they have the potential to decimate the Icelandic horse population rapidly. In 1882, a law was introduced to ban the importation of horses to the island to prevent the spread of disease and dilution of the breed; today, if any Icelandic horse leaves the island, it is never allowed to return. In 1993, a new law was added to further prevent the importation of used horse equipment to try to prevent the introduction of diseases. Despite this, in 1998 there was an outbreak of a viral infection that caused horse fever, and in 2010 a bacterial infection caused contagious coughing and brought Iceland's equestrian industry to a halt for more than three months.

It is only comparatively recently that roadways have come to crisscross the unforgiving volcanic terrain, and until this point the islanders relied solely on their horses for transportation. The Icelandic horse is second to none in terms of its toughness and is able to cover ground that would render most other horse breeds useless at high speed. They are enormously strong and energetic for their size; indeed, if judged on size, they would technically be referred to as ponies, but in no sense of the word are they such. These are small horses, capable of carrying grown men all day, at speed, and across the most difficult terrain. In the past, they were widely used in agriculture in a draft capacity as well as being ridden, though most horses today are kept for leisure purposes. Most towns have large stable complexes where the horses are housed during the winter, but in the summer they are kept on large meadows. Pleasure riding across the stunning landscape is a popular pastime, made even more enjoyable by the Icelandic horse's tremendous gaits. Sporting events and racing are also popular, with the biennial National Horse Show—where the very best Icelandic horses are showcased and judged—the highlight of breeders' and sport riders' calendars.

The horse is held in huge esteem by the Icelandic people, and the small, plucky horses are an understandable source of great national pride. Throughout history, the living conditions of the islanders did not greatly surpass those of their horses, and in great part the people relied on the honesty and bravery of their horses to transport them in adverse conditions. Horses also formed an important part of the local traditions and rituals. During early Icelandic history the horse was worshipped as a deity and considered a symbol of fertility. In many myths and legends horses play an important role, with a consistent theme being that of two powerful stallions battling it out in a ring, often joined by their masters, who offer support and encouragement. These legends were based on fact, and horse fighting formed part of popular entertainment during the early years of settlement. The Icelandic horse was considered the best fighting horse around, and in light of this many of them were gifted by Icelandic chiefs to foreign kings and bishops. The gods, too, were believed to own powerful horses, one of the more well known being the eight-legged Sleipnir, the fastest horse in the world, who belonged to the god Odin.

It was not uncommon for favorite horses to be buried with their dead leaders, and during life horses that belonged to Icelandic chieftains were reputed to be fed a rich diet including grain and milk, which is extraordinary given the frugal lifestyle that the Icelandic people led. White horses have held a special place in the traditions of Iceland, believed to be magical and divine; white horses were often sacrificed during early Norse festivals.

Color is important to the Icelandic horse breeders, and some modern breeding facilities concentrate on producing specific colorings, along with the required Icelandic gaits. That said, breeding for color is never done at the expense of conformational or gait quality. The breed can exhibit more than a hundred color variations, including a beautiful dark chestnut with a pale flaxen mane and tail produced from the Kirkjubaer Stud in the south of the island. It is, however, the performance of the horses and in particular their gaits that are most important in Icelandic breeding programs. The Icelandic horse is naturally gaited, which is a throwback to other ancient breeds, such as the Spanish Jennet and the Asturcian, which probably had Celtic foundations similar to the Icelandic. Gaited horses were highly prized because their smooth, fast gaits allowed travel over great distance in some comfort, a trait still much sought after in Iceland. The horses exhibit five gaits: the walk, a smart trot, the fast gallop, the pace, and the rack, referred to as a *tölt* in Icelandic. The tölt is the most impressive of these and is a four-beat movement equivalent to a running walk but conducted at great speed.

Icelandic horses develop slowly and are normally not started under saddle until they are four years old. Their working life is, however, extremely long, and it is not uncommon for them to be working well into their twenties. They reach sexual maturity at around two years old and have a high fertility rate, although mares are not bred until they are at least three years or older. The horses have adapted to be perfectly suited to their environment. They are able to withstand extreme cold and moisture; now Icelandic horses are often provided with shelter and supplemental feed in the winter, but this was certainly not the case during their history. Because of the relatively sparse vegetation in the winter, they have evolved to gain weight rapidly during the summer months, when grass is more abundant, which then helps them to survive the winter. They are compact horses and tremendously energetic, able to accelerate quickly to a high speed and maintain it for some time. The horses are agile, tough, athletic, and highly intelligent. Such is the popularity of the Icelandic horse that it is bred widely across the world, particularly in Germany, Denmark, Sweden, and the United States. Most Icelandic horses are registered in a central databank called the World-Fengur, and breeding and competition rules are the same in all countries where the Icelandic is kept.

There are approximately 190,000 Icelandic horses in the world today, all of which are the descendants of just 6,000 horses that survived the Móðuharðindin (Mist Hardships) that occurred from 1783 to 1785. This was a natural disaster that happened on the island after the volcanic eruption of Mount Laki and resulted in the death of one-fifth of the human population and three-quarters of the horse population. The horse population was reestablished relatively quickly (within a century), and in the late nineteenth and early twentieth centuries more than 100,000 Icelandic horses were exported, primarily to the British Isles for use in the coal mines and for trotting races, and also to Denmark.

NOBLE BEGINNINGS

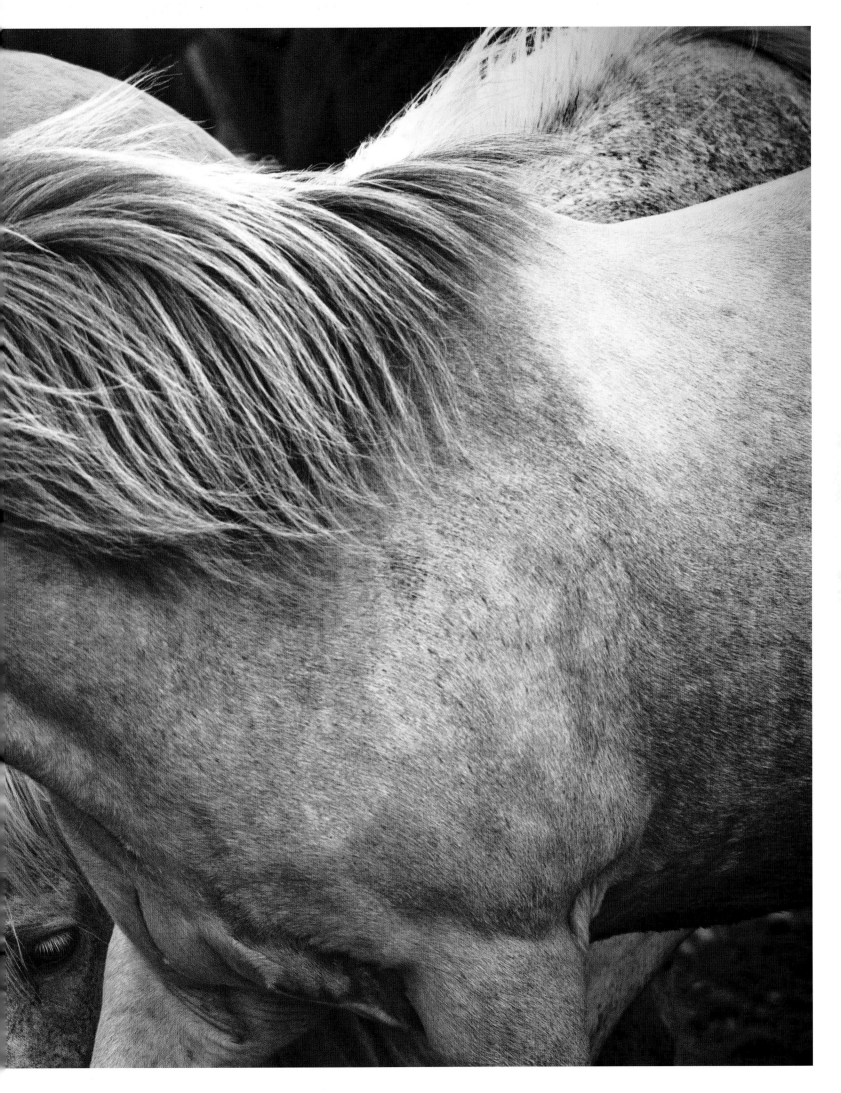

CONNEMARA

ANCIENT – IRELAND – COMMON

HEIGHT
Up to 14.2 h.h.
APPEARANCE
Very attractive, well-defined head with small ears and a large, kind eye. Neck is long, well set to the body, and a good shape, with a flowing mane and tail. Clean, sound limbs, a deep, wide chest, *and a muscular, slightly sloping croup.*
COLOR
Typically gray, dun, black, bay, or brown with very occasional instances of roan or chestnut.
APTITUDE
Riding, light draft, showing, jumping, competitive horse sports

TYPICAL OF NATIVE PONY BREEDS, Ireland's Connemara is a true product of its environment, having developed and evolved through the centuries to be perfectly adapted to its tough habitat. Despite Ireland's international reputation for being a producer of top horses, the Connemara is the only indigenous horse or pony breed to have originated there. The breed takes its name from the area of Connemara, which stretches along the western coastline of southern Ireland across the western part of County Galway and County Mayo. It is a place of striking rugged landscape, where ancient, mysterious Irish bog land meets rocky, barren mountain peaks bordered by the Atlantic Ocean to the west, south, and north, and the Invermore River and Loch Oorid to the east. The coastline is stark and beautiful and without shelter, and inland the landscape is peppered with crumbling stone walls and rocky outcrops. It is here, where the wind blows and the rain strikes down, that the Connemara evolved—a pony of great endurance and hardiness.

The precise beginnings of the breed have been blurred through history, but fossil findings of domestic horse bones suggest that ponies with some similarities to the Icelandic and Shetland have existed in this area since around 2,000 B.C.E. In the fifth and sixth centuries B.C.E., marauding Celtic tribes arrived from the Alps, bringing horses of eastern influence with them. The Celts were renowned for their horsemanship, and horses were central to their daily lives, particularly for transportation and warmongering. They were also great traders and set up active trade links with Celtic tribes across Europe, particularly of Spanish

and Gaulish origin, which would have seen further exchange of horses of Spanish and eastern influence. By the sixteenth century, the superlative Iberian horse, along with horses of Moroccan origin and from Arabia, and the North African Barb, would have been introduced to native stock in Connemara and contributed to the great quality and beauty that is still very much in evidence in the pony.

By the end of the nineteenth century, however, the quality and conformational integrity of the Connemara had started to deteriorate, possibly as a result of widespread poverty among the farming community at that time, and through unsupervised crossbreeding. Official attempts to improve the Connemara by introducing foreign blood, mostly in the form of Welsh stallions, initially met with little success, though eventually a more organized breeding regimen that considered the quality of the native mares as well as the import of new stallions was implemented. Three foundation stallions stand out for their quality and for perpetuating the basic, prized characteristics of the breed: Rebel, foaled in 1922; Golden Gleam, foaled in 1923; and the most charismatic and influential of the three, Cannon Ball, foaled in 1904. Cannon Ball was so highly regarded by the local population that on his death it is said there was a traditional Irish wake that lasted through the night. Later infusions of Arabian, Welsh, Irish Draft, and Thoroughbred were also introduced, and today the Connemara counts as one of the highest quality and most attractive of the native pony breeds.

These ponies are exceptional small athletes and excel at dressage and jumping as well as all ridden and driven activities. They are often used by small adults as well as children and have an alert though trainable temperament. Of particular note is the smoothness of the Connemara's gait, which is long, low, and level, and could reflect an earlier influence of the now extinct Irish Hobby, a gaited horse that was very popular throughout Ireland during the sixteenth and seventeenth centuries.

NOBLE BEGINNINGS

NOBLE BEGINNINGS

WELSH PONY
ANCIENT — WALES — COMMON

HEIGHT
*Up to 12 h.h. in the U.K.,
12.2 h.h. in the U.S. (Section A)*

APPEARANCE
*A beautiful, small head with
large eyes and small ears.
Neck is well formed and
arched. Short back, sloping
croup, and high-set tail. Legs*
*are short, clean, and very
sound and the hooves
incredibly tough.*

COLOR
Often gray but can be any color.

APTITUDE
*Riding, light draft, showing,
dressage, jumping, competitive
horse sports*

THE BRITISH ISLES ARE HOME TO NINE surviving native and ancient breeds of pony, often referred to as the Mountain and Moorland breeds, that developed primarily in the rugged moorlands and highlands of the country. Each exhibits its own distinctive characteristics, but they also share many common traits as a result of the similar, harsh habitat in which they developed; in many cases, they also share similar prehistoric roots.

One of the most influential of Britain's native breeds is the Welsh pony, which has frequently been used with great success to improve and even create other modern horse breeds, such as the American Welara, based on crosses between Welsh ponies and Arabians. Welsh ponies have roamed the moorlands of Wales since prehistoric times and are thought to have descended from the now-extinct Celtic pony. In 1901, the Welsh Pony and Cob Society was established in the United Kingdom by local landowners who recognized the great importance of their ponies, and in 1902 the first studbook was opened. It was divided into four sections to acknowledge the four different types of Welsh pony that had developed: the Welsh Mountain Pony (Section A), the Welsh Pony (Section B), the Welsh Pony of Cob Type (Section C), and the Welsh Cob (Section D).

The Welsh Mountain Pony is the oldest of the four types with fossil evidence suggesting that small ponies existed in the remote hills of Wales before 1600 B.C.E. These animals were small and fine-boned, but they developed great endurance, toughness, and sure-footedness; survival of the fittest and natural selection in wild herds contributed toward the passing on of these innate traits, and the Welsh Mountain pony today has retained its durability.

At some point fairly early in the pony's history there was a significant infusion of Arabian blood, possibly encouraged by Julius Caesar. The ponies were used widely by the Romans, especially in a light draft capacity, and it is possible that Arabian and Oriental blood was introduced to increase their speed and agility. Today the presence of Arabian blood is evident in the Welsh Mountain's extreme quality and often extravagant movement. Welsh Mountains typically have very attractive heads, often with a slightly dished profile that reflects the Arabian influence.

More Arabian blood, in addition to Thoroughbred and Hackney, was introduced to the breed during the eighteenth and nineteenth centuries, with one small early Thoroughbred stallion in particular having a significant effect. Merlin, a descendant of the Darley Arabian—one of the foundation sires of the Thoroughbred breed—had such an impact on the Welsh Mountain that the ponies were sometimes referred to as Merlins. The other great foundation stallion for the breed was Dyoll Starlight (f. 1894), who also had Arabian blood in his breeding. Dyoll was a magnificent gray pony and produced many gray offspring in his likeness. Gray continues to be the predominant color of the breed.

The Welsh Pony (Section B) is a slightly larger version of the Welsh Mountain Pony and can stand up to 13.2 hands high. These ponies have fine, high-quality, beautiful heads with small ears and good width between the eyes. Typically, they have excellent body conformation and a free-flowing action with greater riding-pony qualities. The Welsh Pony can be any color, but they are most frequently black, bay, or gray. They excel as riding ponies and often exhibit a great talent for jumping.

The Welsh Pony originally developed through crossing the smaller Welsh Mountain Pony with the larger Welsh

cob. They share many lines similar to those of the Welsh Mountain, including the early Thoroughbred Merlin and Dyoll Starlight. A significant influence on the breed was the stallion Tan-y-Bwlch Berwyn (f. 1924), who was descended from the Dyoll Starlight line crossed with a Barb. Two further important founding stallions are Criban Victor (f. 1944) and Solway Master Bronze (f. 1959). The Welsh Pony is noted for the elegance and freedom of its movement and is, like all four of the sections, suitable for riding and driving.

The Welsh Pony of Cob Type (Section C) is heavier in frame than Sections A and B and can stand up to 13.2 hands high. Their appearance reflects their cob blood, seen in their heavier frame, majestic bearing, and often-considerable feathering around their lower limbs. They retain all the beauty of Sections A and B, with attractive heads set to a finely arched, muscular neck. They are compact and muscular animals with powerful shoulders that allow for their excellent movement. They are similar in appearance and aptitude to the Welsh Cob, Section D, the largest of the Welsh breeds, which stands at more than 13.2 hands high and has no upper height

limit. These are truly superlative animals that are equally at home being ridden as driven. Both Sections C and D, like their smaller counterparts, exhibit a great talent for jumping and have superb, ground-covering natural movement. Although they can be any color, they are most often black, bay, or gray.

Both Sections C and D developed from the same roots. The cobs originated during the Roman occupation of Britain when the Welsh Mountain Pony was crossed with horses brought by the Romans into the country and later through the infusion of a great deal of Spanish blood. There was also influence from the now-extinct Norfolk Trotter and the Hackney. The Welsh cob was extremely popular, particularly in the Middle Ages, because of its versatility and was used for working the land, riding, and transportation and by the Welsh Militia in 1485 when Henry Tudor won the throne of England. These hardy, energetic horses were and are renowned for their extravagant and smooth trot and are able to traverse difficult terrain quickly and comfortably. The Section D is still famous for its spectacular trot, and for many years breeding stock was selected based on the quality of this gait.

NEW FOREST PONY
ANCIENT – ENGLAND – UNCOMMON

HEIGHT
12–14.2 h.h.
APPEARANCE
A large but fine head set to a muscular neck and good, well-conformed shoulders. The ponies are quite narrow in build but very athletic, with an exceptional long, low, and

smooth stride. Those that are privately bred (as opposed to feral) make fine riding ponies.
COLOR
Any color except cremello, spotted, skewbald, or piebald.
APTITUDE
Riding, showing, dressage, light draft, jumping

THE NEW FOREST PONY has had one of the rockiest histories of Britain's native pony breeds, and also one of the most unusual based on the location of the breed's origin. They hail from the New Forest, a huge area of unenclosed land made up of moorlands, heath, forest, and open pasture that stretches across part of the counties of Hampshire and Wiltshire and also incorporates some of England's southern coastline.

Despite the apparent wilderness of this enormous landscape, it was in fact comparatively busy early in history because of its proximity to the city of Winchester, the capital of the ancient kingdom of Wessex from around 686 C.E. and then of England until shortly after the Norman conquests (1066–c. 1088). Because of the city's importance, there was a continual passage of people and livestock across the surrounding countryside and into the center of commerce. Unlike the other native British pony breeds, which developed in isolated environments, the New Forest pony was in an area subject to a great deal of passing equestrian traffic. As a result, the New Forest pony has been influenced by an extensive range of other pony and horse breeds throughout its development, whereas other indigenous breeds remained largely genetically pure.

The first written accounts of ponies in the New Forest date to 1016 to the Forest Law of Canute, implemented by the Viking king Canute who took the throne of England in the same year. Around 1079, William I of England designated the area a royal hunting ground and granted the rights to common pasture for those individuals who lived

in the forest. At some point the wild little ponies mixed with this domestic stock and moved into private ownership, though they were still kept within the same area.

The New Forest pony has occasionally suffered genetically from a great and often random dilution of the gene pool. Whether encouraged to or not, early travelers' horses would have bred with the ponies, and the effects of indiscriminate breeding soon became apparent. In 1208, the first recorded attempt to systematically improve the breed was made when eighteen Welsh mares were introduced to the herds, and since then Welsh blood has been used with some frequency on the New Forest pony.

One of the more unusual contributors to the New Forest was the Thoroughbred stallion Marske (f. 1750), sire of the famous racehorse Eclipse. Marske was moved to the New Forest in 1765 and helped improve the overall quality of the New Forest pony; although today his influence is not hugely evident, many New Forest ponies do still exhibit high-quality, elegant heads. In the nineteenth century, Queen Victoria instigated a renewed effort to improve the hardy ponies by lending her Arabian stallion Zorah to the forest in 1852, followed by her Arabian Abeyan and her Barb Yirrassan in 1889.

Early in the twentieth century, other native British breeds, including Highlanders, Dales, Fells, Welsh, Dartmoors, and Exmoors, were introduced to the forest with great success. Lord Lucas (1876–1916), who lived in the forest and was a dedicated breeder of the New Forest pony, also used Welsh stock descended from the great Welsh stallion Dyoll Starlight, along with Dartmoors and Exmoors.

A number of New Forest ponies continue to live in semi-feral conditions in the New Forest, and they can exhibit a wide range of characteristics, though they are fairly universally sure-footed and agile. New Forest ponies that are bred in studs and private residences tend to display a far greater quality of conformation and make excellent ponies for children.

FELL

ANCIENT – ENGLAND – AT RISK

HEIGHT
Up to 14 h.h.
APPEARANCE
Small, quality head with intelligent, kind eyes and a well-shaped neck. Long through the back with muscular hindquarters and a sloping shoulder. Deep and broad through | *the chest with sturdy legs and feathering around the fetlocks.*
COLOR
Predominantly black though can be brown, bay, or gray.
APTITUDE
Riding, light draft, packing, showing, dressage, jumping, competitive horse sports

THE FELL, ALONG WITH ITS CLOSE RELATIVE the Dales, is one of the more unique and beautiful native ponies, with an often jet-black coat and a particularly majestic bearing. The breed traces its roots back to the time of Roman occupation in Britain, which first began when the Romans, under the directive of Julius Caesar, landed c. 55 B.C.E., bringing their horses with them (though sustained occupation is generally dated from 43 to 410 C.E.). The Romans constantly battled along their northern border with the fierce Picts, who lived in what is now Scotland, and in 122 C.E. the Roman emperor Hadrian ordered the construction of a massive fortified wall to keep the Picts at bay. The wall would traverse the northern border of England from coast to coast, and at intervals of a mile along the wall there would be sentry stands and armed guards. It was an enormous undertaking and a significant historical event; it also marked a most important development in the establishment of the Fell breed.

The native ponies of that time were small and originally descended from a Tarpan-like pony that bore much in common with the Exmoor. Along the northern and western edges of the Pennines and the open moorland country of Westmorland and Cumberland in the north of England ranged ponies that had developed from these prehistoric ponies and the now extinct Galloway. The Galloway was in effect one of the "superhorses" of history and was the sure-footed and tireless mount of marauding Scottish warmongers and cattle drovers. The Galloway was bred in the Mull of Galloway, the southernmost part of Scotland, and was renowned for its very great trotting ability. Although no longer in existence, the Galloway contributed significantly to a number of breeds, including the Fell, the Dales, the Highland, and, indirectly, the Thoroughbred and the Canadian Newfoundland.

The diminutive size of these ponies roaming along the northern border made it difficult for them to transport the loads required in the construction of Hadrian's Wall. As a result, when building began, around six hundred men from Friesland were sent over to help, and they brought with them their large, black, distinctive Friesian horses, which were crossed with the local native stock. It is thus the indomitable Friesian horse that was most significant in the development of the Fell, and today the stamp of the Friesian is still most evident of all those that influenced the breed. There was the occasional influence of other foreign breeds imported by the Romans, particularly the Arabian and other European horses, but after the Romans withdrew from England, approximately one thousand Friesian stallions were left behind in the northern territories. These horses continued to breed with local stock, thereby consolidating the characteristics of the Fell. Little further outside blood was introduced to the breed, with the exception of the Galloway, and as such it has remained almost untouched genetically.

Fell ponies are very strong for their size and able to carry and pull heavy loads. Because of this, they were greatly suited to riding, driving, and being used as pack animals, and they were used extensively in the north of England for transportation. Roads were few and far between until the eighteenth century, and the Fell was perfect for traversing the difficult terrain at speed and with a very smooth pace. By the nineteenth century, the ponies had started to be used less and less for transportation and in agriculture and instead became popular in trotting races. Today the Fell makes a fantastic riding or driving pony suitable for children and small adults alike.

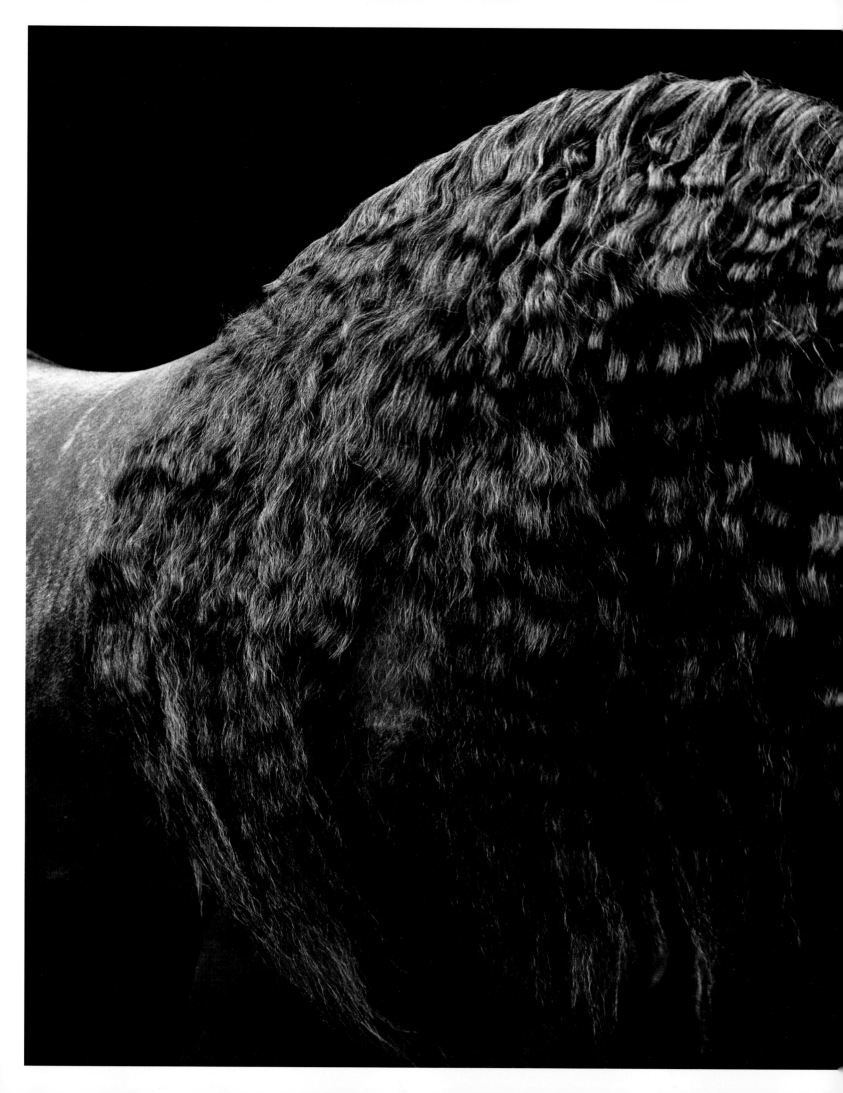

FRIESIAN
PREHISTORIC – HOLLAND – UNCOMMON

HEIGHT
15–16.2 h.h.
APPEARANCE
*Majestic horse with fine,
quality head set to an
elegant and upright neck.
Large, kind, expressive
eyes and small, neat ears.
Compact and muscular*

*through the frame with
powerful quarters and
sound, feathered legs.*
COLOR
Black
APTITUDE
*Riding, light draft, dressage,
classical dressage, jumping,
competitive horse sports*

THE MAGNIFICENT FRIESIAN HORSE is one of the less well-known breeds and also one of the most majestic. There are truly few breeds that can match these stunning black horses, which combine an extraordinary regal air with showstopping movement and unmatched temperament. They are descended from prehistoric roots and have remained extremely pure and true to type throughout their history. This history has seen their fortunes greatly fluctuate, and although they are strongly supported today, numbers of purebred Friesians remain unnervingly low.

The breed originated on the northern tip of the Netherlands in the Dutch province of Friesland, which was first properly settled around 500 B.C.E. Horses existed in this part of Europe many thousands of years before this, gradually evolving along separate lines. Excavations in Friesland have uncovered a variety of prehistoric horse bones of differing sizes that could plausibly belong to prehistoric types such as the Asiatic Wild Horse, the stout and heavy Forest horse (*Equus caballus silvaticus*), the Tarpan, and the large *Equus robustus* (big horse). There is no way of telling to what extent these horses crossbred, but based on type and frame alone, the Friesian is most commonly believed to have developed from the *Equus robustus*, a large animal with substantial bone.

During its early history the Friesian, as with most ancient breeds, was used in all capacities from farming and transport to packing and war. Records show they had been exported to northern England around 122 C.E. along with laborers to work on the construction of Hadrian's Wall, where they influenced local breeds such as the Dales and Fell. They were the favored mount of Friesian mercenaries because of their excellent agility and self-carriage, and by the fourth century they had carried their warring riders to Carlisle in Cumbria, northern England. The presence of these horses at such an early date in the British Isles was most significant in the development of a number of British breeds, including the aforementioned Dales and Fell, the now extinct Old English Black, and the Lincolnshire Black, the last two of which were crucial in the development of the iconic Shire horse. Further Friesians arrived in England during the sixteenth century when Dutch engineers came to drain the fens in East Anglia and brought their beloved horses with them.

During the Middle Ages, the Friesian proved its worth as the mount of knights and was in widespread use in the military, which brought it into contact with horses of eastern origin, particularly the Arabian. It was used again during the Eighty Year War (1568–1648) and came into contact with Iberian horses such as the Andalusian. Both of these breeds had a greatly improving effect on the Friesian and contributed to the development of its characteristic free, high-knee-action trot and the magnificence of its bearing. Other than this, the Friesian has remained very pure genetically and rather than being influenced itself has instead been a significant contributor to a number of other breeds such as the Mérens of the Pyrenees, the German Oldenburg, and the North American Morgan. It has also had a decisive influence on trotting breeds such as the North American Standardbred, the Russian Orlov Trotter, the British Hackney, the Norwegian Døle (Gudbrandsdal horse), the North Swedish horse, and the Finnish Universal.

By the seventeenth century, the Friesian had made its way into the French and Spanish riding academies for classical riding, making its mark alongside the better-known Andalusian, Lippizzaner, and Lusitano, with a number of engravings from this period depicting what are clearly Friesian horses. William Cavendish (1592–1676), one of the preeminent equestrian masters of his time, wrote that the Friesian was very qualified for dressage and High School riding. The breed was also gaining in popularity as a carriage horse, based on its extravagant appearance and movement, and as a trotter for use in short trotting races. Despite its earlier popularity, however, during the eighteenth and nineteenth centuries a fashion arose for the often lighter-framed European warmblood breeds that were bred for sporting events such as dressage and jumping, and the Friesian gradually started to disappear from the international stage, though it retained importance in Friesland. Significantly, today the Friesian horse can be seen competing in dressage events and competitive driving, as well as show jumping and showing.

The Friesian's agricultural role in its homeland was jeopardized by the development and use of larger, stronger draft breeds such as the Bovenlanders and Dutch Draft (from the turn of the twentieth century), and suddenly the numbers of Friesians began to decline. To combat this, breeders bred their horses to be stouter and more draftlike, but this resulted in a loss of their elegance and quality. Simultaneously, there was a decline in breed standard, since the horses were increasingly bred specifically as trotters and started to lose some of their fine and versatile qualities. In 1879 the first studbook was opened for the breed to try to rectify the situation, but by 1913 only three stallions were left in Friesland. The situation rallied somewhat during World War II when there was a demand for the horses for use on the land to save on fuel costs. After the war, though, and in line with the increasing use of machinery on farms, breed numbers again dropped. Farmers were unable to sustain horses for pleasure uses, and the Friesian horse became somewhat redundant. The situation began to change during the 1960s, when a group of dedicated Friesian enthusiasts set about promoting the breed and restoring it to its former glory in both quality and numbers.

Breed numbers are greatly improved today, and Friesians are much admired internationally, particularly in the British Isles and North America. Unique in appearance, they are bred to always be jet black now (though chestnut and brown used to occur) and have a magnificent aspect.

NOBLE BEGINNINGS

ARIÈGEOIS

PREHISTORIC – FRANCE, SPAIN – UNCOMMON

HEIGHT
13–14.3 h.h.
APPEARANCE
*A small, high-quality head,
broad across the forehead and
tapering to a fine muzzle. Short,
muscular neck, broad chest,
well-developed hindquarters,
and sound limbs. Sometimes*
*slightly long in the back, and,
like many mountain breeds,
often cow hocked, though this
does not affect their movement.*
COLOR
A very distinctive black.
APTITUDE
*Riding, light draft,
agricultural use, packing*

THIS GORGEOUS MOUNTAIN BREED OF PONY evolved in the remote Ariège region of southwest France along the eastern edge of the Pyrenees on the border with Spain, specifically between the French county of Rousillon and Spanish Catalonia. Both the breed and the region take their name from the Ariège River, which wends its way down through the Pyrenees and north into France. It is a place of great beauty, but also one notable for the severity of its winters; as a result, the Ariègeois has developed into an extremely hardy pony.

Typical of mountain breeds, the ponies are incredibly sure-footed and able to traverse the rocky and often icy terrain with ease. Like other breeds that evolved in harsh environments, the Ariègeois is also able to exist on meager rations, picking its way through the mountain forage and maintaining body condition where less hardy breeds would fail. The breed is also notably resistant to disease and sports a weather-resistant coat similar to British native pony breeds; the Ariègeois has much in common with the British Dales and Fell pony of the English Pennines, both in appearance and constitution. The ponies also bear more than a passing resemblance to the magnificent Friesian horse of the northern Netherlands, and it is fair to assume that these breeds might have evolved from similar primitive roots.

Evidence suggests that the Ariègeois has lived in its mountain home since prehistoric times. Most striking in this respect are the cave paintings found in the Niaux Cave at the heart of the Ariège in the Vicdessos Valley. These breathtaking painted images depict horses that bear a great similarity to the Ariègeois, but there are also images similar to the Camargue horse, which lives to the north and east of the Ariège. Most distinctive in these images is the Ariègeois' winter coat and characteristic long whiskery beard, which the horses still grow every year.

The first documented evidence of the Ariègeois dates from Roman times to their description by Caesar (100 B.C.E.–15 B.C.E.) in his *Commentaries on the Gallic War*. The Gauls were renowned horsemen and breeders, and had improved many of their native stock through selective breeding—certainly with Spanish stock and possibly horses of Oriental origin—and there can be little doubt that this would have extended to the mountain-bred Ariègeois. The breed was heavily influenced early in its history with horses of Oriental or Eastern blood, though even today this blood continues to have an influence; as recently as 1971, Arabian blood was introduced to improve the breed's quality. With the arrival of the Romans it is likely that the Ariègeois would also have been crossed to heavier, larger Roman-bred horses used for draft and war, increasing their size somewhat.

Over the centuries, the Ariègeois has lost some of its original qualities through persistent crossbreeding, particularly to heavier draft breeds such as the Percheron and Breton. Despite this, the Ariègeois remains a highly attractive and useful animal and is still in widespread use in the agricultural mountain communities of its home area. The ponies work on the steep hillside fields, plowing, harrowing, seeding, and harvesting, and they are able to access areas unsuitable for mechanized vehicles. They are also used for packing (though less so now than traditionally), driving, hauling minerals and timber, and riding. Historically, the Ariègeois was also used for smuggling goods across the Spanish border. They are intelligent and quiet ponies, making them great for children and nervous riders.

CAMARGUE
PREHISTORIC – FRANCE – UNCOMMON

HEIGHT
13.1–14 h.h.

APPEARANCE
Tends toward an upright shoulder, with a large head and a short, thick, muscular neck. Well-defined withers, a short, muscular back, and a deep, wide chest. Legs and feet are strong and robust, with wide hooves adapted to the wetness of their home, but so hard that they are rarely shod. A surprisingly long-striding, smooth walk and "armchair" canter.

COLOR
Gray

APTITUDE
Riding, working livestock

THERE ARE FEW SIGHTS QUITE SO MAGICAL as that of the shimmering white Camargue horses galloping through the saltwater marshes of their home in the Rhône Delta in southern France. Appearing suddenly on the horizon mirrored in the waters and amid streams of foam and clouds of hot breath, these tough, unique horses leave a lasting impression on any visitor lucky enough to see them. They are one of the very few horse breeds to still live a semi-feral existence, roaming across the harsh, unforgiving landscape of their home in small *manades*, or herds. Camargues are born brown or black but mature into their characteristic pure white, a color that accentuates their aura of mystery when they are glimpsed against the wild landscape. The process of changing coat color varies from horse to horse, but it is gradual and can take up to four years or more.

The Camargue is an ancient breed whose roots feasibly trace back into prehistory and to the horse remains found at Solutré. This extraordinary rocky outcrop is far in the south of Burgundy and was discovered to be a Paleolithic

site in the nineteenth century. Many hundreds of horse skeletons have been found here along the southern side of the ridge that have been dated between 32,000 and 12,000 years old and bear great similarities to the shape of the Camargue horse. The site is thought to reflect the scene of mass horse slaughter, presumably for meat with a possible further ritual element, that occurred over thousands of years. Further prehistoric links to this special breed can be seen by comparing its likeness to cave paintings at Lascaux, dated to c. 17,000 B.C.E., and also those at Niaux, c. 11,500 B.C.E., both sites in southwestern France.

The Rhône Delta where the Camargue horse lives is enclosed by saltwater marshes, brackish lagoons, sandbars, and coarse reeds in the south, and to the north on the drier land there are vineyards and handkerchief fields of grain. The landscape is battered by the harsh mistral winds, cold and unforgiving, which hurtle down through the Rhône Valley, and baked in the summer months under a scorching sun. It is home to ferocious mosquitoes and flies, which plague the horses, as well as many other species of flora and fauna, including exotic flamingos and wild boar. This untamed, rugged pocket of land is relatively geographically isolated, which has been a contributing factor to the purity of the Camargue horse. The breed is not without outside influences, but these occurred in large part many centuries ago when armies passed through the area on military campaigns. It is likely that the stocky Mongolian horse found its way to the Camargue under warring Indo-Europeans in pre-Christian times, and Greeks, Romans, and Arab peoples passed through the area, presumably bringing their horses with them. The Camargue was highly prized by the Romans, and Julius Caesar wrote of its fine qualities. The strongest external influences on the breed, however, were those of the Barb horse, itself a majestic animal, and Iberian horses. Barbs and Iberian horses were brought into the Camargue during the seventh and eighth centuries by Moorish invaders from the Iberian Peninsula, and the Barb influence is still discernible in the Camargue, particularly in the shape of its head and its proud bearing. Many of the horse-related traditions of the Camargue, especially those of the French cowboys, the *gardiens*, also still reflect traditions of the Iberian Peninsula introduced by the Moors, including their saddlery with its distinctive metal caged stirrups. Since that time many centuries ago, the Camargue horse has, however, remained almost untouched by other breeds.

The unique and fascinating nature of the Camargue area has led to the development of its own culture, at the heart of which lies the Camargue horse. This is France's equivalent to the Wild West, where the *gardiens* live and where they work the fierce, fighting Camargue bulls from the back of their white horses. The bulls, with their long horns, are bred for their highly prized meat, and also for bullfighting and bull running, a sport in which the *gardiens* excel and in which they must take a cockade from between the bull's horns. The bulls range largely unchecked across the salt marshes, living alongside the Camargue horses, and are renowned for their feisty nature. The *gardiens* use the Camargue horse for working and herding the bulls, carrying a long wooden pole—a trident— to help maneuver the animals. Despite its relatively small size (usually 14 hands high or smaller), the Camargue horse demonstrates extraordinary bravery and an innate ability to work the cattle. In a similar way to the American Quarter Horse, the Camargue instinctively follows and tracks cattle, which greatly aids the *gardiens.*

Such importance is attached to the *gardiens* in the Camargue that each May they are honored along with their horses by the Fête des Gardiens. During the festivities, the *gardiens* parade through the streets with their horses before putting on extensive displays of their equestrian skills. The Camargue horse is an integral part of nearly all of the festivals that occur in this region and is used in a number of riding events, including races in which the *gardiens* jump from horse to horse at a flat gallop—the *saut d'un cheval à l'autre*—and another in which they must snatch an orange at speed from platters held up by girls standing on the ground.

In large part because of the relative remoteness of the Camargue area and the quiet, isolated life of the *gardiens*, the Camargue horse remained relatively unknown until the mid-twentieth century. This was to such an extent that the breed was not officially recognized until 1968, when the Association des Eleveurs de Chevaux de Race Camargue was formed to oversee and protect the breed, including organizing annual stallion inspections. Some

years before this, however, the Camargue horse had crept slowly into public awareness through the release in 1953 of *Crin Blanc* (*White Mane*), a poignant short film by Albert Lamorisse. The film recounts the story of a young boy who tames a wild Camargue stallion he calls White Mane, battling the prejudice of the local ranchers in the process, and ending with boy and horse swimming out to sea. The film, which is beautifully shot on location using local Camargue horses, went on to win the prestigious Palme d'Or at the Cannes Film Festival, and the Prix Jean Vigo. It was released again in 2007 to critical acclaim and has touched the hearts of children and adults alike through the tender portrayal of the relationship between child and horse.

Despite its upright shoulder, large head, and short, muscular neck, when seen moving across their landscape or working the fierce Camargue bulls, the Camargue horses are breathtaking animals. Any criticism of their conformation must be balanced by an appreciation for their incredible hardiness. The Camargue, a product of its environment, is able to subsist on a meager diet, picking its way through the tough grasses and reeds of the saltwater marshes, existing and thriving where many other breeds of horse would fail. Their legs and feet are strong and robust, with wide hooves adapted to the wetness of their home, but so hard that they are rarely shod. Despite their upright shoulder, the Camargue has a surprisingly long-striding, smooth walk, and typically an "armchair" canter, gliding across the ground effortlessly. The smoothness and comfort of their paces has made them a popular choice for riders wishing to explore the Camargue Regional Park.

The Camargue horse is truly one of the more magical horse breeds, and certainly one of the oldest. Their unique character and the profound importance they still have to the local Camargue area sets them apart from many other breeds, and makes them particularly special. Although there are breeders of Camargue horses outside France, as a breed they will always retain a profound relationship with their original home, the wild and rugged saltwater marshes of the Camargue. It is these waters and the horses' propensity to gallop through them with characteristic spirit that has led to their being described as "the horses of the sea" and has lent them such a romantic appeal.

NOBLE BEGINNINGS

KNABSTRUP

ANCIENT — DENMARK — UNCOMMON

HEIGHT
Up to 16 h.h.
APPEARANCE
Beautiful, well-conformed horses that can exhibit quite some variation in size and type due to breeding for color. In general, they have attractive heads set to a well-arched and set neck, with

defined withers, muscular backs of medium length, and muscular hindquarters.
COLOR
Spotted.
APTITUDE
Riding, light draft, showing, dressage, jumping, competitive horse sports

ALTHOUGH THE ACTUAL HISTORY of the beautiful Knabstrup horse is relatively short and dates back only to 1812, the spotted horses of Europe have ancestors that go back to prehistoric times. There can be little doubt that these horses, so highly prized for their coat coloring, were the distant relatives of the modern Knabstrup and other spotted breeds. Spotted horses are included in the paintings in the French cave of Pêche Merle, which date to approximately 25,000 years ago and are among the earliest extant depictions of horses. Although there is no proof that these spots were a representation of the actual horses and not the painter's addition, perhaps for spiritual reasons, it is widely accepted that the spotted coat coloring, like the dun coat, has extremely primitive origins and probably developed as a form of camouflage.

Artifacts from Austria and Italy reveal decorative details of spotted horses dating to around 800 B.C.E., while there is a great deal of evidence for spotted horses heralding from Central Asia at a much earlier date, with the much sought-after horses of Ferghana often exhibiting this prized coat. By around 800 C.E., monks in Scotland were keeping and breeding spotted horses, and by the turn of the first millennium they had arrived in Denmark, as indicated by the Viking fresco at Skibby Church not far from Knabstrupper Hovedgaard. In the fresco, a procession of fine spotted horses carries three young princes, reflecting the very early association of these magnificently marked animals with nobility. Many centuries later they would be highly prized by the elite classes for their extravagant looks.

A spotted stallion appears on a fragment from a thirteenth-century tapestry in the Baldishol Church in Oslo, Norway, ridden by an eleventh- or twelfth-century knight; an equally majestic spotted horse ridden by one of the horsemen of the four seals is depicted in the Spanish Silos Apocalypse manuscript. By this time, spotted horses were popular across Europe, from Spain to Constantinople. Though it is rarely seen in the modern Iberian breeds, Spanish horses in particular exhibited the coat coloring, and they were in great demand in Austria, where they were highly regarded for use in the Spanish Riding School in Vienna, opened in 1572.

In 1562, King Frederik II of Denmark established the Royal Frederiksborg Stud to breed magnificent horses befitting a king, ones suitable for use in displays and ceremonies as well as in the cavalry. The Frederiksborg breed was one of the great successes of the stud, but it was also here that the Knabstrup started to take shape. The stud housed a number of Spanish horses in which the spotted coat coloring was prevalent, and later additional Spanish blood was introduced during the Napoleonic Wars when Spanish soldiers were stationed in Denmark and brought their horses with them. In 1683, the stud purchased a majestic black stallion called Superbe from the Spanish monastery and breeding facility at Jerez de la Frontera, again primarily to improve the Frederiksborg horse, but it was through Superbe's line that the foundation for the Knabstrup was laid.

In 1812, a direct descendant of Superbe was bred to a spotted mare called Flaebehoppen (the Snivel Mare) who came to Denmark from Spain during the Napoleonic Wars. The mare was bought by Judge Lunn, owner of the Knabstrupgaard Manor in Holbaek, and once proved her worth by allegedly pulling a cart about 18.5 miles (30 km) in 105 minutes to transport Lunn's son to the doctor in an emergency. The other horse that was in harness with her is said to have died, but Flaebehoppen was apparently back at

NOBLE BEGINNINGS

work the following day. Whether or not the story is true is a matter of some debate, but it is clear that the mare was a horse of great endurance and speed. The foal she had from the Superbe line in 1813 was called Flaebestallion, and he became one of the foundation stallions for the Knabstrup breed. All of Flaebe's foals were born with a distinctive spotted coat pattern, including her son Mikkel, who was famed for his racetrack record—he was apparently made to pull a farm cart carrying his owner to the track before he raced under saddle.

The Knabstrup is an extraordinarily versatile breed and was originally used in harness on small farms for pulling coaches, riding, and racing, as well as being used as a cavalry animal and later in the circus. They were used by Danish officers during the war in 1848–1850 but were not ideal cavalry mounts, as their eye-catching color made them easy targets. The breed then suffered in 1891 when twenty-two of the breeding Knabstrups at the Lunn's stud were killed in a fire.

With the creation of the modern circus in the eighteenth century by the Englishman Philip Astley, the Knabstrup found a new role. Its smooth gait and tendency to have a broad, flat back made it an excellent horse for use in the circus, particularly for vaulting, and in this capacity Knabstrups traveled widely across Europe and even to Australia and America during the nineteenth and early twentieth centuries. They are highly intelligent horses, which added to their aptitude for life in the circus and helped endear them to the modern rider.

Today the Knabstrup is a high-quality, beautiful horse. It is strong through the frame, and compact, and should be nicely put together with strong, clean limbs and hard feet. Unusually for horse breeds, the Knabstrup can be found in all sizes because of systematic breeding for color over other considerations such as size. This method of breeding has not always served the breed well, however, and did lead to a loss of quality in the late nineteenth and early twentieth centuries; during this time, the breed suffered a deterioration in conformation and athleticism, though this has now been fully rectified. Today the horses are all-rounders and highly regarded athletes, equally suitable for pleasure and competitive riding.

NORIKER +
SPOTTED PINZGAUER
ANCIENT – AUSTRIA – COMMON

HEIGHT	*abundance of mane and tail.*
15.2–16.3 h.h.	**COLOR**
APPEARANCE	*The Noriker displays a range*
Heavy but well-proportioned	*of coat colorings from dark to*
frame with a well-set head	*light chestnut, dappled and/or*
and neck and muscular	*brindled.*
hindquarters. Exceptionally	**APTITUDE**
strong limbs with a small	*Heavy draft, riding, meat*
amount of feathering and an	*production*

THE NORIKER IS ONE OF THE OLDEST heavy draft breeds of Europe and most probably descended from the prehistoric Forest Horse and the postulated Pony Type 2. The horses take their name from the ancient Roman vassal province of Noricum, which roughly equates to modern-day Austria south of the Danube River, and were bred by the Romans in this mountainous Alpine region. However, the horses are thought to have originated in the Pindus Mountains of Thessaly in northern Greece where they were bred by the Greeks as warhorses.

The Greeks were superior horse breeders and equestrians to the Romans and placed great stock in their horses. Although Greece does not have a particularly favorable habitat for breeding horses because of the climate and resulting poor grasses, Thessaly is more productive, and consequently many of the ancient Greek horse activities were based there. Thessalonian horses were greatly admired and bred along different lines for riding, packing, draft, and war.

During the Roman conquests, these heavy Greek warhorses from which the Noriker would later develop were taken across the Alps into what is now Austria. Following Greek precedents, the Romans established a number of systematic horse breeding programs to breed horses for purpose, and through this the Noriker developed. The horses were kept and bred at high altitude among the valleys and peaks, where they became very sure-footed and hardy. A major center for the early breeding of the Noriker was the Roman Juvavum stud farm, situated close to what is now Salzburg. Many centuries later, the Salzburg area remained strongly identified with the Noriker breed, primarily through breeding programs that were implemented in local monasteries.

Very early in its history, the Noriker was developed as a versatile heavy horse capable of pulling great weights, packing goods in mountainous areas, and even being ridden. Despite its size and bulk, it remains a very versatile breed and, because of the unusual smoothness and length of its stride, also makes a useful riding horse. Its marvelous temperament, paired with great intelligence and spirit, has made it an extremely popular horse through the centuries. Today the Noriker breed accounts for approximately 50 percent of Austria's horses, and it is still widely used in mountainous forest areas for hauling timber.

By the Middle Ages, the Noriker had developed to be a small, compact, but incredibly strong horse for its size. From around 1565 most of the Noriker breeding activities were managed by monks in the monasteries around Salzburg, and in 1574 the Archbishop of Salzburg established the first public breeding facility and the studbook. Subsequently, a rash of stud farms sprang up, and there was some introduction of Spanish, Italian, and French blood to improve the Noriker's height and elegance. This proved successful, and the horses became extremely popular for use in jousting tournaments.

The influence of Spanish blood in the breed is apparent in the Noriker's great quality and the freedom of its movement, but the Spanish horses also significantly introduced the spotted coat. The spotted Norikers, particularly prevalent around Pinzgauer, became known as Pinzgauer-Norikers and are now often called Spotted Pinzgauers. These horses are essentially the same breed as the Noriker, but they have a specific leopard-spotted coloring that was officially acknowledged in 1903 when a studbook for the Pinzgauer-Noriker was opened.

2 | MARTIAL GRACE

In modern times, the horse has become largely, but by no means universally, part of the leisure industry. Throughout history, however, it was primarily as a means of transportation and a tool for warfare that the horse reigned supreme. Its role as a warhorse ultimately led to the development of numerous different types and breeds—from the fine, wiry, and agile Arabian horses of the Moorish armies to the larger, heavier weight-carrying steeds of the armored knight, and the fast, tough horses of the Mongol warriors. The various battles for land domination meant that horses of different breeds were spread across the world, particularly during the Roman Empire (c. 27 B.C.E.–c. 476 C.E.) and the sixteenth century, when Spanish conquistadores descended on South America, taking their Spanish horses with them. Today, the majority of South and North American horse breeds trace their roots back to the influence of the Spanish horse. Of great interest in this respect is the American Indian nation, which had never seen horses before it was assailed by white warriors on horseback. In fewer than one hundred years, American Indians adopted the horse into their culture and became expert equestrians.

In warfare, the development and use of the saddle and stirrup had a profound impact on the effectiveness of cavalry soldiers. Some of the earliest saddles date to the Scythians, and were felt or cloth pads. The Romans are thought to have developed the first solid tree saddle, which had the great advantage of dispersing weight across the horse's back. This allowed the horse to be used harder and for longer periods without becoming unduly sore. The first stirrup took the form of a toe loop and is thought to date back to around 500 B.C.E. and to India. After this came the single stirrup, which aided mounting, and the first pair of stirrups originated in China in around 322. The Mongols rapidly adopted the paired stirrups because these gave a great advantage during battle. They rode with their stirrups short, which allowed them to stand in the saddle and shoot arrows, as well as giving them great downward thrust with a sword for use against the enemy. The use of stirrups probably spread to Europe through invaders from Central Asia from around the eighth century.

Horse breeding took on entirely new significance under the impetus of the Prophet Mohammed (570–632), the founder of the Islamic religion. To spread the word and power of Islam, he needed horsemen on swift desert horses ready to mobilize into action. The horse was treated as a reverential being, called the "supreme blessing" in Islam, and was looked after and bred accordingly. By the eighth century, the Islamic Empire had spread to incorporate North Africa, the Iberian Peninsula (Spain and Portugal), India, and Indonesia, eventually reaching the Great Wall of China. The conquests were almost universally won from the back of the desert-type Arabian horses.

In Europe, there was a renewal of Christian faith and a concerted effort by the Germans and French to develop new methods of warfare to halt the spread of Islam. This focused on their cavalry, which was reorganized by Charles Martel (c. 688–741), first minister to the Frankish king. In contrast to the Moors' light cavalry, made up of swift desert horses, Martel designed a heavy cavalry incorporating large bodies of armored knights and horses to attack in close formation and present an impenetrable "wall" of soldiers. Native French horse stock, such as the early Percheron, Boulonnais, Ardennais, and Limousin, was bred to fine Asian horses acquired during the Crusades to produce a more agile warhorse. These horses were weightier in frame than the light cavalry of the Moors but were also agile during battle maneuvers. Martel's defeat of the Moors at the battle of Poitiers in 732 was one of the earliest occasions when European soldiers used stirrups. His victory represented a change of fortunes that saw the beginning of the Moors' expulsion from Europe. It also marked the beginning of the Age of Chivalry, a time inextricably bound to the ideals of moral order and to the mounted knight.

The principles of heavy cavalry were continued by Martel's grandson, Charlemagne (c. 742–814), who founded the Holy Roman Empire in 800, and expelled the Moors from northern Spain. There was a continued demand for warhorses and a need to increase their size and weight-carrying abilities in line with the increasing weight of armor. The European warhorses of the Middle Ages tended to be described by type, rather than by specific breed. The most expensive and sought after was the destrier, the medieval charger. These horses were kept as stallions and were noted for their power, size, and speed. They were only ridden during battle. The knight would ride his palfrey to the battle, leading the destrier, then change horses at the last minute. Palfreys were also expensive and were a lighter weight riding horse. Palfreys were bred and trained to pace, a trot where the legs move in lateral rather than diagonal pairs. This results in a much smoother ride, which was appreciated by the knight in his unwieldy and heavy armor. Coursers were also used in battle and for hunting, and were lighter than the destrier and faster than the palfrey. Rounceys were a more general-purpose horse suitable for riding or for warfare. They were cheaper than destriers, palfreys, and coursers, and were used by soldiers of more restricted means.

Two hundred years after Charlemagne's endeavors, the knights of Christendom renewed their activities with the start of the Crusades in 1095. These military campaigns were waged to restore Christianity across Europe and the Holy Land, but it seems political and geographic power played an increasingly significant role. One of the great heroes of the Crusades was Rodrigo Díaz, better known as El Cid (c. 1040–99). El Cid was a valiant warrior whose victories against the Moors saw him heralded as the savior of his country. Almost as famous is El Cid's horse, Babieca, who came from the Spanish horse breeding area of Jerez de la Frontera and was in all probability one of the ancestors of the Andalusian, also referred to as the Iberian Warhorse. Spanish- and Portuguese-bred horses were among the most highly prized of warhorses. They had been bred to an improved size, and combined a weight-carrying capacity with tremendous agility and athleticism, which, when complemented by their trainable temperament, placed them at the top of their league.

As the knights of Christendom sped across Europe on their mighty warhorses to meet in battle the Moors on their desert-bred Arabians, an entirely different scenario was playing out across central Asia. Here, the indomitable Mongol Hordes, riding their far from elegant Mongol horses, were rapidly claiming territory to left and right. Led by Genghis Khan (1162–1227), these warriors—on their tough, fast, and thrifty Mongolian horses—cut a swath through central Asia, taking what they wanted and destroying everything else. Genghis Khan mobilized one of the largest and most effective cavalry of all time, completely reliant on an endless supply of Mongolian horses. Eventually, his bloody empire stretched from the Mediterranean to the Pacific—won and ruled on horseback. The Mongolian horse, which is unprepossessing to look at, but incredibly tough and quick, was dispersed widely through this area and has had an influence on many of the desert-bred breeds.

By the late sixteenth and early seventeenth centuries, the requirement for extensive heavy cavalry in Europe had decreased, but the skills, horsemanship, and bravery associated with the knights of chivalry persisted.

The Riding School, or High School, became an essential component of every nobleman's education. Alongside the Riding School, there was also the popular sport of jousting, which had similarly and more obviously developed from the battlefield. Jousting activities began in around the eleventh century, first as a means for practicing battle skills, but by the fifteenth century it had turned into a sport full of pageantry.

The earliest Riding School was opened in Naples in 1532 by Federico Grisone. He sought to train horse and rider to perform athletically in perfect harmony and balance, deploying classical nimble movements that had been developed and utilized in battle (side stepping, twirling, backing up, rearing, and controlled kicking out). His school was extremely popular and led to a demand for suitable horses, ones that were agile and noble, while also having a calm and forgiving temperament. The Iberian breeds fit this mold perfectly. The most famous of the Riding Schools and the oldest still in existence is the Spanish Riding School of Vienna, which was established in 1572 as part of the Hapsburg Court. The school uses only the regal Lipizzaner horse, bred especially at the Piber Stud near Vienna. These magnificent white horses are exercised daily in the baroque splendor that is the Winter Riding Hall, built in 1735.

The pinnacle of the Riding School endeavors lay in the exercises above the ground, or the airs above the ground. These maneuvers were loosely based on those used on the battlefield, and the Iberian breeds that excelled in battle also excelled in these exercises. There were originally a number of these movements, but today only three are performed: the levade, the courbette, and the capriole. In the levade, the horse must sit back on its haunches with its front legs bent; for the courbette the horse maintains this position and springs forward on its hind legs; and to achieve the capriole the horse must then leap from this position into the air vigorously extending its hind legs out behind it. The agility of the Iberian breeds is second to none, and it is in this respect that these horses also surpass others in the dangerous arena of bullfighting. The Iberian or Spanish horse is the mount of choice for the Spanish and Portuguese cowboys because it is able to move swiftly and smoothly after cattle in the working place and nimbly avoid the bull in the arena. In fact, many of the exercises performed in the bullring are an extension of those seen in the Riding School.

The development of gunpowder weapons from the mid-sixteenth century saw a decrease in the deployment of heavy cavalry and a move toward professional infantry-led armies. The Hungarian Hussars were among the most famous and effective of light cavalry units. They relied heavily on their fast horses and were known for their frequent use of "lightning strikes," sudden and deadly surprise attacks on the enemy. Hungary has an established tradition of breeding top quality horses that dates back to the Magyar horsemen of the ninth century, when they settled in the Carpathian basin. Through subsequent centuries, Hungary built a reputation for producing the finest horses for use in the military, based on native stock with heavy Arabian influence. During the eighteenth century, this was centered on the studs of Bábolna and Mezohegyes. From Bábolna came the Hungarian-bred Shagya Arabian; Mezohegyes produced the Nonius and Furioso, and from the former Kisber Stud came the Kisber Felver, developed during the mid-nineteenth century.

Although the costs of supporting a heavy cavalry were prohibitive, it was still deployed occasionally. Termed cuirassiers, the "modern heavy cavalry," which replaced the knights of the Middle Ages, was seen in French, British, Russian, and German armies to the twentieth century, although in small numbers. As armies became more organized, specific horses were bred as army riding horses, commonly called "remounts." The Russian Don, for example, earned great fame during the Russian/French wars in the winter of 1812. Napoleon's army and horses could not withstand the Russian climate; those that survived fled back to Paris, pursued by the Russians on their wily Don horses, which had thrived.

The Boer War (1899–1902), fought between the British Empire and the Dutch-speaking Boers of the South African Republic and the Orange Free State, saw horrific loss of equine life, thought to number approximately 400,000 horses on the British side alone. These included the native South African horses, the Boer Horse and Basuto, British horses, and huge numbers of the Australian Waler. World War I also had a devastating effect on many horse breeds and resulted in the death of millions of horses. However, they were used to great effect on the Eastern Front, where the Australian Waler was deployed in its thousands. The Indian Marwari fought bravely at the Charge of Mughar Ridge at Haifa, Israel, 1917, but were also heavily relied on across the Western Front where they were used as pack animals, for transportation, draft purposes, and fighting. Significantly, too, the horse was used by nearly all the nations involved, including, but not limited to, Germany, Russia, Poland, Japan, Turkey, North Africa, Australia, France, and the United States. Horses were used again during World War II, although less so in the face of improved vehicles.

The spread and exchange of breeds from east to west during wars and conflict is hugely significant in relation to the development of modern horse breeds. However, regardless of the specific breed, the feats of bravery and heroism exhibited by horses during warfare are quite extraordinary, and indeed humbling. There are many honorary monuments scattered across the globe that pay homage to our most loyal and indispensable friend.

NORTH AFRICAN BARB
PREHISTORIC — NORTH AFRICA — COMMON

HEIGHT
14–15.2 h.h.
APPEARANCE
An attractive head with a ram-like profile and almond-shaped eyes. Neck is well-arched and shoulders are sloped and powerful. Withers are well-defined, the back is short, *and the croup is sloped with a low-set tail. Chest is wide and hindquarters are muscular.*
COLOR
Gray, bay, brown, black, or chestnut.
APTITUDE
Riding, dressage, classical dressage, endurance, cavalry

THERE ARE FEW HORSES AS ANCIENT, mysterious, and important as the North African Barb (also known as the Moroccan Barb), one of the foundation breeds for many of the modern light horse breeds. Because of the Barb's very great antiquity, there is little documented history and a great deal of myth surrounding its origins, but what is clear is the enormous role it has played in the development of other breeds.

The Barb is said to have originated in North Africa in prehistoric times, but there were no indigenous horse breeds there, so its ancestors must have come from the east or traveled across prehistoric land bridges from the Iberian Peninsula. There is a widely debated connection to the Arabian horse, with some sources citing the Barb as the ancestor to the Arabian. Considering the dominant physical differences between these two breeds, differences with which they stamp their progeny, this seems unlikely. The two breeds' most distinctive trait is their unique morphology: the Barb is typified by its ram-like profile, sloping croup, and low-set tail; the Arabian is almost the opposite and displays a concave profile, level croup, and high-set tail. What is more probable is that the Barb and the Arabian shared a similar prehistoric heritage and then developed their particular characteristics as a result of being bred differently in different geographic locations.

The Barb shares similarities with the postulated Horse Type 3, a prehistoric desert animal whose nearest modern equivalent would be the Akhal Teke. These desert horses that lived in Central Asia—the ancient Turkmenian, the now-extinct Tarpan, the Mongolian, and the Caspian, with its very Arabian characteristics—must have formed the early basis for the Barb in some combination. It can be conjectured that the ancient superhorse used by the Persians, the Nisean, might also have contributed to the Barb. The Nisean, which is thought to have been related to the ancient Turkmenian, often exhibited the classic ram-like profile seen in the Barb and the horses of the Iberian Peninsula. There is further speculation that the primitive Sorraia, which could have traveled from the Iberian Peninsula into North Africa, also contributed to the Barb, and the two breeds also share similarities in the shape of their heads.

Warring nomadic peoples like the Hykos and the Hittites traveled with their horses from Central Asia down into the Middle East in the sixteenth and seventeenth centuries B.C.E. Nomadic tribes spread across North Africa, and there was a great exchange of equine blood, particularly in Algeria, Morocco, and Libya. The Barb played a central role in these cultures and was widely used as a warhorse because of its incredible speed and endurance. The horses were particularly prized by the Numidians, semi-nomadic Berber tribes who occupied part of Algeria and Tunisia from around the second century B.C.E. The Numidian riders were famed for their great skills and were said to ride their horses with no restraints, using just a piece of string around the horses' necks to guide them. The Carthaginians later used Numidian cavalry, mounted on Barbs, as mercenaries.

Julius Caesar (100 B.C.E.–44 B.C.E.) is reputed to have used Barb horses in his battles, especially against the Gauls, and this could have contributed to the spread of the Barb horse across Europe. Certainly the Barb was well known and greatly appreciated in southeast France and the Mediterranean countries by the Middle Ages and was bred at special stud farms. By the sixteenth century, Barbs had arrived in England, and Henry VIII (1491–1547) kept a number of Barb mares at his stud at Eltham.

Barbs were popular for use in the Classical Riding Schools, trained alongside Iberian horses, and were used by William Cavendish Duke of Newcastle (1592–1676), the British Master of Equitation. The first French Master of the Horse, Antoine de Pluvinel de Baume (1555–1620), with whom Cavendish trained, also kept a number of Barbs at his academy. Louis XIV (1638–1715) continued the royal patronage of the Barb horse in France, breeding the horses at the royal stud of Saint-Leger en Yvelines. Although there are conflicting accounts, it has been suggested that one of Louis XIV's illegitimate children acquired two important Barb stallions from the sultan of Morocco. These were subsequently imported to England and contributed to the foundation of English running stock that eventually developed into the Thoroughbred. Barbs were of crucial importance to the development of the Thoroughbred, and it was a Barb, the Godolphin Barb (f. 1724), who was one of the three foundation sires of the great British horse breed. (The Godolphin Barb is also frequently referred to as an Arabian, and his exact bloodlines remain extremely contentious. However, a painting of the horse by David Morier done from life reflects an animal of distinctly Barb appearance.)

The Barb also played an integral part in the development of the modern Iberian horse breeds, particularly the Andalusian. Although the Andalusian type was already established when Barbs were taken into Spain during the Moorish conquests in the eighth century, the Barb greatly influenced its further development. The Irish Connemara undoubtedly has Barb blood in its foundation, as do many of the French breeds, including the Camargue and the Limousin, a horse specifically bred during the Middle Ages to be a military charger. Indeed, it is in a military capacity that the Barb horse has most served humans, from its first domestication through to World War II. Of particular note is the Barb's use by the Spahi, the light cavalry regiments of the French army sourced from across North Africa.

The Barb is extremely resistant to heat and able to subsist on minimal rations. It is incredibly sure-footed and able to traverse inclines and declines at great speed and to maintain its speed over considerable distances. The Barb is noted for its fiery spirit when required, which is matched by a calm and kind nature when at leisure. Like Arabians, Barbs are also characteristically loyal to their owners and riders and form strong bonds with their handlers.

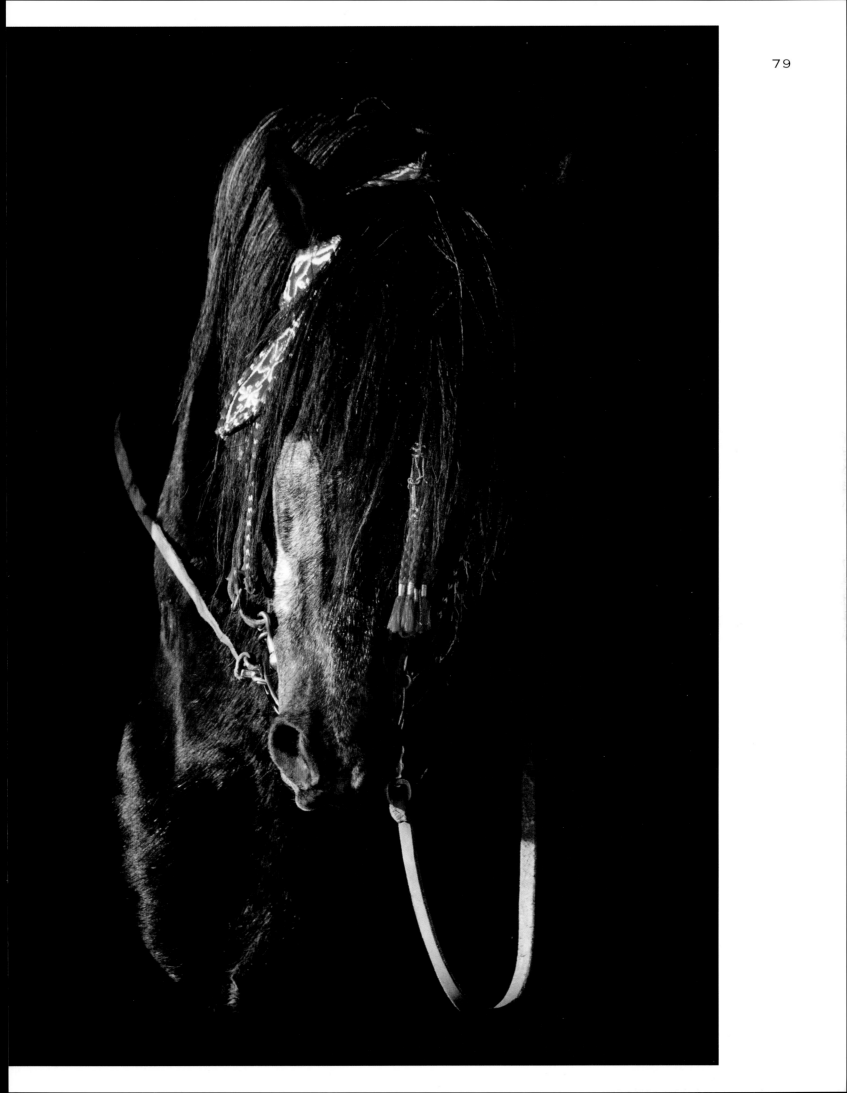

ANDALUSIAN
(PURA RAZA ESPAÑOLA)
ANCIENT — SPAIN — COMMON

HEIGHT	*frame compact with a deep chest*
15–15.3 h.h.	*and very muscular quarters.*
APPEARANCE	*Moves with great freedom.*
Athletically built and	**COLOR**
tremendously muscular with	*Mostly gray or bay but other*
strong, sound limbs. Beautiful	*colors accepted.*
head with a straight or ram-like	**APTITUDE**
profile, alert ears, and large, kind	*Riding, classical dressage,*
eyes. The neck is well set, the	*dressage*

ACCORDING TO ANCIENT FOLKLORE, the Spanish horse was the offspring of Zephyr, the ancient Greek god of the west wind who fathered Balius and Xanthus, two immortal horses who pulled Achilles' chariot during the Trojan War. Although the truth may be slightly less exotic, the Andalusian, or Pura Raza Española (pure Spanish breed), remains a superlative horse. One of the most respected and widely used warhorses, it was the mount of kings and noblemen, as well as of bullfighters and cowboys. Today the Spanish horse is highly sought after as a competitive athlete.

The term Spanish (or Iberian) covers various different breeds of the Iberian Peninsula that have much in common. The Andalusian, from Andalusia in southern Spain, was historically, and confusingly, also called the Iberian Warhorse, Jennet, Carthusian, Lusitano, or Alter Real, all of which are recognized today as different breeds. Technically, the Andalusian horse, as referenced in this book, should be referred to as a Pura Raza Española, or PRE. These are purebred Spanish horses registered with the National Association of Purebred Spanish Horse Breeders of Spain, as opposed to just any horse of mixed heritage from Andalusia.

The roots of the Iberian horse can be traced to the indigenous *Equus stenonius*, which roamed the peninsula thousands of years before the end of the last ice age. The Sorraia is the modern equivalent of this prehistoric horse and contributed significantly to the development of the modern Iberian breeds, along with other indigenous ancient breeds such as the Asturian, the Galician in its original form, the Garrano, and the Pottok pony of the Pyrenees.

However, the indigenous horses of Iberia were subjected to a substantial and fairly continual genetic influence from outside during continual invasions of the peninsula.

Trade routes were also established from 500 B.C.E. all along the Mediterranean coast, with gold, silver, and, in all likelihood, horses being exchanged. At this early date the incoming equine influences fall into two specific groups: Oriental horse breeds (hot-blooded desert horses from Western and Central Asia), and the heavier, cold-blooded horses of Europe. Among the earliest of the desert horses to reach Iberia were those belonging to the Hyksos, an Asiatic nation that ruled Egypt from 1674 to 1567 B.C.E. The Hyksos were a horse-oriented people and would have taken their prized desert horses, ancestors of the ancient Turkmene, with them into Egypt. It is likely that these horses would then have spread across North Africa into the Iberian Peninsula.

Oriental blood was again introduced to the Iberian stock when Visigoths from Sweden invaded the Iberian Peninsula in 414 C.E., ruling there until the arrival of the Moors in 711 C.E. The warring Visigoths had traveled through Germany and Poland in 200 B.C.E. before settling near the Black Sea in western Russia for around a century. While there, the Visigoths' horses were subjected to the influence of Central Asian breeds, which was passed on to the Iberian breeds many years later. Similarly, the Moors brought desert-bred horses, including the Arabian, with them.

Early European influence came via the Celts, who moved into the northern and central parts of Spain and parts of Portugal and Galicia from 800 to 600 B.C.E. During this period, eastern and southern Spain retained their ancient Iberian cultures, and where the two cultures overlapped they were referred to as Celtiberian. After a visit to Spain, the Stoic philosopher Posidonius recounted in 90 B.C.E. that both the Iberians and the Celtiberians had horses of great quality. Those of the Iberians were highly trained and used by the cavalry. Posidonius described how the Celtiberian horses were "starling-colored," probably meaning that they were a flea-bitten gray. This early mention of coloring is interesting since there was also a great exchange of Spanish and Camargue blood. The tough little Camargue is nearly always born dark and turns gray, a trait also found in the Lipizzaner, another of the Iberian breeds, and gray is the predominant color in the Andalusian.

The Romans were responsible for the spread of many equine gene pools throughout Europe as their empire expanded, and the Andalusian is no exception. Roman historian Tacitus (56–117 C.E.) wrote that Rome provided all the cavalry regiments of European origin with Iberian horses, since they were bigger than their contemporaries, as well as being strong, noble, obedient, and loyal. Roman accounts and earlier indications offer irrefutable evidence of the Andalusian's existence before the Moorish invasion in 711 C.E.; by this date a fine horse of antiquity already existed.

Just as horse breeds passed from outside into Iberia, so too did the indigenous Iberian breeds migrate outward, particularly into North Africa, where they were fundamental to the development of the North African Barb. When the Moorish invasions of Iberia began, great numbers of Barb horses passed back into the peninsula and crossed again with the native Iberian stock; the hot-blooded Barb lightened the frame of the Iberian horse and helped to generate a breed of greater speed and elegance.

The Andalusian reigned supreme as the ultimate warhorse, swifter and more agile than the massive types being bred in northern Europe, yet larger than many of the desert breeds and able to carry more weight. With its combination of hot Oriental and calm cold blood, the Andalusian became a horse worthy of, and sought after by, kings and leaders alike, and it was used by the knights of the Reconquista against the Moors on their Arabian horses. Indeed, the famous mercenary El Cid (c. 1040–99), who battled against the Moorish occupation of Spain, is said to have ridden an Andalusian; his loyal horse, Babieca, came from the Carthusian monastery at Jerez de la Frontera.

Around the time that El Cid and Babieca were crushing Spain's foes, the first Andalusians were recorded in England, ridden by William the Conqueror (c. 1028–87). Many of the numerous horses that appear in the Bayeux Tapestry, which records the Norman conquest of England (1066), also clearly reflect Andalusian qualities. Centuries later, the Andalusian was among the first of the horses reintroduced to the Americas when it was taken by the conquistadores into South America. Today, the influence of the Andalusian and other Spanish breeds can be seen in nearly all American horse breeds.

The horses of knights in medieval Europe had to be highly skilled and agile, able to turn and twist quickly and smoothly in close combat, to rear up, kick out, back up, and even leap in the air to avoid injury or aid attack, and it was from these movements that the concept of High School dressage evolved. Horses of Iberian breeding served as ideal mounts for use in the High School, where the arts of horse training and dressage became part of the education of noblemen. Of the many depictions of horses in Renaissance paintings, a large proportion strongly exhibit Andalusian characteristics, providing compelling visual evidence of the extent to which the breed was used and prized.

Early in the seventeenth century, the Andalusian suffered briefly under King Philip III (1598–1621), who appointed Juan Jeronimo Tiuti, a Neapolitan horseman, as director of the royal stud at Córdoba. Tiuti imported massive Neapolitan, Danish, Flemish, and Norman stallions and used them on the Andalusian mares. The result was disastrous and quickly apparent: the Andalusian lost its elegance and agility, becoming larger in frame and less athletic.

That situation was addressed, but disaster struck again after the Peninsular Wars (1808–14) when there was a sudden, greatly misguided attempt to introduce Arabian blood to the already magnificent Andalusian breed. The Arabian, itself an undeniably beautiful breed that generally has an improving effect on others, had suddenly become the horse of choice. A fashion developed for horses with small, Arabian-like heads, rather than the majestic and noble head of the Andalusian. The Arabian's influence had a weakening effect, and the Andalusians started to lose the power that had made them the best warhorses of old.

Fortunately, the integrity of the breed was saved by a handful of dedicated breeders, including Don Pedro Jose Zapata, founder of the Hospital de Arcos de la Frontera, and Carthusian monks at Jerez de la Frontera. The monks bred a special type of Andalusian called the Carthusian, considered by some to be the purest form of the breed. Don Pedro also bred the Carthusian line, and it is still bred in the Jerez region, while more generally the Andalusian horse is now widely bred across the world.

MARTIAL GRACE

SORRAIA

PREHISTORIC – PORTUGAL, SPAIN – RARE

HEIGHT
12.2–13.2 h.h.

APPEARANCE
Large head, often with a ram-like or straight profile and broad forehead. Ears can be quite long and curve inward at the tip. Long, elegant, well-set neck, defined withers, and a short, strong back.

Sloping croup and low-set tail. Legs and feet are extremely tough.

COLOR
Clearly primitive colorings, often a mousy dun, red dun, or grullo, with dark zebra markings on the legs and a dorsal stripe.

APTITUDE
Riding, packing, working livestock

THE STRIKING LIKENESS OF THIS LITTLE HORSE appears in the prehistoric cave paintings of Spain, Portugal, and France, indicating the very great antiquity of this important equine. The Sorraia is thought to be the modern representation of *Equus stenonius*, one of the few identified prehistoric horses, and also bears much in common with the now extinct Tarpan and its modern, reconstructed form. Some theorists have suggested that the Sorraia has further links to the Asiatic Wild Horse, but this remains highly debatable and there are few apparent similarities to be seen. It is, however, a vestigial primitive horse and has not been subjected to human interference or "created" by selective breeding.

Despite its relatively diminutive size and its now great rarity, the Sorraia can be considered one of the most fundamentally important groups of horse. The Sorraia, along with its close neighbors the Garrano and the Asturian, was significant in the development of the Iberian horse breeds, including the Andalusian, the Alter Real, and the Lusitano, which have directly or indirectly influenced many of today's modern horse breeds. It is thought that Sorraias formed part of the early cargo of horses to the

Americas, taken by the conquistadores in the sixteenth century; as a result, Iberian blood runs at the foundation of many of the modern American breeds, such as the Argentinean Criollo or Peruvian Paso.

The breed's name comes from the rivers Sor and Raia, which run through Spain and Portugal and form the boundaries of their natural habitat. The horses evolved on the wide, sparse plains that fall between the two rivers, and consequently they are able to exist on minimal rations. The Sorraia is also resistant to extreme heat and cold, having evolved in an area with little shelter, and is a very hardy, tough animal. The Garrano, which descended from prehistoric stock similar to the Sorraia, developed farther north along the lush Portuguese valleys of Garrano do Minho and Traz dos Montes. This breed is less hardy than the Sorraia and has been subjected to a far greater influence of foreign blood, particularly Arabian. Today the Garrano bears little in common with its ancient ancestors and is a small, high-quality riding pony.

In contrast, the Sorraia has changed little and has remained relatively untouched by other breeds, based primarily on its isolated habitat. It is one of the few horses never to have been influenced by Arabian or Oriental blood, or even that of the Northern European breeds. It bears a striking similarity in conformation to the reconstituted Tarpan in all respects, apart from the profile of its head, which has a characteristic ram-like appearance. Despite its small size, the Sorraia is a small horse and not a pony, based on its conformation. It is long in the leg, compact through the body, and typically has a well-set neck. In most respects the Sorraia has the appearance of an Andalusian in miniature, although it lacks some of the Andalusian quality. The Sorraia also has great strength for its size and was used for centuries by local Spanish and Portuguese cowboys to work the cattle and also for packing.

The Sorraia owes its survival in large part to the efforts of Ruy d'Andrade, a well-known Lusitano breeder who discovered a herd of feral Sorraias in the region of Coruche in the lower Sor Raia area in the 1920s and quickly realized their importance. D'Andrade moved a small number of the horses to his own land, beginning a long and continuing connection between the breed and the d'Andrade family.

MARTIAL GRACE

LIPIZZANER

HISTORIC – AUSTRIA – RARE

HEIGHT
15–16.1 h.h.
APPEARANCE
A large, noble head with either a straight or ram-like profile. The neck is extremely muscular and arched, well set and carried. They are deep and wide through the chest, quite flat through the

withers, and with a long, strong back. The hindquarters are muscular, the croup slightly sloping, and the tail carried high.
COLOR
Predominantly gray.
APTITUDE
Light draft, dressage, classical dressage, riding

THERE ARE FEW SCENES QUITE SO SPECTACULAR as the gray (white) Lipizzaners of the Spanish School of Riding, Vienna, performing their extraordinary "airs above the ground," the highest level of dressage movements. These amazing athletes combine great power and spirit with incredible calmness, making them one of the few breeds able to cope with such physically and mentally challenging training. They are a breed apart and have suffered through a tumultuous history that has nearly seen their total destruction. It is testament to the great historic importance of both the breed and the Spanish School of Riding in Vienna that they still survive today, and their histories are inextricably bound together.

The breed traces its roots back to the sixteenth century, when there was a demand for a majestic type of horse suitable for battle, for carrying kings, and for performing complicated movements in the Riding School. Equestrian training in the school formed an important part of the education for the royals and for noblemen, but it required a special type of horse, one with brains and beauty and a tractable temperament. The Iberian breeds, led by the Andalusian, were such an animal and were in great demand across Spain and Portugal as well as much of Europe.

The all-important Spanish blood found its way to Austria when Maximilian II (1527–76) founded the court stud at Kladrub around 1562, stocking it with Spanish horses. In 1580, Maximilian's brother, Archduke Charles II (1540–90), founded another stud based on Spanish horses at Lipizza in present-day Slovenia, near Trieste in Italy. The stud at

Lipizza was situated on the harsh, limestone Karst plateau, an unforgiving area that contributed greatly to the characteristics of the Lipizzaner. The rocky terrain and lack of shelter produced horses with exceptionally strong and sound limbs and feet, able to exist in a difficult environment to such an extent that fertility rates in Lipizzaners fell when they were bred in more clement circumstances. The horses are also extremely long lived; they mature late, but they will continue on in an athletic capacity into their twenties and consistently improve with age.

A final, third court stud was established at Halbturn, Austria, in 1717, and the three—Kladrub, Lipizza, and Halbturn—provided horses for the Spanish School of Riding in Vienna, so called because of the horses' Spanish origin. The Spanish School in Vienna is the jewel in the crown of equestrian establishments and is the oldest school of its type. It was formed in 1572 and furnished with Spanish horses with the purpose of teaching the gentry classical riding skills.

The very specific Lipizzaner horse developed initially from a combination of horses being bred at the three court studs, with Spanish stock at their foundation. The Halbturn stud closed in 1743 and the stud at Lipizza became the major breeding center for the white horses. As well as the original stallion lines perpetuating, many of the original mare lines are still in existence.

The fate of the Lipizzaner stud farms has been consistently threatened during times of war, and in extreme circumstances the breeding stock was moved away. During World War I, breeding stock from Lipizza was moved to Laxenburg near Vienna, and some of the foals were relocated to Kladrub. From 1920 the main breeding activities were moved to the Piber stud in western Austria, and it is from Piber that the horses for the Spanish School are still sourced. During World War II the Spanish School and its horses faced serious threat. The breeding stock from Piber was moved to Hostau in Czechoslovakia by the

German High Command in 1942, and the stallions from the Spanish School were taken from Vienna to St. Martins, Austria, in 1945 when Colonel Alois Podhajsky, head of the Spanish School, feared for their safety. General George Patton (1885–1945) of the U.S. Army, who was a keen horseman, was near St. Martins at the time and learned of the Lipizzaners housed there. Podhajsky put on a display of his horses for Patton and after the routine asked him to take the fate of the Lipizzaners into his hands. He did so, and the stallions finally returned to the Spanish School in Vienna in 1955. Meanwhile, the U.S. Second Cavalry Unit commanded by Colonel Charles Reed (1900–79) had discovered the Lipizzaner horses at Hostau, alongside large numbers of Allied prisoners. Reed instigated a rescue strategy that saw 375 Lipizzaners taken temporarily to the Bavarian town of Kotzting before being relocated to Wimsbach in Austria and finally returning to Piber in 1952. The Lipizzaner is now also bred in state studs in Hungary, Romania, and the Czech Republic, as well as privately in the United States and the United Kingdom. Numbers for the breed remain fairly low, however, and it is considered a rare breed.

Lipizzaners are bred to be gray (white) although they are born dark and lighten over time. Some may be bay, and it is traditional for the Spanish Riding School to keep one bay Lipizzaner there at all times. The Spanish Riding School uses only gray stallions and follows a regimented and very slow training program to allow the horses to mature naturally and increase in strength and mental ability without undue stress. The horses begin their training at around three and a half years old, and it can take five to six years of training before they are performing airs above the ground at the top of their sphere.

The airs above the ground are the ultimate expression of classical riding and represent the apogee of dressage riding. Traditionally, there were around seven different exercises performed in the air, but today only three tend to be practiced: the levade, the courbette, and the capriole. To achieve these extraordinary feats, the horses must be incredibly agile, highly intelligent, and calm, and these are the predominant features of the breed. Along with the Andalusian, the Lipizzaner is among the most breathtaking and spectacular breeds to behold.

LUSITANO
ANCIENT – PORTUGAL – RARE

HEIGHT
15–16 h.h.

APPEARANCE

An extremely muscular horse with a well-set, arched neck and a wide, deep chest. Withers are well defined and long, back is muscular, and croup is rounded and slightly sloping. Strong, sound limbs and abundant mane and tail hair.

COLOR

Gray; occasionally bay or chestnut.

APTITUDE

Riding, working livestock, dressage, classical dressage

THE GREEK POET HOMER (c. eighth century B.C.E.) described Iberian horses as "fast as the wind and sons of Podargo, the harpy that was impregnated by the wind Zephyr while grazing at the borders of the River Oceanus." Centuries later, Roman historian Pliny the Elder (c. 23–79 C.E.) reinforced this legend, writing that mares from Lusitania were "impregnated with the West Wind, and brought forth an offspring of surprising fleetness."

The magnificent Lusitano horse takes its name from Lusitania, the Latin word for Portugal, where this branch of the Iberian horse family developed. All the Iberian breeds, including the Andalusian and the Alter Real, share very similar foundations, but throughout their history the different breeds developed along varying lines according to their geographic homes. The Lusitano and the Andalusian in particular share many similarities, although the Lusitano can sometimes retain a slightly more ram-like profile and a more sloping croup with a lower-set tail. The Lusitano is arguably the purer of the two breeds and has remained relatively free from outside influence. This is most notable with regard to Arabian blood, which was introduced to the Andalusian to produce a horse with a finer, smaller head. Portuguese breeders of the Lusitano rejected this approach and remained true to their original stock.

Iberians were the most sought-after warhorses in early history, but those from Portugal were singled out as being superlative. The Greek historian Strabo (c. 63/64 B.C.E.–24 C.E.) wrote that during the Punic Wars (264–146 B.C.E.) the Lusitano riders were mounted on horses that would climb escarpments that no other horse would attempt. The Carthaginian military commander Hannibal (c. 248–183 B.C.E.) is said to have traveled from the Iberian Peninsula over the Pyrenees and the Alps with 12,000 of these prized horses. The Lusitano soldiers with their horses proved exasperating opponents for the far less skilled Roman cavalry, but once the horses were captured, the Romans recognized their worth and used them throughout their expanding empire. Their role as the ultimate warhorse continued throughout much of their early history and well into the Middle Ages, and they were sought after across Europe to improve the heavier, slower-moving European breeds.

It was not just as a warhorse that the Lusitano excelled, however. These horses are extraordinarily versatile, thanks in large part to their excellent combination of athleticism and obliging temperament. They were particularly noted for their ability to learn and perform complicated movements that were used at first on the battlefield and later in the Riding School as the concept of equestrian training took off during the sixteenth century. Despite the Lusitano's great skill and nobility in this respect, it was also highly prized as a working stock horse and was used by the Portuguese cowboys for working cattle and bulls. It is perhaps most famous as a bullfighting horse, combining enormous bravery with dexterity and calmness. In Portugal, all bullfighting is conducted on horseback and the bull is not killed in the arena. The horse must avoid the bull's charges, and between charges it performs a series of high dressage movements with absolute grace and calmness.

Lusitanos were transported to the Americas during the sixteenth century and have contributed on a founding level to the development of the vast majority of American breeds. Today, Brazil is an important center for Lusitano breeding and produces some of the best examples of the breed. It is still bred in Portugal, as well as North America, the United Kingdom, and across Europe, yet in spite of this, numbers for the breed remain low.

ALTER REAL
HISTORIC – PORTUGAL – RARE

HEIGHT
15–16.1 h.h.
APPEARANCE
A large but attractive head with a ram-like or straight profile and small, alert ears. Neck is muscular and well set and chest is particularly deep and wide. Reasonably long, broad back and very muscular hindquarters. Limbs are strong and sound, with longer cannon bones than other Iberian breeds.
COLOR
Bay or brown.
APTITUDE
Riding, dressage, classical dressage

THE BEAUTIFUL TOWN OF ALTER DO CHÃO sits along the shores of the Lake Verde lagoon in central eastern Portugal. It is an idyllic spot, home of the regal Iberian breed the Alter Real. The breed, which has had the most troubled history of all the Iberian horse breeds, takes its name from the town and from *real*, the Portuguese for "royal."

Although the breed's foundations are ancient and based on the same stock that gave rise to all of the Iberian breeds, the specific qualities of the Alter Real were not developed until the eighteenth century. In 1748, the Braganza family, Portugal's royal family, began a breeding program at the Vila de Portel stud to supply the royal stables with carriage horses and horses for use in the High School. The program was initiated by King John V (1689–1750), who placed his son José I (1714–77) in charge of the stud's administration. After several years, the breeding activities at Portel were moved to the area around Alter do Chão, where the climate and terrain were particularly suited to horse breeding and which already had a number of highly regarded horses.

The stock was based on three hundred pure Andalusian mares brought from Jerez de la Frontera in Spain and bred to the local Spanish and Portuguese stallions, with the stud activities overseen by the Marquis of Marialva (1713–99), Portugal's most respected Master of the Horse. Under Marialva's direction the stud reached its pinnacle, and the classically trained horses were greatly admired for their athleticism and temperament. The royal stud began to produce distinctive horses of great quality that excelled in the demanding High School exercises.

With the turn of the century, however, the stud's fortunes changed. The Napoleonic invasions began in 1807 and the breeding stock was greatly undermined. The same year, the Braganzas, who had been so instrumental in the stud's development, fled to Brazil, taking some of their Portuguese horses with them. Many of the horses left behind were either killed or taken by the French troops, and numbers of purebred Alter Reals dropped dramatically. In an effort to restore the breed, large quantities of Arabian, Hanoverian, English Thoroughbred, and Norman stock were introduced, with disastrous effects. The introduction of Arabian blood in particular was most detrimental to the Alter Real, which coincides with a similarly diminishing effect that Arabian blood had on the Andalusian around the same time. The Alter Real recovered only when pure Andalusian blood, including some from the highly regarded Zapateros line, was used to restore it.

In 1910, Portugal abolished its monarchy and the government closed the royal stud. The property was integrated into the Ministry of War, and from 1911 to 1941 it was run as a military stud farm. During this time, nearly all of the stud records for the Alter Real were lost, and many of the horses were dispersed and the stallions gelded. It could have spelled the end for this talented and noble breed were it not for the efforts of Portugal's greatest equestrian authority, Ruy d'Andrade, who was also instrumental in the preservation of the Sorraia. D'Andrade managed to obtain a small number of pure Alter Real horses, including two stallions, and with great perseverance and time he rebuilt a small breeding herd.

In 1942, D'Andrade was able to present the ministry of agriculture with a small but stable herd of Alter Real horses that has perpetuated to the present day. Since 1996, the stud has undergone extensive restoration and now houses around sixty Alter Real mares and a number of the finest stallions, as well as Lusitanos and Sorraias, and operates a careful breeding program.

FREDERIKSBORG
HISTORIC — DENMARK — RARE

HEIGHT
15.1–16.1 h.h.
APPEARANCE
An attractive head with a straight or marginally convex profile set to a well-shaped and muscular neck. They are deep and wide through the chest with muscular

hindquarters and a good sloping shoulder that allows for their excellent, free-flowing movement.
COLOR
Predominantly chestnut.
APTITUDE
Riding, light draft, dressage, jumping, cavalry

THE ELEGANT FREDERIKSBORG, DENMARK'S OLDEST horse breed, traces its history to the sixteenth century. Combining striking looks with versatility and athleticism, typical of Danish breeds, it is a rare but iconic part of Danish cultural history. The breed was developed with three rather different purposes in mind—cavalry horse, carriage horse, and horse suitable for use in the High School—and proved itself eminently capable of all three. Although its numbers are now very low, the Frederiksborg continues to excel as a light driving horse and in the competitive fields of dressage and show jumping.

By the mid-sixteenth century, Denmark was already home to a large number of impressive horses, many of Iberian origin. After the 1536 Count's War, which marked the Reformation in Denmark and a move from Roman Catholicism to Lutheranism, King Christian III (1503–59) took possession of all the breeding stock from the abbeys. These horses were among the best in the country, and much of the stock was relocated to the beautiful manor house of Hillerødsholm, later renamed Frederiksborg after King Frederick II (1534–88), who established the royal stud there. When Frederick's son Christian IV (1577–1648) took over the running of the stud, specific breeding programs were established. More purebred Iberian stallions were brought to the stud, along with horses from central and eastern Europe, which were crossed with the existing stock. Christian was interested in developing a Danish horse to match the hallowed Iberian and based much of his breeding stock on these same horses.

The horses were bred along two loose types: a lighter, more agile horse for cavalry and High School work, and a heavier type for use with the royal carriages and ceremonial purposes. Mares were divided into herds of between ten and twenty, and each herd was kept in a fenced area of wooded countryside. In the spring, a stallion would be introduced and allowed to run with the mares through the breeding season. By the seventeenth century, the horses of Frederiksborg had become famous for their elegance and their very great merit as both riding and driving horses, and they began to be exported all over Europe.

By the mid- to late seventeenth century there was a call to produce an even flashier horse to keep in line with the pomp and ceremony of the French courts. The Frederiksborg began to be bred for color, particularly those carriage types that needed to exactly match each other in color and markings to create the best effect. The breeding herds were divided and named according to their color, resulting in the chestnut, black, and gray studs. For almost a century the Frederiksborg was one of the most sought-after horses and was sold in great numbers abroad as well as being used to upgrade other Danish breeds such as the Jutland. The magnificent Frederiksborg stallion Pluto even went on to become one of the foundation stallions for the Lipizzaner breed. The tremendous success of the breed ultimately led to its downfall, however, since much of the best breeding stock left the country; the quality of Danish stock began to fall, eventually resulting in the closure of the stud.

Some horses remained in private homes where breeding activities continued, and in the early to mid-1900s there was a concerted effort to reconstitute the breed. Neapolitan, Friesian, Oldenburg, Thoroughbred, and Arabian blood was introduced to the surviving Frederiksborg stock, resulting in the production of a supremely elegant and versatile horse. Sadly, numbers of Frederiksborg horses remain low, despite their admirable qualities.

PERCHERON
ANCIENT – FRANCE – COMMON

HEIGHT
15.2–16.2 h.h.
APPEARANCE
Highly attractive head and lively expression. Short, muscular neck well set to a short, broad, muscular back. Very deep and wide in the chest, with a fairly sloping shoulder. Short in the leg

but with dense, substantial bones. Legs are mostly free from feathering, though they have an abundance of mane and tail.
COLOR
Gray or black.
APTITUDE
Heavy draft, agricultural work, riding, cavalry, meat production

FEW DRAFT BREEDS ARE QUITE AS ELEGANT, versatile, and widespread as the gorgeous Percheron. Most notable about these horses is their very great quality, which is especially evident in their heads but also in their unusually free-flowing action. The breed has been heavily influenced by Arabian blood, which has given the horses their particular attractiveness, and they are often described by aficionados as Arabian horses influenced by climate and their working history over the centuries. Although this might be a slight exaggeration, they are nonetheless most majestic creatures.

The history of the Percheron has become greatly dimmed through the centuries, and there are a number of plausible but unsubstantiated explanations for its emergence. What is known is that a horse similar in build to the Percheron existed in a region of Normandy called Le Perche as far back as the last ice age (ended c. 10,000 years ago). Le Perche is an area much given over to producing horses: the land is fertile, the soil rich in calcium, and the climate temperate. The landscape is pocked with lush valleys and crossed by the Huisne River, which wends its way through the richly agricultural area. It is also an area that has been traversed back and forth throughout its history by warring factions, and it is as a warhorse that the Percheron first garnered such acclaim.

The horses are believed by some to be related to the second of France's superlative draft breeds, the Boulonnais, and indeed the two breeds do bear some striking similarities, particularly in their quality. The Boulonnais was used by Caesar's legions as they advanced on Brittany

(58–51 B.C.E.), and it is possible these horses may have mixed with the stock at Le Perche. However, the Perche horses had developed long before the Roman invasions, possibly based on the heavy Flemish horses of northern Europe that had been brought to the area by Celtic invaders approximately four hundred years earlier. Although no actual evidence remains, it seems apparent that the small, heavy horses from Le Perche were again influenced during the eighth-century Moorish invasions by the Moors' desert-bred Arabian horses. This influence is especially seen in the vigor and spirit of the Percheron along with the smoothness of its action (for a heavy draft horse) and often in the shape and appearance of its head. It was during this time, too, that Charles Martel (688–741 C.E.) implemented the use of organized heavy cavalry—armored knights on substantial mounts riding in close formation to create an impenetrable wall of force—in a bid to stop the Moors from penetrating Europe further. His soldiers probably rode heavy European types such as the early Friesian, and possibly horses from Le Perche. It is further suggested that the horses of Le Perche were greatly influenced at this point by Arabian stallions and Barb horses captured from the Moors after Martel's victory at Poitiers in 732. Certainly the Arabian influence in the Percheron goes back to an early date and has remained most apparent.

There is evidence that one of the early Counts of the area, Robert Count of Rotrou (c. 1080–1144) brought Arabians and Spanish horses back to Le Perche with him after the First Crusade in 1096–1099. This influx of Arabian and Spanish blood is believed to have been instrumental in the early development of the Percheron, which has since been periodically subjected to further Arabian or Eastern influence, most notably from the Arabian stallions Godolphin and Gallipoly in the eighteenth century. These two stallions stood at the national stud of Le Pin, and Gallipoly went on to father Jean le Blanc (f. c. 1823), the most famous of Percheron stallions.

The local breeders of this magnificent horse have historically been incredibly clever with their breeding policies, which has led to the continued success of the breed when many other draft breeds have declined in numbers. Most significantly, the Percheron has always been bred to fill "market need," and consequently several different types of Percheron exist that can generally be divided into a heavier draft and agricultural type, and a lighter riding and coaching type. Their early worth was as a weight-carrying warhorse, but they also have an impressive turn of speed for an animal of their bulk. Percherons were also able to pull heavy loads, for which they were used during wartime and in industrial and agricultural capacities.

A finer, lighter type of Percheron was bred for pulling coaches and carriages before being replaced by the swifter coaching breeds like the Cleveland Bay and the Norman Cob. The lighter Percheron also makes a lively and comfortable riding horse and has been widely used for crossbreeding to light horse breeds to produce competition animals.

Percherons have been exported all over the world, particularly to North America, Canada, Australia, and the United Kingdom. They were used extensively by the British army during World War I as cavalry remounts and artillery horses, as well as by the French forces. The Percheron remains one of the most popular and versatile draft breeds, based in large part on its wonderful, equable temperament.

DON

HISTORIC – RUSSIA – RARE

HEIGHT
15.3–16.2 h.h.
APPEARANCE
An attractive, high-quality head that can display Oriental or Arabian-like features. The neck is generally muscular and quite long, and the back long and flat with a sloping croup and
sometimes a low-set tail. Long in the leg, occasionally with sickle hocks, and very strong hooves.
COLOR
Chestnut or brown, coat tends to have a metallic sheen.
APTITUDE
Riding, light draft, endurance, light agricultural work, cavalry

THE GRAND DON RIVER WENDS ITS WAY ACROSS the steppes of southwest Russia for 1,200 miles (1,930 km) before flowing into the Sea of Azov. Its river valleys and those of its tributaries can be fertile and richly grassed, but as the steppe stretches away on either side, there unfolds a harsh and unforgiving environment in which only the toughest animals survive. This is the home of the Don horse, Russia's most famous native breed and one of the hardiest breeds in the world. What these horses might lack in conformational excellence they more than compensate for with their extraordinary resilience.

The specific Don horse did not develop until the eighteenth and nineteenth centuries, but the stock the breed was based on has roots tracing to nomadic tribes such as the sixteenth-century Nogai that lived east of the Caspian Sea. Even before the Nogai, the area was home to the rugged Mongolian horse and its relatives, and to horses of desert influence from Kazakhstan, Turkey, and the Ukraine. The Nogai were skilled in animal husbandry and prized their tough little horses, a combination of the south Russian steppe animal and those finer, more fiery desert-bred horses such as the ancient Turkmene and its descendant the Akhal-Teke, Persian horses, and the Karabakh of Azerbaijan. The first recorded mention of these horses is from 1549, when they were originally referred to as the Old Don horse or the Don Kazakh. Though small in stature, they could survive year-round on the steppes, working all day long and living in open-range herds (called *taboons*) with no extra rations.

Organized breeding of the Don did not truly start until the eighteenth century when Orlov, Arabian, and early Thoroughbred blood was introduced to the core stock of tough mares from the steppes. The primary objective was to produce a cavalry horse that could survive the extreme conditions of the Russian steppes, and in this respect the development of the breed proved to be a resounding success. The horses achieved their greatest fame as mounts for the Don Cossacks who fought Napoleon's army during the campaigns of 1812–14. In a feat of unparalleled endurance, the Cossacks pursued Napoleon's defeated troops as they headed back to France, then turned and rode back to Moscow on their Dons in the most severe weather conditions. The French army lost thousands of their horses during the campaigns, particularly in the winter of 1812, but Don horses are quite at home in terrible conditions. They will paw the ground to remove snow and expose forage and can survive on minimal rations with very little care and attention. On top of this, they have enormous reserves of stamina and have frequently broken endurance records during performance testing. In 1899, for example, a cavalry officer rode two Don mares 1,636 miles (2,633 km) from Luben in southern Russia to Paris in just thirty days.

By the twentieth century, the Don was being bred in huge numbers in Russia and was extremely popular not only as a cavalry remount but also as an all-around horse. The breed suffered devastating losses, however, during World War I and the Russian Civil War (1918–20) and a concerted effort was then made to stabilize the breed at the Budyonny and Zimovnikovski studs in the Rostov region of southern Russia and at the Issyk-Kul stud in Kirgizia. The Budyonny stud was also home to the Budyonny horse, another highly successful breed developed primarily as a cavalry animal and based on Don, Cossack, and Thoroughbred stock. The Budyonny is essentially the Russian Warmblood and has enjoyed recent success in competitive horse sports, whereas the Don excels at endurance racing.

MARTIAL GRACE

TRAKEHNER

HISTORIC – WEST GERMANY, EAST PRUSSIA (PRESENT-DAY LITHUANIA) – COMMON

HEIGHT
16–16.3 h.h.

APPEARANCE
A high-quality, refined head; a long, well-set and well-arched neck; defined withers; a short, strong back; and muscular hindquarters. The shoulder is well conformed with a good slope that

allows for a smooth, long stride.

COLOR
Most commonly black, chestnut, bay, or brown, but can be gray and very occasionally parti-colored.

APTITUDE
Riding, light draft, cavalry, dressage, show jumping, eventing

THE TRAKEHNER IS ONE OF THE MOST MAGNIFICENT of the present-day warmblood breeds and a top equine athlete in numerous competitive fields. Between the two world wars, Trakehners won Olympic medals in dressage and eventing, and also won the prestigious Prix des Nations for show jumping. Trakehners won the arduous Pardubice Steeplechase, one of the most grueling races of its kind, a total of nine times between 1921 and 1936, and today they continue to win at the highest level in many disciplines, including dressage, show jumping, and three-day eventing.

The origins of the breed and the stock from which the Trakehner ultimately developed go back to the Scythians, a great horse people who inhabited tracts of land in Eastern Europe from approximately the sixth century B.C.E. to the first century C.E. The Scythians practiced sophisticated methods of horse management and raised horses of Central Asian origin, including the mighty Turkmenian ancestor to the Akhal Teke and horses of Mongolian descent that they brought with them from Persia. This Central Asian blood influenced the notable early stock in the Eastern European area, including the Hucul and Konik (closely related to the primitive Tarpan), and the now-extinct Schweiken pony of East Prussia, also a descendant of the Tarpan. These breeds formed the early basis from which the Trakehner would eventually develop.

In the thirteenth century, the Teutonic Knights conquered East Prussia and established a horse-breeding policy based on the versatile Schweiken. The Schweiken was a small farm horse suitable for riding, light draft, and light agricultural

work, but with the spirit and tenacity of the ancient Turkmenian. They were tough and hardy with great endurance—qualities still evident in the Trakehner.

Centuries later, under King Friedrich Wilhelm I of Prussia (1688–1740), the true foundations for the Trakehner were laid down. Friedrich saw a need to produce a faster, tougher cavalry horse and established the Royal Trakehner Stud Administration between Gumbinnen and Stallupönen in Eastern Prussia. This vast stud eventually covered around 15,000 acres and become the principal center for horse breeding in the country, based at first on carefully selected examples of existing cavalry horses to which Arabian, Turkmenian, and early Thoroughbred blood was introduced.

Meanwhile, East Prussian farmers continued to breed light agricultural horses strong enough to work in the heavy soils of the area all day long yet elegant enough to ride. These animals were introduced to the royal breeding stock, adding to the hardiness of the horses. In 1787, the royal stud activities were taken over by an administrator who further improved the stock by introducing Danish and Mecklenburg blood, as well as more Thoroughbred and Turkish blood. Breeding was divided by color, with distinct qualities developing in each group. Mares from the black herd kept at Gurdzen, for example, were noted for their strength and endurance and were slightly heavier in frame than others. Horses of the chestnut herd, developed through breeding to the Thoroughbred stallion Thunderclap XX and kept at Trakehnen, were prized for their elegance and performance; it was from this chestnut herd that the great Trakehner stallion Abglanz (f. 1943) originated. Abglanz went on to produce some of the great dressage lines and influenced the development of the Hanoverian horse. A mixed herd, which included grays, was kept at Bajorgallen and the mares bred to Arabian stallions. This herd produced two famous foundation mares, Kassette (f. 1937) and Donna (f. 1938), who were two of only a very few Trakehner mares to survive the onslaught of the Russian army during World War II.

The top stallions were kept at Trakehnen itself, where each horse was assigned a special groom and they were rigorously performance tested. Their education began at the age of three, when they were started under saddle and the horse's future would be decided: whether for cavalry, riding, or breeding. Stallion testing could last for a year, during which time the horses were thoroughly evaluated for performance, temperament, and rideability. Only the very best stallions were used for breeding, resulting in horses of an extremely high quality.

The Trakehner was used widely during World War I and greatly lauded for its endurance and spirit under duress. The breed suffered substantial losses during the war, but breeding was successfully continued afterward. The most devastating blow to the Trakehner occurred during World War II in the winter of 1944. As the Russian army advanced into East Prussia, the Trakehnen stud was evacuated and eight hundred of the best of the stock, mares, foals, and stallions, were loaded on trains to take them to safety in the west. The majority of the horses did not survive the trip, however, and many of them were captured and shipped to Russia. Private breeders were not able to leave until 1945, by which time it was almost too late. They packed up wagons with their belongings and took their horses with them, fleeing in the thousands. This excruciating eight-hundred-mile exodus to safety in extreme weather and severe conditions resulted in a catastrophic loss of human and equine life. Only twenty-one of the original mare stock from Trakehnen survived the journey.

In 1947, the West German Association of Breeders and Friends of the Warmblood Horse of Trakehnen Origin was established and with the help of dedicated breeders managed to relocate and catalog the scattered Trakehners to try to rebuild the breed. In 1950, breeding centers were established in both East and West Germany, and after the unification of Germany in 1991 the two breeding factions were united. Those horses transported by the Russians back into Russia were also bred, and today there is a distinct Russian Trakehner—like its German counterpart, a horse of enormous talent. Today the Trakehner is thriving once again. It is no longer a cavalry animal, but instead has stormed the arena of competitive riding and is a worthy contestant for the crown of king of warmbloods.

MARTIAL GRACE

WALER
HISTORIC – AUSTRALIA – RARE

HEIGHT
15–16 h.h.

APPEARANCE
A supremely elegant horse, well balanced through the frame. Quality, attractive head, well-set and carried neck, defined withers, and a deep, broad chest and rib cage. Muscular hindquarters with a good sloping shoulder.

COLOR
They are generally any solid color, being bay, black, chestnut, brown, or gray.

APTITUDE
Riding, light draft, working livestock, dressage, jumping, competitive horse sports, cavalry

AUSTRALIA, A COUNTRY OF CONTRASTS AND EXTREMES, has produced some of the finest horses on record since they first stepped onto its shores in the eighteenth century, and it now supports a thriving equestrian industry. Its first and arguably greatest horse breed, the Waler, is, however, now one of the least known beyond its shores.

The Waler's story begins in 1788, when the first horses to land on Australian soil arrived with the First Fleet that set sail from Cape Town in South Africa to establish a new colony. The fleet arrived in what became known as Port Jackson (Sydney Harbour) in New South Wales and is believed to have consisted of Barb horses: a stallion, three mares, two fillies, and a colt. Over the following years a large number of horses were imported, including early Thoroughbreds; British native pony breeds; trotters and coaching horses like the Hackney and Cleveland Bay; heavier working breeds such as the Suffolk Punch, Clydesdale, Shire, and Percherons; Arabians; and Indonesian breeds like the Timor pony. From this widely diverse pool of horses, a distinctive type started to emerge, in great part shaped by the unique Australian environment. The journey for horses to reach Australia was long and arduous, and only the strongest and hardiest actually survived the trip. From the start, then, the developing Australian horse breed was based on the very toughest genes.

Horses were indispensable to early settlers. They could cover long distances at a steady speed and were used for working the land and transporting goods, both in a draft and packing capacity, as well as for pulling lighter coaches. By crossbreeding the horses that had been imported, a general-purpose type of horse began to emerge, one that could fill any required role. Gradually this early Australian horse, now known as the indomitable Waler, developed into different types: a heavier type suitable for harder draft work and a lighter riding type. Overriding characteristics that developed early in the Waler's history and which are still dominant are its very great stamina, its ability to withstand hardship and survive on minimal rations, and its tenacity, bravery, and affable temperament. The Waler proved its worth so rapidly that it began to be used as a cavalry remount for the British army in India, and in this capacity it earned even greater respect.

The first Walers to be shipped to India were bought by a private British family in 1816, beginning a demand among private buyers for the horses. By the 1830s they had come to the attention of the British army, and by the 1840s there was a steady and lucrative trade of Walers to India. As well as being used by the British army and private homes, the Waler was also fundamental to the development of the Indian Half Bred, used by the Indian cavalry, and in improving the Indian Country Bred pony. Walers were also used for the traditional and ferocious Indian game of pig sticking and in the breeding of polo ponies.

Over time and with selective breeding, the heavier and lighter types of Waler further developed into four types, based primarily on their roles in the army, that still exist in the breed today. These are the Officers Horse, a lightweight and flashier type with a higher percentage of Thoroughbred blood; the Troopers Horse, a heavier-weight horse suitable for carrying soldiers and their equipment; the Artillery Horse, the heaviest of the four types, containing the most draft blood, used for pulling guns and ammunition loads; and the Scout Horse, the smallest of the four, containing the most pony blood, used for relaying messages quickly and also for polo and sporting events.

Walers were widely used during the Anglo-Boer War (1899–1902), with a recorded 16,357 horses shipped from Australia to South Africa. The horses were sent straight into battle as soon as they arrived, with no time to rest or acclimatize, but they rose to the challenge and worked tirelessly. Walers that remained in South Africa had a huge influence on the Boer horse and later the Basuto. They again proved their mettle during World War I, when Australia provided an entire cavalry division made up solely of Walers to fight the Germans and Turks in the North African deserts. The mounted infantry brigade earned fame as the "Desert Column" when they stormed enemy lines to take the wells of Beersheba in 1917, a surprise attack whose effectiveness was due in no small part to the courage and endurance of the soldiers' horses.

Walers were used again during World War II, and afterward the trade for Waler remounts to India did continue for a time, but by the 1950s it had dried up. This coincided somewhat with the Waler's being replaced at home by finer, flashier horses or by vehicles as the horse's role as a key part of human life diminished; meanwhile, in sporting endeavors the faster Thoroughbred had largely taken over. The pure lines of the old Waler horse gradually began to be diluted through crossbreeding to Thoroughbred horses, Arabians, and other imported breeds, resulting in the Australian Stock Horse, a beautiful and talented breed that is based on the old Waler lines but has been greatly infiltrated by outside blood.

There were just a few canny families who maintained pure Waler breeding lines, and it is thanks to their belief in the original Waler's great strengths that the breed still survives. It was not until 1986, however, that the Waler was really thrown any kind of lifeline, when two women in Tasmania set about to look for any Waler descendants. A herd was discovered near Alice Springs, where the Waler remounts had once been bred, and through studied research other similarly isolated herds were located and brought to New South Wales to be managed. Today the Waler is protected by the Waler Horse Owners and Breeders Association Australia and also the Waler Horse Society of Australia. The latter accepts only horses and their progeny derived from the old bloodlines of isolated Waler herds, with no bloodlines after 1945 being recognized. Careful management has seen this treasured Australian gem slowly reestablished.

MARTIAL GRACE

MARWARI

ANCIENT – INDIA – RARE

HEIGHT
14.2–15.2 h.h.
APPEARANCE
An elegant head well set to an arched and muscular neck. Mobile ears curl inward at the tip. Withers are defined and the body compact with a well-sprung rib cage and a long, muscular

croup. Tail is set and carried high. The natural ambling gait is called the "revaal" or "rehwal."
COLOR
Any color except albino; bright bay with a metallic sheen is most prized.
APTITUDE
Riding, dressage, jumping, competitive sports, cavalry

THE MARWARI, ALONG WITH ITS CLOSE RELATIVE the Kathiawari, is India's most respected horse breed and was historically closely affiliated with the ruling families. They are most famous as India's warhorses of the Middle Ages, and legends were written of their fearlessness and heroic exploits in battle. The horses' role in war continued right up to the twentieth century; their last great efforts were seen in 1917 in Haifa under General Allenby as part of what is today the 61st Cavalry Regiment. Significantly, this regiment is the only mounted cavalry regiment in the world to remain unmechanized.

The earliest origins of the Marwari are unrecorded. It is likely that the breed developed from the desert horses of Turkmenistan and Afghanistan, with probable Mongolian, and later Arabian, influence. Certainly the Marwari exhibits many similarities to the descendants of the ancient Turkmenian, although it has its own unique appearance and character. The Marwari is a classic desert-bred horse and thrives in the extreme climate and poor conditions of its home, namely Rajasthan, and particularly the state of Marwar (Jodphur). It is fine skinned with a very silky coat, slender framed, and has a high-quality, refined head. The Marwari is generally small, quick, and agile—the qualities that made it so useful in warfare—and has incredibly strong, sound limbs and feet, which rarely need to be shod. Most striking on first inspection are the Marwari's ears, which curve inward to touch or even overlap at the tips. This trait is also present in the Kathiawari; in fact, if the ear tips do not touch, the

horse is considered to be a poor example. This curling of the ears was almost certainly achieved through consistent and specific breeding early in the breed's development and could possibly have derived from Arabian strains. The Marwari's ears are also highly mobile, and the horse is believed to have exceptional hearing. In all respects the best examples of the Marwari breed are truly majestic animals.

Legend recounts that the Marwari was so respected that only those of royal blood, or from ruling families or warrior castes, were allowed to keep them. The early breeding of Marwaris is closely linked to specific powerful families, in particular the Rathores, who bred the horses from around the twelfth century. In 1193, the Rathores lost their Kingdom of Kanauji and retreated to the Great Indian and Thar deserts to reformulate their strategy. Their horses were absolutely essential to their survival in these remote and inhospitable areas, and without the horses for transport they would have faced certain death. Bred in the desert, the Marwaris evolved to be not only incredibly tough and hardy, but also very loyal to their riders. The loyalty of the Marwaris forms the center of nearly all the legends surrounding the breed. They were said never to leave their rider's side, and never to fall in battle, despite their own injuries, until they had carried their rider to safety. Marwaris are also reputed to have leaped city walls and taken on elephants to aid their riders in battle, allegedly standing over their injured riders to bite and kick any assailant attempting to reach them. The horses were declared "divine and superior to all men."

In 1576 Maharana Pratap (1540–97), the fiery Rajput leader of Mewar, led his soldiers to victory against the Mughals at the famous battle of Haldighat in present-day Rajastan. By all accounts he was greatly aided by the efforts of his much-loved horse Chetak, a Marwari (or Kathiawari) who launched an attack on the elephant carrying the Mughal commander Man Singh. During the attack Chetak

sustained a leg injury, but in spite of this he managed to carry his master away from the battle before staggering and falling to the ground, whereupon he died. Maharana Pratap was devastated and erected a small monument at the spot to honor his much loved horse. Today Chetak's bravery is recounted in many poems and legends. During the same period, the Mughal emperor Akbar (1542–1605) was expanding his empire across India; he also favored the Marwari and furnished his extensive cavalry with many thousands of the horses, as did the Lion of Punjab, Ranjit Singh (1780–1839), who became the first maharaja of the Sikh Empire. Ranjit Singh was passionate about horses, and when his favorite mare, Leili, thought to have been a Marwari, died, he wept inconsolably and organized a ceremonial burial with a twenty-one-gun salute.

By the twentieth century, warhorses were no longer so important and the breed's numbers had dropped dramatically. In the 1930s the late Maharaja Umaid Singhji of Jodphur, with great foresight, acquired good remaining examples of breeding stock and began a program to try to save the breed. At around the same time, Maharana Bhagwat Singh of Mewar in Udaipur started the Chetak Trust to preserve the Marwari and to work toward prevention of cruelty to animals. Several of the best stallions, including Mor, Kanaiya, Pratap, Peelo, and Rajhans, were sent to cover Marwari mares, and the efforts of a few dedicated breeders and enthusiasts have done a great deal to restore the noble Marwari breed.

However, it is the efforts of the Indigenous Horse Society of India that have truly saved the Marwari from disappearance. The society was established in 1999 by Raghuvendra Singh Dundlod, a leading authority on the breed; Francesca Kelly, a British Marwari expert; and Raja Bhupat Singh of Jodhpur, who owned Rajtilak (f. 1982), one of the best stallions of modern times, and was also a working president of the society. The tireless work of Dundlod and Kelly to preserve and promote the Marwari has seen a significant increase in the breed's numbers. Thanks also to Kelly's work, Marwari horses have now been exported to the United States, Spain, and France. Today these charismatic, beautiful horses are used for pleasure riding, by the police force, in competitive sports, and at ceremonial events, and they remain an important part of India's rich cultural heritage.

3 | SUBLIME POWER

The horse has been at the epicenter of human endeavors from prehistoric times to the mid-twentieth century, carrying cultures across the world, breaking new frontiers, winning wars, transporting produce, and working the land. Horses provided the majority of inland transport; they worked in the mining, timber, farming, and cattle industries (where they are still used today); and they packed wild game, fish, heavy-cut peat, and the illicit goods of smugglers along coastlines and borders. Throughout history, the horse has worked tirelessly in a huge range of capacities, and frequently to death; it is only comparatively recently that the horse's role as a working tool has diminished. This shift in use and priority has led to some working breeds suffering a great decline in numbers, while others have adapted to a changing lifestyle.

A significant invention in the history of the working horse was the development of the padded collar harness in China, first thought to have come into use in the East around the first century B.C.E. This form of harnessing replaced earlier, much less successful methods, which exerted enormous pressure on the horse's windpipe, making hauling heavy loads extremely difficult. With the vastly improved padded breast collar, the horse was able to pull considerable loads, and it is testament to those early Chinese inventors that this system has changed comparatively little to the present day. However, despite the collar system of harnessing, the horse was not widely used in agriculture for many hundreds of years; instead, this role was largely filled by oxen. In the Middle East and Asia, where great spiritual reverence was attached to the horse, it was maintained as a vehicle of war, for transport, and for conveying messages, whereas oxen, mules, and donkeys were made to work the land. One of the earliest mail systems was developed in Persia around the third century B.C.E., and through the use of the swift, spirited desert-bred horses a messaging system was established that ran from Egypt to Asia Minor, and India to Greece.

The Romans used their horses primarily for warfare, people passage, and transporting produce, as well as racing. Horses were used for threshing grain, but not for plowing; this remained the domain of the slow-moving oxen. The padded collar harness is thought to have arrived in Europe by the seventh century, and reference is made to horses being used for plowing and harrowing by the ninth century. In general, however, the stronger oxen were used for the heavy plowing work and the still relatively small horses used for harrowing; it was several hundred years before the enormous draft horse breeds evolved.

Although oxen were cheap to maintain, they were much slower than horses, and it is not insignificant that by the fifteenth century oxen were being phased out in the eastern region of England, East Anglia, in favor of horses. This fertile region had a long history of progressive farming, so it was unsurprising that the local farmers turned to the swifter horse to work their land. It was also in this area that the Suffolk Punch, the oldest of Britain's three heavy draft horse breeds, developed, with the earliest written accounts of this powerful horse dating to 1586. It was not until the eighteenth century, however, that oxen were replaced by the horse for heavy farm work. This change was partly driven by the development of a three-field system of crop rotation, which allowed for greater crop production in a single year and so produced enough spare grain to sustain working horses.

The majority of horses were relatively small in stature, which led to a sustained effort to increase their size. The need for larger horses in Europe was initially driven by a requirement for warhorses to create a heavy cavalry that could deflect the light cavalry tactics of Moorish horsemen during their conquests and the ensuing Crusades. This led to a policy of breeding for size and suitability for war. The horses of Belgium, the Great Horse, Flemish Horse, or Flanders Horse, were prized for their size (although still relatively short in height compared to modern equivalents) and strength and were widely exported through Europe, particularly to Britain to improve native stock. The same was true for the mighty Friesian and for the Great Warhorse of France, later known as the Breton. These sublime powerhouses were almost certainly descended from the Forest Horse of prehistory. This was a "heavy horse": a slow-moving, large-bodied, and large-boned animal that lived in the cold, damp climate of northern Europe. It was coarse-haired and had large, wide feet—a product of its marshy environment.

Henry VIII of England (1491–1547) implemented a number of laws to try to increase the size of the British horse. He ordered that "nags of small stature" be eliminated, banned the grazing of stallions under 15 hands high on common land, and decreed that every substantial landowner should own at least two mares that stood more than thirteen hands high. Working horses are not all about size, however, and they are best considered historically in three groups. The first group is made up of small utility working stock, which accounts for some of the native British pony breeds and the small horse breeds of Europe—the Icelandic, Noriker, Haflinger, and Fjord, to name a few. The second group is that of the light draft, which historically were midsized cob types and today are best represented by the Irish Draft. The third group is the heavy draft, which were developed for their size and strength and include by the Clydesdale, Shire, Suffolk Punch, Percheron, Breton, Boulonnais, and Belgian Brabant. All three types of working horse are noted for their innate strength and power, irrespective of their size.

For the most part, the small utility working breeds developed in very specific and generally isolated environments. These include the Shetland pony—whose diminutive size belies its enormous strength—which evolved in the remote Shetland Isles; the Highlander, also of Scottish origin; the Dales, from the northeastern side of the Pennines in northern England; and the Dartmoor, from southwest England. These pony breeds survived a long tradition of breeding for size, primarily because of the remoteness of their environment and because they were perfectly equipped to work within the difficult conditions of their habitat. They were easy and inexpensive to maintain and yet enormously strong. All of these breeds were adapted to cross difficult terrain while laden with heavy, packed goods: they would work all day and traverse uneven country where large horses would struggle. These small, plucky breeds were used in all areas of rural life, they worked the land, and they were ridden. Highlanders in particular were used for packing dead game animals from their point of kill back to base, while the Shetland pony, the Dales, and the Dartmoor were widely used in mining. Shetland ponies were used extensively as pit ponies, particularly after the Child Reform Law of 1847 banned children from working in the mines. Many of the ponies lived most of their lives underground, rarely seeing

daylight. Several of the smaller working breeds of Europe, such as the Norwegian Døle Gudbrandsdal and Fjord, the North Swedish, and the Finnish, were used for forestry work, and in many cases still are. Although machinery has overtaken the role of horses in most instances, there are some situations, such as forestry, in which horses are able to access areas that are unsuitable for vehicles.

In the eighteenth century in Britain, substantial improvements were made to roadways, which meant produce could be transported more quickly and in heavier loads, and personal transport could be undertaken at greater speeds. The effects of this were twofold. Firstly, the role of packing horses, where produce is transported on their backs, started to decrease and there was an increased requirement for larger, heavier, and faster draft horses able

to haul bigger loads. Secondly, there was a huge demand for lighter weight draft horses that could pull private coaches and vehicles at speed, and also work the land if required. These versatile light draft horses included the spectacular trotting breeds, such as the Norfolk Roadster, Yorkshire Roadster, and the Shales horse (all extinct), the Welsh Cob, and the Hackney. Possibly the best known of the light draft horses is, however, the superlative Irish Draft. This middleweight horse developed to excel at light draft work and as a ridden horse, making it an eminently versatile animal for the smallholding owner. The eighteenth century saw the beginnings of the agricultural and industrial revolution, which peaked during the nineteenth century. This period of enormous growth in Britain and also the United States was reflected in the development of horse breeds. Horses, which had always been pivotal to life, suddenly became crucial. A telling mark of this was the opening, in 1791, of the Veterinary College, purely for the study and treatment of equine diseases. It was not until 1872 that this was expanded to cover all animals, and the name changed to the Royal College of Veterinary Surgeons.

There were great advances in the design of horse-drawn agricultural machines during this time, such as seed drills, corn grinders, threshers, and plows. At the same time, the size of farms had started to grow, and horses provided almost all the power on farms, with some 800,000 horses working in farming in Britain during 1812. The increased size of farms led to a demand for larger, heavier, more powerful horses, which resulted in the development of breeds such as the Clydesdale, Shire, Suffolk Punch, Breton, Boulonnais, and Percheron. These giant horses were specifically bred for their hauling capabilities (although some can also make suitable riding horses), and they were second to none in this capacity, working in the fields and hauling goods on the roads. The massive machines designed to cope with the vast tracts of arable land in the United States were so huge that some were pulled by teams of more than forty horses, no doubt an extraordinary sight to behold.

The same period saw the construction of Britain's network of canals across the country, which provided passage for both people and freight. Huge barges were pulled by equally robust horses, some of which needed to be smaller than fifteen hands high to pass beneath the bridges along the tow path. These gentle and powerful horses led a hard life; traversing the tow paths was frequently difficult and sometimes they were required to jump fences, stiles, and obstacles in their way while continuing to haul heavy loads. The construction of the railways also saw a big demand for horses that could haul goods and raw materials between the trains and the depots. Heavy draft horses were used for the largest loads, while the lighter Irish Draft type hauled lighter goods more quickly; a further express service was based on the swift trotting breeds, including the Welsh Cob. Huge draft horses were employed in the rail yards to shunt rolling stock, with the last of its kind retired from service in Newmarket in 1967, and equally massive horses were used to haul the horse-drawn trains, which operated through Britain and in parts of Europe.

As populations increased, horses were employed exponentially in cities for transport and delivery services, with an estimated 175,000 horses working in New York City in 1880. The life of these urban draft horses was largely miserable, and they were worked almost to death. The working life span of horses pulling trams, for instance, was just four years. Horses continued to be used into the twentieth century, although their role was starting to decrease with the advent of electric trams and motorized machinery. Hundreds of thousands of horses were used by the military during World War I, not only for riding but also large quantities of draft horses (and mules and donkeys) were used to haul equipment. After the end of the war and with advances in technology, there was a gradual decrease in the number of draft horses used in farming, industry, and transportation, and after World War II their role became all but obsolete as motorization became the norm. The massive draft breeds suffered most, because they are the least versatile for the modern horse owner. Fortunately, concerted efforts by enthusiasts and breed societies continue to try to maintain these magnificent horses, and they are still used on a small scale by breweries, rural farmers, and for displays and showing. The lighter and smaller draft breeds have fared better in changing times. These horses have been adapted to become noteworthy riding animals, while some breeds are still worked in rural farming and forestry.

FJORD

ANCIENT — NORWAY — COMMON

HEIGHT
13.2–14.2 h.h.

APPEARANCE
A short but arched neck and a very attractive head with a slightly concave profile and wide-set eyes. Flat withers, short, strong back, and short, sturdy legs. Quarters are
rounded and muscular and the chest is deep and wide.

COLOR
One of five kinds of dun: brown, gray, red, white, or yellow.

APTITUDE
Riding, light draft, light agricultural work, packing, dressage, jumping

THE STUNNING NORWEGIAN LANDSCAPE, with its jagged mountains and deep, glistening fjords, was shaped by prehistoric glaciers, and it is to this same age of ice and bitter cold that one must turn to discover the origins of its most famous equine, the Fjord. This beautiful and versatile small horse—it is a small horse, not a pony, despite its height—is native to Norway, and it was in this rugged land that the breed evolved its particular characteristics. However, as with so many horse breeds, the ancestors to the Fjord were undoubtedly the primitive horses of Central Asia, specifically the Asiatic Wild Horse and the Eurasian Tarpan of Eastern Europe and western Russia. The Fjord has the distinction of having retained its primitive appearance to a very great degree, and, with the exception of its high-quality head, it still bears a striking physical resemblance to the Asiatic Wild Horse.

Precisely when the primitive horses of Central Asia and Eurasia crossed into northern Europe is unclear, but it is known that the ancestor to the Fjord had arrived in Norway by the time of the last ice age (approximately 10,000 years ago). Once there, the horses remained essentially genetically pure because of the isolated nature of their environment, and they have been subjected to little outside influence throughout their history. As a result, the physical characteristics of the Fjord are quite uniform and distinctive throughout the breed. They are highly attractive small horses and are always one of five different variations of dun in color, normally retaining the primitive dark markings associated with dun horses, namely dark legs, sometimes

with zebra stripes, and a dark dorsal strip. Fjord horses have a centerline of dark hair that grows down the middle of the mane bordered on each side by blonder hairs. Although the mane will grow to a normal equine length, traditionally it is trimmed short enough to allow the coarse hairs to stand upright and to reveal the dark line of hair growth in the center, exaggerating the horse's naturally impressive crest. This tradition of trimming manes can be dated back to the Vikings from the eighth century C.E., and there are many stone carvings from this time that depict Fjords in this way.

The Fjord was the Vikings' warhorse and carried them on many warring excursions, though the horses were also used to pull carts and pack heavy loads. Over the centuries, the Fjord's strengths as a working animal continued to be greatly appreciated by the Norwegians, and these small, enormously strong animals worked the land in all capacities, from plowing heavy soils and dragging logs for the timber industry to pulling carts and wagons and trekking sure-footedly through treacherous mountain terrain. They also made excellent riding horses.

Although Fjords are used less now in agriculture and industry than they were in the past, they are still used for transporting tourists and are particularly noted for their use with disabled riders and therapeutic schools. The horses are also used extensively in competitive driving competitions with great success and are prized for trekking and riding schools because of their wonderful temperament. Indeed, its incredible temperament is one of the most outstanding features of the Fjord; the horses are calm, quiet, and loyal, but will also respond with spirit and energy when being ridden.

Thanks to its very great qualities and versatility, the Fjord has smoothly made the transition from a working animal of yesteryear into a modern-day all-rounder. It is Norway's best-known horse and an important part of Norwegian culture, and has now been exported widely, enjoying considerable popularity in the United States, Canada, and Great Britain in particular.

DALES
ANCIENT – ENGLAND – ENDANGERED

HEIGHT
14–14.2 h.h.
APPEARANCE
A middle weight and muscular animal. Exceptionally attractive head set to a finely arched and muscular neck. Strong shoulders, a short back, and muscular hindquarters.

The legs are stout and sound, and the feet incredibly tough.
COLOR
Black, brown, bay, or gray.
APTITUDE
Riding, light draft, light agricultural work, packing, dressage, jumping, competitive horse sports

THE DALES PONY SHARES MUCH OF ITS ANCESTRY with its smaller relative the Fell but originated in the northeast rather than northwest of Britain. It was along the northeastern side of the Pennines—from the High Peak in Derbyshire to the Cheviot Hills near the Scottish border and throughout the upper dales of Tyne, Allen, Swale, Wear, and Tees—that the Dales pony developed. This was an area that from Roman times boasted a flourishing

mining industry, and it was for use in the mines, primarily as a pack pony, that the Dales was originally bred. Coinciding with the construction of Hadrian's Wall (c. 122 B.C.E.) there was an influx of Friesian blood to the area, and the Friesian influence remains evident in the modern Dales pony, particularly in its proud carriage and extravagant knee action at the trot. During the seventeenth century— and undoubtedly long before—the tough Scottish Galloway ponies (now extinct) were brought to the area and allowed to mix with native stock, upgrading it in size and strength.

The Dales pony was indispensable to the mining industry of the north and highly prized for its incredible stamina, ability to pack and haul huge weights at speed, and sure-footed passage over steep, rocky terrain. The ponies were used to transport the mined lead cross-country to the ports on the northeast coastline and to

transport fuel and coal back to the mines, and they became famous for their endurance and tremendous strength. A pack load weighed approximately 240 pounds (110 kg), and the ponies commonly traveled up to or even more than 100 miles (160 km) a week carrying these loads. Their value was not lost on local farmers, and the Dales became a popular agricultural animal used for light plowing, tilling, transporting crops, and other farming activities. They were much prized as riding horses, too, for their flashy appearance, comfort, and ability to cover great distances at a spanking trot.

During the eighteenth century, particularly with the advent of mail and stagecoaches, demand for faster road horses increased greatly. In order to shape the Dales to meet this new requirement, blood from the now extinct Norfolk Trotter (Roadster) was introduced to the breed. The Norfolk Trotter was the preeminent trotting horse of the day along with the also extinct Yorkshire Roadster. Both of these trotting breeds traced their heritage to the horse Shales the Original (f. 1755), a horse predominantly of early Thoroughbred blood who passed his very great trotting ability on to all his progeny. The Norfolk and Yorkshire infusion improved the Dales'

already impressive trot, which was then further enhanced through the use of the Welsh stallion Comet (f. 1877).

Early in the twentieth century, Clydesdale blood was introduced to the Dales with moderate success, and many Dales were subsequently used by the British army in World War I. The Dales Pony Improvement Society was formed in 1916 to protect and preserve the breed, and a studbook opened. The ponies were again greatly used during World War II, and many of them traveled overseas with the British army. This, combined with indiscriminate breeding and the loss of their owners, led to a catastrophic decline in the number of Dales after the war. In 1964, the Dales Pony Society was restructured and a concerted effort was made to increase the numbers of Dales while maintaining their high standard.

Although the requirement for Dales in an industrial or agricultural capacity has dropped sharply away, this supremely versatile animal continues to be one of the most useful and elegant of Britain's native breeds. The Dale excels at most ridden events and makes an excellent driving pony. The pony is a "good doer" and a thrifty eater, exhibits an exuberant trot, and has the added advantage of a particularly quiet and trainable nature.

HAFLINGER
ANCIENT – AUSTRIA – COMMON

HEIGHT
13.3–14.3 h.h.

APPEARANCE
A high-quality head that reflects its Oriental heritage, with a well-proportioned and well-set neck. Back is muscular and the croup strong and sloping. Deep and wide through the chest, with exceptionally strong limbs and feet.

COLOR
Varying shades of chestnut with flaxen mane and tail.

APTITUDE
Riding, light draft, packing, dressage, jumping, competitive horse sports, cavalry

THE BEAUTIFUL AND DISTINCTIVE HAFLINGER developed in ancient times in the picturesque southern Austrian Tirol, specifically around the village of Hafling. This mountainous area has a long tradition of horses and is home also to the Noriker horse, which developed slightly to the east.

The Tirolese valleys saw a heavy passage of people and cultures through the centuries. The descendants of the Ostrogoths brought their small Oriental horses to the area in the sixth century, and the horses are thought to have benefited from the introduction of a stallion brought to the area from the kingdom of Burgundy in the fourteenth century, but more than these early influences, it was the geography of the area that truly shaped the small horses. Away from the passes and valleys, the mountainous areas provided an isolated habitat in which the horses developed. They are hardy and tough, able to thrive in the extreme cold and to live on sparse rations, while the thin mountain air contributed to the Haflinger's developing a strong heart and lungs. Even today young stock is still reared on the Alpine pastures at high altitude, which perpetuates the breed's desirable qualities.

The Haflinger's character was cemented in the nineteenth century, primarily through Arabian blood. In 1874, Josef Folie bred the Oriental stallion 133 El Bedavi XXII to a local mare, which resulted in an exquisite colt foal later named 249 Folie. The foal was a brilliant golden chestnut with a flaxen mane and tail and described as being the best combination of solid native stock with Arabian features. Folie became the foundation sire of the modern Haflinger,

with seven of his sons founding Haflinger lines. It was from Folie that the Haflinger derives its distinctive coloring, which ranges from chestnut to golden chestnut or palomino, though during the early years of the breed's development other colors such as black did occur, as did the occasional dark dorsal stripe. White markings should not be present on the legs, but horses can have a white star, snip, blaze, or stripe on the face. These horses were extremely popular in the Tirol for their versatility and were highly sought after by local farmers for use in agriculture and the timber industry, for packing, and for riding, and were particularly famed for their sure-footedness, able to traverse their mountainous and often treacherous habitat with ease and speed.

Systematic, organized breeding of the Haflinger truly began in 1921 with the formation of the North Tirolean Horse Breeders' Cooperative. The Haflinger had suffered during World War I when many of the horses were drafted into military use and other valuable breeding stock was lost after the Treaty of Saint Germain, signed in 1919, which resulted in South Tirol—including Hafling, where many of the best brood mares were—coming under Italian authority. The cooperative established the first studbook for the breed in 1926, and consistent selective breeding with emphasis on quality resulted in its continued improvement. Added to this, at the end of the 1920s, one hundred high-quality Haflinger mares from South Tirol were purchased and distributed among the North Tirol breeders and those of Upper Austria and Styria.

The Haflinger stock that remained in South Tirol and is found throughout the Italian Alps and Apennines is known as the Avelignese. There is some debate over whether the Haflinger and Avelignese are the same breed. What is clear, however, is that these two horses share extremely similar ancestral roots and bear a striking physical similarity to each other. The Avelignese is generally bred to be slightly larger and more draft-like than the Haflinger and is still widely used for light agricultural work.

DARTMOOR
ANCIENT – ENGLAND – VULNERABLE

HEIGHT	COLOR
Up to 12.2 h.h.	*Bay, black, brown, or gray;*
APPEARANCE	*piebalds and skewbalds are*
Attractive head with small	*not allowed.*
ears and an intelligent eye. A	**APTITUDE**
sturdy, muscular build and	*Riding, light draft, light*
long, sloping shoulder, which	*agricultural work, packing,*
lends them a particularly	*dressage, jumping, competitive*
long, low, smooth trot.	*horse sports*

THE MOORLANDS where the plucky Dartmoor pony evolved stretch across southwest England, running through the center of the county of Devon and encompassing spectacular countryside, rushing rivers, rocky tors, valleys, wetlands, and bogs. The first mention of ponies on Dartmoor was in 1012 in the will of Saxon bishop Aelfwold of Crediton, though fossil evidence indicates that ponies roamed across England more than 10,000 years ago. Unlike the Exmoor—the oldest of the British breeds and a close neighbor to the Dartmoor though one that remained very pure and unchanged through its history because of the isolation of its environment—the ponies that arrived on Dartmoor were subject to enormous external influences from the high volume of traffic through this area.

Tin mining on Dartmoor, which dates back to before the Roman occupation of Britain and continued to the twentieth century, was largely responsible for this heavy traffic, and the horses and ponies required as transport and pack animals for the mining industry would have crossbred with any native stock. The ponies on Dartmoor were themselves widely used in the mining industry, mostly to transport the mined metal off the moors and to the nearest towns. Whenever the industry waned, many of these ponies would have been turned loose onto the moors, where they maintained a semi-feral existence. Even then, however, the Dartmoor continued to be eminently useful as a farm animal, its relative strength for its size and need for less feed than larger animals making it popular with farmers. During the Industrial Revolution in the eighteenth century,

Dartmoors began to be used for coal mining, and a number of Shetland stallions were released on the moors to breed with Dartmoors in an attempt to improve their usefulness as pit ponies. Unfortunately, this resulted in a loss of quality in the pony, though this has since been rectified.

As the interest in sports, in particular polo, grew through the nineteenth and twentieth centuries, the Dartmoor enjoyed a resurgence in popularity. The National Pony Society was formed in 1893, soon after becoming known as the Polo Pony Society, and the Dartmoor was initially entered into their studbook. In 1925, the Dartmoor Pony Society was established and a more specific type was set for the Dartmoor; subsequently the Dartmoor pony kept in studs and private homes has become an extremely high-quality riding pony. A few Dartmoors still live a semi-feral existence on the moors, and although these ponies exhibit excellent hardiness and an ability to survive on minimal rations, they are not generally of the same quality.

The elegance of privately bred ponies and their agility and endurance made them excellent polo ponies, particularly when crossed to small Thoroughbreds and Arabians, which Prince Edward (Edward VIII) (1874–1972), who kept Dartmoor ponies near Princetown, did in 1920. It was around this time that the Arabian stallion Dwarka (f. 1892) was used on Dartmoor mares to improve the stock, and Dwarka's son The Leat (f. 1918) had a significantly positive effect on the ponies. It was through The Leat's line that the Dartmoor stallion Jude (f. 1941), one of the most famous Dartmoor ponies, was bred.

The breed was decimated during World War II, with only a few registered ponies remaining after the war. There has since been a concerted effort to restore the breed, and today, although still listed as vulnerable, the Dartmoor is very much evident. Dartmoors make excellent children's riding ponies and dominate in the show ring. They have also proved to make fantastic competition ponies when crossed with small Thoroughbred and Arabian horses and Welsh ponies.

MAREMMANA
HISTORIC — ITALY — RARE

HEIGHT
15–16.1 h.h.

APPEARANCE
A large, noble head with either a straight or ram-like profile. Extremely muscular, arched, well-set neck. Deep and wide through the chest with well-defined withers. A long, strong back, muscular hindquarters, and a slightly sloping croup. Exceptionally strong limbs and feet.

COLOR
Any solid color.

APTITUDE
Riding, light draft, classical dressage

THE MAREMMA IS A LARGELY UNDISCOVERED and totally unspoiled coastal area of Tuscany that comprises rocky peninsulas hiding sandy bays, rugged salt marshes, great swaths of pine forest, and huge tracts of cattle-rearing land. Tucked away in relative isolation is one of Italy's best-kept secrets, the Maremmana horse, which is the mainstay of the Italian cowboys, or *butteri*. Just as the golden light of Italy infuses the atmosphere with a sense of wild romance, so too does this extend to the Maremmana, which retains a compelling mystique not unlike that of the white Camargue horse of France.

Indigenous to Italy, the Maremmana is based on ancient stock, with the first evidence for the presence of horses here dating to the Etruscans around the seventh century B.C.E. The horses evolved in the wild marshes between Pisa and Caserta, where they established their hardiness and ability to thrive on meager rations. It is highly probable that these tough native horses were greatly influenced early in their history by the North African Barb, and the shape of the Maremmana's head and its incredible endurance would seem to confirm this.

During the fifteenth, sixteenth, and seventeenth centuries, horse breeding in Italy flourished, and there was great demand for talented dressage horses for use in the High School. To meet these demands, Spanish, Arabian, and Barb horses were imported, and there was emphasis on the improvement of the grand Neapolitan horse. (The Neapolitan, now extinct, was an Italian horse largely based on Spanish blood and was extremely popular for classical dressage.) Although the Maremmana was not used in the High School, it is highly likely that the breed was influenced by these horses, evidence of which could be seen in the breed's modern quality and majesty. Maremmanas were also used widely on small farms in a light agricultural capacity, as well as for working cattle, a job at which they continue to excel. The breed was also popular as a cavalry remount and was widely used by both cavalry and police.

During the nineteenth century, the breed was greatly refined through the introduction of Thoroughbred blood as well as that of the now-extinct English Norfolk Roadster; at the stud at Grosseto, the Maremmana was bred to be an energetic saddle horse. The modern foundation sires of the breed, however, are from the twentieth century and include the Maremmana stallion Othello (f. 1927) and the Thoroughbreds Ajax (f. 1926) and Ingres (f. 1946). These influences have produced a refined version of the Maremmana that is more elegant in appearance than the old agricultural type but has retained all the valued qualities of stamina, toughness, and agility. The horses are extremely talented at working cattle and are still widely used in the ranching industry. However, Maremmanas and Maremmana crossbreds have proved to make exceptional competition horses, particularly in the sphere of show jumping; the purebred Maremmana Ursus del Lasco, ridden by Graziano Mancinelli, won the 1977 Italian jumping championship.

Many Maremmanas are still bred in semi-feral conditions, which has greatly contributed to the perpetuation of their hardiness. Typically a small group of ten to fifteen mares is allowed to run with a stallion through the breeding season, allowing for a process of natural selection. As long as the quality of the mares is carefully maintained, this unregulated breeding still results in high-quality stock. Other stud farms in the Maremma breed purebred and crossbred horses specifically for jumping.

BRETON

ANCIENT — FRANCE — COMMON

HEIGHT	COLOR
15–16 h.h.	*Chestnut with a flaxen*
APPEARANCE	*mane and tail, though*
Square head, often with a	*can also be red or*
slightly dished profile, is well set	*bay roan.*
to a muscular neck. Short and	**APTITUDE**
wide in the back with massive	*Heavy draft, agricultural*
hindquarters, a deep, wide	*work, riding, cavalry,*
chest, and short, strong limbs.	*meat production*

THE LOVELY BRETON, INSTANTLY RECOGNIZABLE as a high-quality draft and riding horse with a well-proportioned and balanced frame, is an iconic feature of cultural life in Brittany and has for centuries been a great source of pride for the region's people. From around 900 B.C.E. Brittany was inhabited by the Veneti, a Celtic seafaring tribe famed for its horse-breeding skills. The horses of the Veneti could have influenced the early development of the Austrian Noriker and Haflinger, as well as being the ancestors to the Breton horse. Other possible origins for the horses of Brittany are the primitive horses from the steppes of Central Asia, which were brought to the area by early warring nomads of Indo-European cultures, though a link to the prehistoric Forest Horse cannot be discounted.

Brittany's rugged, breathtaking landscape gave rise to a hardy, stout, muscular horse that was bred early on to be versatile. There is a long tradition of specialized breeding in Brittany to produce horses to fill market need; this has led to the continued success of the Breton, and to a number of different types. In the Middle Ages, Bretons were highly sought after for their weight-carrying abilities. The native stock was crossed with Oriental horses to improve their speed and agility, giving rise to the Bidet Breton. The Bidet Breton was small in height, topping out at around 14 h.h., but was strong and highly prized for its comfortable but swift ambling pace. Many centuries later, the Bidet Breton is said to have been the only French breed of horse to have survived Napoleon Bonaparte's (1769–1821) retreat from Russia in 1812.

Throughout the Middle Ages, the Bidet Breton evolved into two types, the Sommier and the Rossier. The Sommier was the larger of the two and was bred for packing and heavy draft work in an agricultural capacity, though even this massively framed horse was still suitable for riding. The Rossier retained the Bidet's smooth gait but was a lighter riding horse able to traverse the countryside quickly and comfortably.

With continued selective breeding, a further three different kinds of Breton horse were developed: the Cheval de Corlay, the Postier, and the Heavy Breton (Trait). The Cheval de Corlay was produced by crossing Bretons with Arabians and Thoroughbreds and is a small, lighter-weight riding horse that is also used for racing. The Cheval de Corlay has largely disappeared today, however, and in its place is the jewel of Brittany's breeding, the Postier, originally developed to pull the mail coaches. The Postier was produced by crossing lighter Bretons with the now-extinct trotting breed the English Norfolk Roadster, resulting in a superior type of Breton that is both elegant and energetic; the Postier has a superlative trot and yet is still heavy enough to perform light draft work. The final type is the Heavy Breton, bred primarily on the northern coastal areas of Brittany. The Heavy Breton was developed through crossing with the Boulonnais, Percheron, and Ardennais to create a massively framed, powerful horse.

The only types of Breton horse recognized today are the Postier and Heavy Breton. Beginning in 1909, they each had their own studbook, but in 1912 the two were combined in one volume with separate sections, and since 1926 there has been a single studbook for both types. Although the Breton has been used to improve the base stock of other breeds, there have been no further influences of foreign blood on the Breton since 1920, and as such the breed remains very pure and true to type—a heavy yet athletic horse with excellent conformation.

BOULONNAIS
ANCIENT – FRANCE – RARE

HEIGHT
15.1–16.2 h.h.

APPEARANCE
The head reflects its Arabian ancestry, with a long, elegant neck and fine frame. Well-defined withers, a reasonably sloping shoulder, and a deep, wide chest. Legs are long and very strong with little feathering. A short, thick mane and often quite bushy tail.

COLOR
Predominantly gray, but can be bay, black, or chestnut.

APTITUDE
Heavy draft, agricultural work, riding, cavalry, meat production

THE MAJESTIC POWERHOUSE OF NORTHWEST FRANCE and the Boulogne-Calais hinterland is the Boulonnais, one of the most elegant and attractive of all draft breeds. The Boulonnais is an extraordinary combination of cold-blood and hot-blood characteristics, with all the strength and size of a draft horse but clothed with the quality and spirit of the Arabian. Noted for the freedom of its stride, excellent temperament, and great stamina, it is a truly impressive breed, but one whose numbers are sadly diminished.

In Roman times, the Boulonnais lived in the area around the Boulogne coastline, but it probably originally descended from the primitive Forest Horse. The most significant early influence on these French horses was from North African Barbs, which were brought through the area when Caesar (100–44 B.C.E.) camped with his army near Cape Gris-Nez in 54 B.C.E. on his way to invade Britain. The next major development in the breed's history occurred in the Middle Ages during the Crusades. This was a fundamentally important period for the evolution of modern horses because of the exchange of Eastern and Western blood between so many breeds; in particular, large quantities of Oriental and Arabian blood were introduced to the heavier European breeds. During this period, two noblemen—Eustache, Comte de Boulogne (c. 1015/20–c. 1087) and Robert, Comte d'Artois (1287–1342)—improved the French horses by using Arabian stallions on the native stock at their stud farms to produce a more elegant and spirited horse suitable for draft work and riding.

In the fourteenth century, Mecklenburg horses from Germany were crossed with the Boulonnais to increase its size and make it suitable for carrying armored knights. In the sixteenth century there was substantial crossbreeding to Andalusian and other Spanish breeds as Flanders came under Spanish occupation. The breed was not actually named until the seventeenth century, though it had already earned an admirable reputation for its elegance and power. Boulonnais horses were bred in large numbers and traded extensively with dealers coming from Picardie and Haute-Normandie.

Eventually, the breed developed into two distinct types, each bred for a specific purpose. The first type, which has sadly all but disappeared, was a smaller Boulonnais that stood up to around 15.3 hands high and was known as the Mareyeuses or Petite Boulonnais. These strong but fast horses were used to transport fish from Boulogne to Paris in carts filled with ice. The horses had to travel quickly enough to arrive before the ice melted and the fish were spoiled, and they were greatly prized for their spanking trot. The second type is heavier and still exists today, although in greatly reduced numbers. This larger horse has a greater draft capacity but still exhibits an extraordinarily active and free trot for a horse of its size. These heavy Boulonnais can stand up to around 16.2 hands high and are also raised for their meat.

World War I had a devastating effect on the Boulonnais; the breed's use in active military service and the destruction of much of its homeland almost completely wiped it out. The Boulonnais suffered a further reduction in numbers during World War II, which caused an interruption to breeding programs. By this time, too, its role was largely superseded by motorized vehicles and advances in farm technology. Despite these setbacks, the horses can still be found in small numbers working on smaller farms and continue to be bred for the meat industry, as well as by a number of enthusiasts.

BELGIAN BRABANT

ANCIENT – BELGIUM – RARE

HEIGHT
15.2–17.2 h.h.
APPEARANCE
A particularly fine, elegant head and well-arched neck set to sloping shoulders. The back is short, wide, and muscular and the hindquarters rounded and very powerful. Legs are short but noted for their strength and soundness.
COLOR
Bay, black, and chestnut; sometimes roan or gray.
APTITUDE
Heavy draft, agricultural work, riding, cavalry

ONE OF HISTORY'S "SUPERHORSES," THE Belgian Brabant developed around the region of Brabant and across Flanders in the north of Belgium. It is one of the most ancient heavy draft breeds, preceded by its close relative the Ardennais, and both breeds trace their roots back to the heavy, prehistoric Forest Horse.

The great merit and quality of these horses had already been established by Roman times; Julius Caesar (100–44 B.C.E.) even mentioned their endurance and biddable temperament in his writings on the Gallic War. In fact it was war that first shaped these horses, as they were the mount of choice for knights and soldiers during the Middle Ages. At that time, horses from the region were referred to as the Flanders horse (sometimes the Flemish horse) or simply the Great Horse, and were heavy, high-quality riding horses also suitable for pulling vehicles. Such was their reputation that they were exported all over the world and have consequently had a significant effect on the development of many other draft breeds, including the Shire, Clydesdale, Suffolk Punch, Irish Draft, and Percheron.

Whereas the Ardennais lived in the forested, hilly areas of southern Belgium and northern France, the Brabant developed primarily in the lush agricultural areas of central Belgium and was bred to be able to fulfill many roles: warhorse, carriage animal, and agricultural worker. The Brabant, which is now called the Belgian Heavy Draft, was kept largely free from external breed influences as efforts were made to maintain and improve on the horse's esteemed qualities, leaving it very pure. By the 1860s, three separate types of this Belgian horse had developed, the first being the line of *Gros de la Dendre* founded by the stallion Orange I (f. 1863). These horses were the most massive of the three types and generally bay in color. Orange I produced a series of champions, including his son Brilliant and his grandson Reve d'Or (f. 1890). The second line was the *Gris du Hainaut*, founded by the stallion Bayard (f. 1890), predominately gray, red roan, dun, and sorrel in color; the third was the *Colosses de la Mehaique*, founded by the stallion Jean I and esteemed for the toughness and soundness of their legs. Today, however, the three lines are barely distinguishable.

The Belgian government realized the worth of this homegrown asset and established a number of regional breed shows that culminated in championships at the National Show in Brussels. This became a showcase for the breed and attracted a large measure of international interest. In 1903, the Belgian government sent some of their best Brabants to the St. Louis World's Fair, which generated much U.S. interest in the breed and began a healthy trade in horses from Belgium to the United States. This came to an abrupt halt with the onset of World War I, leaving American breeders responsible for establishing their own breeding stock of horses from Belgium, fostering the emergence in America of a very distinct type of draft horse, based on the Belgian Brabant, but bred to be finer and lighter in build, taller in height, and with clean limbs. This breed is officially called the American Belgian and is now quite different in appearance from the Belgian Brabant. It is predominantly chestnut with a flaxen mane and tail, is one of the most popular draft breeds in the United States, and has enjoyed a healthy resurgence.

The Belgian Brabant was used widely during both world wars, but as with all draft breeds it suffered an enormous decline with increasing mechanization. More recently there has been a renewed interest in the breed, which is still bred for meat production and driving competitions.

CLYDESDALE
HISTORIC – SCOTLAND – VULNERABLE

HEIGHT
16–18 h.h.

APPEARANCE
A noble head with large, wide-set eyes and a well-formed neck. Defined withers and a short, strong back leading into long, muscular hindquarters. Long in the leg with sound feet and long, silky feathering on the legs.

COLOR
Bay or brown; sometimes black, gray, roan, or chestnut, with white markings on face and legs.

APTITUDE
Heavy draft, agricultural work, riding, showing, cavalry

ALTHOUGH THE CLYDESDALE is a heavy draft horse, it has all the attitude and elegance of a much lighter-weight horse. It is a large creature, among the tallest of horses, and has a huge pulling capacity, but despite this the Clydesdale is not a massive horse. It does not have the weight and bulk of the northern European heavy breeds such as the French Breton and the Ardennais, and it is beautifully proportioned, as well as being one of the most athletic breeds for its size.

The modern history of the Clydesdale dates to the eighteenth century, although the stock from which the breed developed is much older and could have had the prehistoric Forest Horse at its roots. There has also been a long tradition of hardy, working horses in Scotland that dates back to pre-Roman times and to the Picts, a Celtic people who lived in northern and eastern Scotland until around the tenth century. The Picts were primarily farming people who raised crops and kept livestock. The quantity and quality of their cattle and horses were a sign of wealth, and it is likely that they operated a selective breeding process to increase the size of both these animals. Later, the Romans brought a substantial number of horses to England from northern Europe particularly during Julius Caesar's invasions of 55 and 54 B.C.E., but also in subsequent years and throughout Roman domination

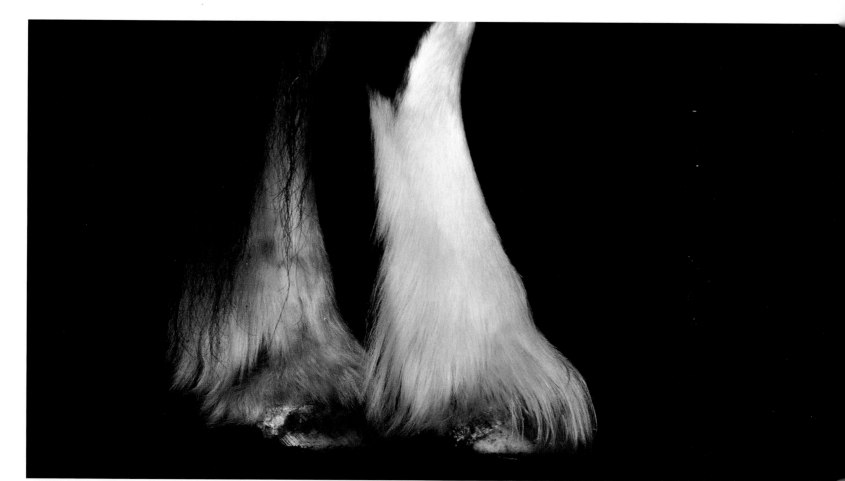

of the island, which were of influence on English horses and those over the borders in what is now Scotland—particularly from 71 to 213 C.E., when the Roman Empire had a huge influence in Scotland.

These horses, which included Friesians brought over during construction of Hadrian's Wall begun around 122 C.E., bred with local native stock and developed characteristics based on their environment, and further qualities were fixed through deliberate breeding. This was the base stock from which the Clydesdale was originally developed. The horses needed to be hardy to cope with the inclement weather and sure-footed to travel across the difficult terrain; they were used for farming and transport, riding, and packing and were tough, versatile animals.

The breed developed specifically in Lanarkshire, which was traditionally called Clydesdale after the river Clyde, which flows through the area. The local farmers wanted to improve the quality, size, and strength of their native horses, particularly to produce a horse that was capable of hauling coal from the developing coalfields. Roadways had improved significantly by this time, allowing for the more efficient transportation of hauled rather than packed goods.

The first step toward developing the breed was the introduction of the great Flemish horse, or Belgian Draft, to the local stock, which occurred between 1715 and 1720 when the sixth Duke of Hamilton imported a number of Flemish stallions. Flemish horses were not new to Scotland—they had been imported for some years for use on the land because of their strength and size and had also been popular as warhorses—but this appears to be an early occurrence of a considered breeding program between the Flemish stallions and local mares as the duke, a major landowner, made his stallions available to his tenants. Meanwhile, one John Paterson of Lochlyoch brought a Flemish stallion up from England who would have a particular influence on early stock. This stallion was black with a white face and white markings on his legs and gave rise to a number of impressive offspring, which rapidly became very popular as word of these large, strong, beautiful horses spread.

Another black horse with white markings who was important to the early breed development was Blaze, a native stallion who came to Lanarkshire from Ayrshire and had won a gold medal in 1782 at the Edinburgh show. Although his heritage is unclear, it is widely believed that

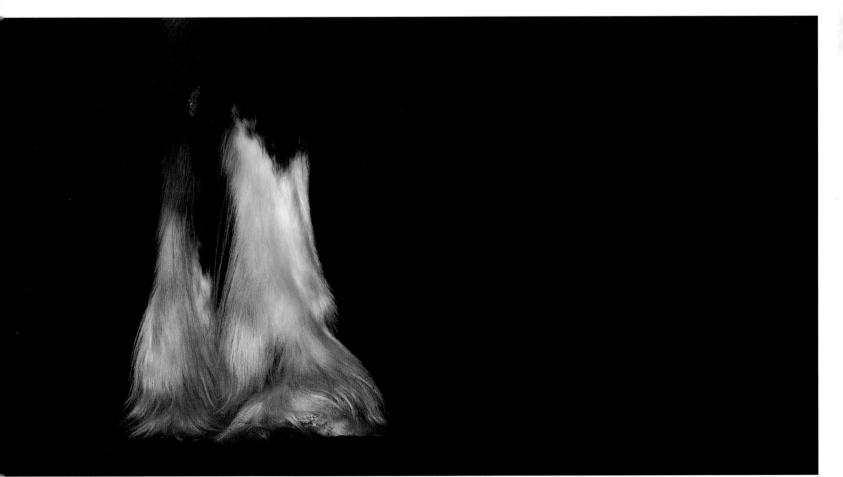

Blaze had some coaching blood, which might explain the great freedom of movement inherent in the Clydesdale.

A defining year for the emerging Clydesdale was 1808. It was during this year that a gentleman breeder, Mr. Somerville, purchased what later came to be known as the Lampit's Mare, and it is to this mare and her progeny that many Clydesdale lines are traced. Among others, she produced Farmer's Fancy and Glancer (also known as Thompson's Black Horse), a foundation stallion for the Clydesdale breed. His descendant was Broomfield's Champion 95 (f. 1831), a great horse who in turn had a son called Clyde (or Glancer 153), who is said to have contributed many of the characteristics seen and appreciated in the modern Clydesdale.

The popularity of the Clydesdale rose during the nineteenth century as the horses proved their extraordinary worth within agriculture and industry. Their strength was unmatched, but alongside this phenomenal power they were also agile, moved well, looked good, and had superb temperaments. They were used primarily for farming in Scotland and for work in the coalfields, eventually replacing the Shire horse in this northern area. Word of the Clydesdale's merits extended far beyond its Scottish homeland, with an amazing twenty thousand horses recorded as being exported internationally between 1880 and 1945. Many Clydesdales were shipped to Australia and New Zealand, as well as Russia, Austria, and the Americas, and it is in North America in particular that the breed still flourishes. The horses were used extensively during World War I, but their numbers began to decrease after the war. In England, there were two hundred licensed Clydesdale stallions in 1946, but by 1949 this had dropped to eighty.

As with all heavy horse breeds, their decline mirrored advances in mechanization when they were largely replaced in the workplace by vehicles. There has been a recent renewed interest in these beautiful horses, which has seen a concerted effort to improve breed numbers, and the UK Rare Breed Survival Trust has moved their listing from rare to vulnerable. Because of their athleticism, Clydesdales are now being used as heavy-weight riding horses or for crossbreeding to lighter stock to produce competition horses.

SHIRE

HISTORIC – ENGLAND – AT RISK

HEIGHT
16.3–18 h.h.
APPEARANCE
An attractive head, large, kind eyes, and well-formed, alert ears. A well-set and arched neck of good length leads to defined withers and a short, muscular back. Chest is wide
and the barrel well-sprung. Hindquarters are long and muscular, with the tail set high.
COLOR
Black, bay, brown, gray, or roan, often with white leg markings.
APTITUDE
Heavy draft, agricultural work, riding, showing, cavalry

THE MAJESTIC SHIRE HORSE IS AN ICONIC PART of British heritage. Like all of the draft horse breeds of western Europe, the Shire's roots are in the great horses of Belgium and France—the Brabant (Flanders Horse or Flemish Horse) and Ardennais—which in turn trace their development to the prehistoric Forest Horse of northern Europe. Strong-bodied horses from Europe, particularly Friesians, were taken into Britain during the Roman occupation (43–410 C.E.), and during the Norman Conquest of 1066 there was again a substantial influx of large, weight-carrying horses.

The demand for the heavy horses that developed into the Shire originated with their use in a military capacity. There was a concerted effort to increase the size of British horses to make them more suitable for use in heavy cavalry, as well as to breed a horse that could remain calm on the battlefield. This breeding for size continued through the Middle Ages and led to the emergence of what would now be termed a heavy cob type, called the Great Horse—later to be the Shire. These horses were substantial and proud in bearing but were still relatively small compared with the modern draft horse. During the sixteenth century, there was another influx of Friesians brought over with Dutch engineers during the reclamation of the fens in the eastern counties of Lincolnshire and Cambridgeshire. Friesians undoubtedly had a positive effect on the Great Horse, adding refinement and freedom of movement, as well as contributing their black coloring, which was predominant in the early Shire.

The Shire truly developed in the cold, wet, marshy landscape of the fens. Flanders Horses, German drafts,

and Friesians were all bred with local stock, and over time a classic type of heavy horse began to emerge, characteristically black with feathering on its legs. The horses were solidly built, strong animals and became known as the Old English Black in the seventeenth century.

By the eighteenth century, as breeding became more focused, two types of black horse emerged. The first was called the Bakewell Black after the agriculturalist Robert Bakewell (1725–95), who made great advancements in selective breeding of farm animals. Bakewell used Flanders Horses to improve his stock, which was noted for its elegance and endurance. The second was the Lincolnshire Black—heavier, stronger, and larger than the Bakewell, with greater feathering. These increasingly massive horses went from being predominantly warhorses to being versatile agricultural and industrial tools. Their great strength and placid nature made them ideal for anything from working the land to transporting goods and pulling canal barges.

The term *Shire* is thought to have first been used to describe these equine powerhouses during the seventeenth century, but the foundation sire of the breed is generally recognized as the Packington Blind Horse, a black horse from Leicestershire active during the mid-eighteenth century who seems to have stamped much of his extensive progeny with his characteristics. The English Cart Horse Society, established in 1876, published its first studbook in 1878 and became the Shire Horse Society in 1884. The Shires, as they were thus officially known, were extremely popular. They also earned a growing respect in the United States, where a breed society formed in 1885. Numbers began to fall after World War I and decreased sharply after World War II as they were largely replaced by vehicles. More recently there has been a revived interest in the Shire, leading to renewed efforts to preserve this important breed. They are still used on a small scale on some farms, but they are perhaps best known for their use as dray horses by the large brewing companies.

SUFFOLK PUNCH
HISTORIC – ENGLAND – CRITICAL

HEIGHT
16–16.3 h.h.
APPEARANCE
An extremely solid, muscular body set upon short, sturdy legs with very little feathering. Attractive head with great width between the eyes and small, alert ears. Muscular, *well-set neck with a good arch. Powerful, rounded hindquarters and low-set shoulders.*
COLOR
One of seven shades of "chesnut."
APTITUDE
Heavy draft, agricultural work, showing, cavalry

THE SUFFOLK PUNCH IS ONE OF THE MOST ENDEARING and charming of all draft horse breeds; the horses are quite simply delightful and have an indefinable charisma that is all their own. They are instantly recognizable—the most distinctive and uniform of draft breeds—and they have remained morphologically virtually the same throughout their history. Sadly they are also one of the rarest, although numbers are gradually starting to improve.

Like many of the older horse breeds, the Suffolk has been greatly shaped by its environment, and the relative geographic isolation of the Suffolk's home in particular has contributed to its purity. They developed in the eastern county of Suffolk bordered to the east by the North Sea, to the north by Norfolk, and partially by the wet fenlands to the west. The early history of the Suffolk is not documented, although it is possible that the horses arose from those brought to the area by the Vikings around the ninth century. These in turn were the native horses of Denmark, which eventually became the heavy Jutland, a breed that ironically much later in its history was then substantially influenced by a Suffolk stallion. Certainly the Suffolk is a very old breed, with the earliest recorded account of it appearing in William Camden's *Britannica*, published in 1586. Camden's description refers to the Suffolk as having existed for eighty years, and it is likely that it far predates even this. More significant, however, and unusual, is the fact that the Suffolk would appear to have changed little since this date, implying perhaps that perfection was attained early and maintained vigorously.

There is no mistaking a Suffolk Punch. They are always chesnut in color (the traditional spelling of the word), and can be one of seven shades: bright, golden, red, yellow, light, dark, and dull-dark, but it is their body shape that is most distinctive, with its massive bulk and short legs. The breed developed to fulfill a very specific purpose—as an agricultural animal—and this is what they do best. They have tremendous, almost unequaled pulling power, making them giants in the fields of plowing and hauling crops. In traditional strength competitions, the Suffolk was made to pull a fallen tree and was expected to go down on one knee in its effort to do so. Their limbs are free from feathering, which makes working in the heavy clay soil of their East Anglian home easier, and they should be built to allow them to walk cleanly along the furrow. They are hardworking horses, exhibit great stamina, and are long lived despite maturing relatively early. The Suffolk fulfilled all of the needs of the East Anglian farmer and was bred, raised, and worked on private farms with little exchange outside the counties of Suffolk and Norfolk, which contributed further to the purity of the breed at its foundation.

All "modern" Suffolks can be traced to a single foundation sire who was foaled near Woodbridge, Suffolk, in 1768. Known as Crisp's Horse after his owner, Thomas Crisp of Ufford, he stood at just 15.2 hands high and was chesnut, short legged, and big bodied, with a handsome head. Crisp described him as "able to get good stock for coach or road," and he covered mares across the area from Woodbridge to Saxmundham and Framlingham. Crisp's description indicates the coaching blood in the horse and also alludes to the tradition for coaching horses within the wider region, particularly Norfolk, which gave rise to the flash Norfolk Trotter and the Norfolk Cob. A Norfolk stallion called Blakes Farmer, foaled in 1760 and chesnut in color, was also influential in the Suffolk's development, and along with their use in agriculture, they were also used for transportation.

The Suffolk Horse Society was established in 1877, mostly because of the efforts of Herman Biddell, the society's first secretary. Biddell spent some years collating and researching the history of the Suffolk Punch and compiled the first studbook, *The Suffolk Horse History and Studbook*, in 1880, which was also the first year that Suffolks were exported to the United States. The American Suffolk Horse Association formed and published its first studbook in 1907, and although the association closed for some years after World War II, it reopened in 1961 and is very active today. Suffolk Punch horses have also been exported to Canada, Russia, New Zealand, Australia, Pakistan, and all across Europe.

Because of their great strength, Suffolks were also popular for use in the military to pull heavy artillery and were widely exported to Pakistan to use for breeding cavalry remounts, improving local stock, and breeding mules. Despite its slightly unconventional conformation, the Suffolk has been used extensively to improve other breeds, as well as for crossbreeding with lighter-weight stock to produce fantastic competition horses. A Suffolk stallion, Oppenheimer LXII, was exported to Denmark in the 1860s, where he was a significant influence on the Jutland breed, which bears a slight physical resemblance to the Suffolk. They have also had a pronounced effect on the Russian Vladimir Heavy Draft.

Because of the Suffolk's very great qualities, it remained extremely popular and was widely used throughout the two world wars, though after World War II it experienced a sudden and dramatic decline. Their usefulness was eclipsed by vehicles and large farm machinery, and many of them were sent to slaughterhouses during food shortages. Such was the decimation of the Suffolk Punch that in 1966 only nine foals were registered, which was catastrophic for the breed. Since then, there has been an incredible effort by devoted enthusiasts to improve breed numbers. The Suffolk is still, however, registered as critical. It is hard to comprehend the decline of this wonderful breed, known for its incredible temperament and traditionally described as having "the face of an angel, the body of a beer barrel, and the bottom of the farmer's daughter," though it is reassuring that they are making a comeback.

IRISH DRAFT

HISTORIC – IRELAND – COMMON

HEIGHT	*chest with a long, slightly*
15.1–17 h.h.	*sloping croup. Clean, strong*
APPEARANCE	*legs with substantial bone.*
Well-shaped head set to an	**COLOR**
average length, well-set neck.	*Any solid color.*
Powerful through the frame,	
with well-defined withers and	**APTITUDE**
a gently sloping shoulder and	*Medium draft, agricultural*
strong back. Deep through the	*work, riding, dressage,*
	jumping, showing, hunting

FOR A SMALL NATION, IRELAND HAS one of the best reputations for the production of first-class horses. The country is perfectly suited to raising horses, particularly the inland areas, and evidence of horses in Ireland can be traced back approximately three thousand years. The foundations for horse breeding in Ireland are most commonly traced to the fifth and sixth centuries B.C.E., however, when the Celts arrived from the Alps with their Eastern-influenced horses. Early Irish horses are mentioned in the pre-Christian epic the *Cuchulainn Saga*, which describes swift, slender chariot horses with long, curly manes and forelocks of heavy curls.

By around the tenth century C.E., the Irish Hobby had developed, based largely on the Spanish Asturian, which may have been brought to Ireland by the Romans. This small, agile horse rapidly became very popular, thanks in large part to the extreme smoothness of its ambling gait. When the Normans invaded Ireland in 1172, they brought their mighty warhorses, the Great Horse and the French warhorse, which towered above the Irish Hobby. These French and Belgian horses bred with Hobby mares to produce a larger, heavier riding horse that was further influenced by horses imported from Britain and France, and especially Spain and Portugal, including the Andalusian. By the Middle Ages, the Irish Hobby had been exported across much of Europe.

The Irish Hobby eventually disappeared, for reasons that remain rather unclear. The horses had started to be bred increasingly for size and agricultural purposes, and they developed into what became known as the Irish cart horse or cob. The ambling gait, once so highly prized, disappeared along with the Hobby, but the Irish cob would eventually become one of Ireland's finest horses, the Irish Draft. The Irish cob made an excellent riding horse, was hunted and jumped and utterly fearless, worked in a light draft capacity, and could pack goods. Still relatively small in height, the Irish cob required little maintenance, cost little to keep, and appeared to have an inherent intelligence and sense. It bore little resemblance to the massive draft breeds of Britain and Europe and yet was still able to work tirelessly in the fields or on the roads. This was the early Irish Draft, a horse approximately 15.2 hands high with excellent bones, solid structure, and great agility.

During the nineteenth century there was an effort to increase the size of the Irish Draft by introducing Clydesdale and Shire blood to the breed. The results were disastrous, with the Clydesdale in particular blamed for introducing a conformational fault of the lower leg bone that has since been bred out. The long, feathery leg hair of the British draft breeds was also unsuitable for the heavy Irish clay soils because of the huge clods of mud that it would trap. Farmers quickly realized that the best way to increase the size of their stock was to use the largest of their own animals for breeding, and the size of the Irish Draft has increased significantly.

Big improvements to the horses occurred in the early twentieth century when stallion subsidies were made available and a premium scheme for approved stallions set in place. Numbers of Irish Draft horses boomed, and many were used by the military during World War I. As with all draft breeds, there was a decline in numbers after World War II, but efforts by breeders have reestablished the Irish Draft, and today they are extremely popular horses, though used more often for riding than for draft purposes. They make excellent heavyweight hunters and riding horses and have been used increasingly to produce competition horses by crossing them with Thoroughbreds.

SHETLAND

PREHISTORIC — SCOTLAND — COMMON

HEIGHT
Up to 42 in. (Shetlands are always measured in inches)

APPEARANCE
Attractive head with small ears and alert, intelligent eyes. Short in the leg with a sloping shoulder and a well-set neck. Strong and muscular through

the frame and particularly sound in wind and limb.

COLOR
Any color except spotted.

APTITUDE
Riding, light draft, light agricultural work, packing, showing, jumping, competitive horse sports

THE SMALLEST PONY BREED OF THE BRITISH ISLES is also one of the oldest and strongest relative to its size and is a true product of its environment. The breed developed on the rugged, picturesque Shetland Islands approximately 100 miles (160 km) off the northeast coast of Scotland. The windswept beauty of the archipelago is matched by the ferocity of its legendary winter weather and the scant forage available for livestock. This extreme environment and its geographic isolation were fundamental in shaping the development of these little ponies.

Ponies may have first crossed to the Shetland Islands from Scandinavia more than ten thousand years ago when there were still land bridges in Europe; it is thus possible that they are linked to the same foundation stock that gave rise to the small Icelandic horse. Although unproven, it is possible that they can also trace their roots to the little-known and now-extinct Tundra, a prehistoric pony that evolved in northeast Siberia at a time similar to that of the Asiatic Wild Horse and the Tarpan. The Tundra is also believed to be the ancestor of the Siberian Yakut pony, whose extraordinary imperviousness to cold is very similar to that of the indomitable Shetland.

Excavations on the Shetland Islands have revealed small pony bones that date back approximately four thousand years, by which time the ponies are thought to have been domesticated. Much like the Icelandic horse, the extreme geographic isolation of the Shetland Islands greatly contributed to the early purity of the pony breed, though the native stock is thought to have been infiltrated toward

the end of the Bronze Age by some eastern influence introduced by the Celts, and then later from ponies shipped over by the Vikings.

The Shetland's ancestors were small in stature, and the ponies that arrived on the islands subsequently remained small because of the difficulty of transporting them in boats; their size was then further cemented by environmental conditions. According to the Shetland Pony Stud-Book Society, the ponies did not become smaller as a result of the harshness of the environment; rather, it was only the small ponies that survived the harsh environment. Interestingly, however, Shetlands raised in more favorable conditions do not show any significant increase in height.

What is beyond doubt, however, is the impact the environment had on the development of certain characteristics within the breed, such as their ability to subsist on extremely sparse rations. Stories abound of how Shetlands would pick out an existence during the winter by feeding on seaweed washed up on the shores when other forage was absent. The Shetland pony's toughness and endurance is legendary, as is its ability to withstand extreme cold. Its feet and limbs have also evolved to become incredibly tough and sound from picking across the rocky landscape, but perhaps its most important trait is its uncanny sagacity and talent for survival.

For most of its history the breed has been used in a light agricultural capacity, fulfilling a wide range of roles on the small farms and crofts of the islands, and by fishermen. Despite their small size, the ponies are enormously strong: they are capable of packing heavy loads and can even be ridden by grown men. With the onset of industrialization during the eighteenth and nineteenth centuries, the ponies became extremely popular for use in mines and were sold into England and across Europe, and even to the United States. Demand for their use in mines rose dramatically in 1847, when a law banning children from working in mines was put into effect. The ponies were the perfect size for working underground, and many of them spent the majority of their lives in the dark, coming above ground only infrequently. Many of the miners forged strong and affectionate relationships with these brave little ponies.

Early in the breed's history, two distinct types developed, one being heavier and sturdier with a large head, the other finer with a high tail carriage and longer length of stride. These two types still exist today, with the former most suited to driving and the latter to riding. As the Shetland's worth as a working animal was recognized, concentrated efforts were made to maintain and improve its qualities, beginning with the establishment of the Shetland Pony Stud-Book Society in 1890. The quality of registered ponies was strictly monitored, greatly aiding the modern development of the breed. One early breeder who made a great contribution to the Shetland was Lord Londonderry, who formed a stud in the 1870s to produce Shetland ponies for his collieries in County Durham. Through a process of rigorously selective breeding, Londonderry quickly made a dramatic impact on the quality and substance of the ponies, with one stallion in particular—Jack 16, f. 1871—passing on his admirable conformation to a number of lines.

When Londonderry's stud was dispersed in 1899, the stock was distributed among the leading breeders of the day, including to Ladies Estella and Dorothea Hope of Hopetoun House in Scotland. The Hope sisters had begun a breeding program in the 1870s when they acquired several top mares and they were highly regarded breeders in their time; they even sold ponies to Queen Victoria (1819–1901) for driving. The stud has remained in the family and is now run by Anne De La Warr at Buckhurst Park in East Sussex. Most significantly, they still own the same original six lines of ponies, all named with the initial of their dam (B, C, F, I, R, and V), thereby preserving these important historic bloodlines.

Although the Shetland's role as an agricultural or industrial animal has changed, the ponies have remained extremely popular and have not suffered the devastating drop in numbers experienced by other working breeds such as the Suffolk Punch or the Shire. The ponies have made the transition into the leisure industry with hardly a hair turned and are now sought after as children's ponies or for competitive driving events.

HIGHLAND
PREHISTORIC – SCOTLAND – AT RISK

HEIGHT
13–14.2 h.h.
APPEARANCE
*Muscular through the frame
with a well-set and often
crested neck. A beautiful
head, wide between the eyes,
with small, alert ears.
Exceptionally strong, sound*

*limbs, and great strength
through the frame.*
COLOR
*Predominantly dun, but can
be gray, black, brown, bay, and
occasionally liver chestnut.*
APTITUDE
*Riding, light draft, packing,
showing, dressage, jumping*

LIKE THE SHETLAND, THE HIGHLAND PONY originated in Scotland, this time amid the rugged peaks of the Scottish highlands and on the Western Isles (Outer Hebrides) off the northwest coast of the Scottish mainland. The two areas originally supported slightly different types of Highland pony, with those on the islands smaller and lighter in frame than their mainland counterparts; recent breeding, however, has seen these two types merge into one.

The ponies, whose ancestry goes back to prehistoric times, are thought to have evolved from crosses between the Asiatic Wild Horse and ancestors of the Exmoor pony. During the Bronze Age, around 2,000 B.C.E., horses from Scandinavia and possibly Iceland were brought over, impacting the native stock. As is so often the case with ancient breeds, the Highland's defining characteristics were shaped by its environment; like the Shetland, the Highland is tough, hardy, and very resourceful. Highlands also have a double-layered, weatherproof coat and are able to survive on minimal rations. Thousands of years of picking their way across treacherous rocks, up and down hills, and across boggy land has made the ponies incredibly sure-footed and imbued them with an innate sense for finding safe ground; they can travel across these unforgiving landscapes with speed, safety, and dexterity.

The breed has been subject to a number of influences through the years, including from Arabian stallions that were introduced to the native stock on the islands of Barra and Mull in the sixteenth century. This Arabian blood had a pronounced positive effect on the breed, with the Arabian stallion Syrian in particular stamping his mark on the ponies of Mull. In the same period, French and Spanish horses are said to have arrived in Scotland and crossed with the Highlands, having swum ashore after galleons from the Spanish Armada were sunk off the coast. Further Spanish blood was introduced in the early eighteenth century by the chief of Clanranald to his ponies on Uist. There was also some influence of Clydesdale blood from the Bains Horse stallion in the nineteenth century, which saw the ponies increase in size and mass. During this time, some trotting horse blood in the form of the Norfolk Roadster was also brought in, and, significantly, today's Highland has very good, smooth paces.

Throughout its long history, the Highland has proved to be one of the most versatile utility breeds. Their size makes them suitable riding animals for both children and adults, and they are strong enough to carry a grown man all day. Highlands were used in all capacities, from working the land and riding to pulling heavy loads and packing game. The ponies were also used extensively in military capacities, both by warring clans and the army. King Robert the Bruce (1274–1329) allegedly rode a Highland, and Bonnie Prince Charlie (1720–88) rode a Highland stallion bred on Uist during the Jacobite uprising of 1745. More recently, Highlands were a part of the mounted Scottish Horse Regiment, a yeomanry regiment of the British Territorial Army from 1900 to 1956, and they were used by the Lovat Scouts during World War II.

Today, Highlands are still used in an agricultural capacity in some of the more remote parts of the highlands and for cattle driving and packing game such as deer and wild fowl. With the establishment of pony trekking in the 1950s, the Highland found a perfect new niche, and it continues to be used in this capacity and is even exported to France to work in trekking centers. It is a popular riding pony for both children and adults in a competitive sphere and is frequently used for competitive driving.

4 | NEW WORLD SPLENDOR

Archaeological evidence indicates that the ancestor of the modern horse evolved in North America around sixty million years ago, yet horses became extinct across this vast continent toward the end of the last great ice age, approximately ten thousand years ago. The horse was only reintroduced to the Americas around five hundred years ago, and yet in that relatively short timespan horses have flourished here; numerous breeds have developed and the United States has become one of the foremost producers of horses in the world. The history of horses in the United States is an extraordinary and intense success story, and one that inexorably affected both the native cultures and the exploration of the New World by white settlers.

The story of the horse in the Americas is bound to that of the Spanish conquistadores, who were left kicking their heels and seeking new adventures following the end of the Moorish occupation of the Iberian Peninsula at the close of the fifteenth century. Christopher Columbus (1451–1506) "discovered" the New World in 1492 when he landed on one of the islands of the Bahamas. The following year, he set sail again from Spain, this time with a fleet of ships, people to colonize the new lands, livestock, produce, and a number of horses. By order of King Ferdinand the Catholic (1452–1516), these were to be the finest warhorses available, but when they arrived it transpired that the finest horses had been exchanged for a collection of inferior quality stock. In all likelihood, however, this supposedly inferior quality stock comprised the ancient Sorraia, Spanish Jennet, Asturian, and Garrano, all of which are important Spanish breeds. The horses were left on the island of Hispaniola, and within ten years—through the addition of more horses brought on subsequent voyages—breeding farms had been established here and on the larger islands of the West Indies. Additional voyages of discovery set sail loaded with horses, but such was the death rate in transit that the stretch of ocean between Spain and the Canary Islands was named the Gulfo de Yeguas, or the Gulf of Mares. The severity of

the voyages for the horses resulted in only the hardiest stock surviving, and it was this tough, noble, Spanish stock that gave rise to the new horse populations in the United States.

Royal stud farms developed through Cuba and the West Indies based on huge importations of Andalusian, Barb, and other fine stock from Spain, while in Brazil the Portuguese settlers imported their beloved Lusitano. In 1519, Hernán Cortés (1485–1547) set about his exploration of Mexico, taking sixteen horses with him, including his black stallion, El Morzillo. The native Mayans, who had never seen horses before, were terrified by them and believed them to be gods. After El Morzillo became lame and could not continue, Cortés left the horse with the Mayans; the local people fed him and erected a shrine in his honor, but he died in spite of their efforts. Some years later, in 1532, Francisco Pizzaro (c. 1471–1541) arrived with his men and horses and ravaged the Inca, while elsewhere white explorers arrived to the east of the Andes. Before long, the Spanish had reached the vast Argentine grasslands with their superlative horses.

The first horses to arrive in North America did so in 1521 with the explorer Juan Ponce de León (1474–1521), who landed off the coast of Florida . His expedition was a mitigated disaster, however; the Calusa people attacked the colonists and Ponce de León was shot in the leg with a poison arrow. Those that survived the attack fled to Havana, Cuba, and it is unlikely that any of the fifty horses he shipped there survived for long.

As the Spanish continued to extend their colonization of the West Indies and Mexico, and their explorations into South America, the horse population of Spanish stock rapidly took hold. Meanwhile, further exploration was taking place along the east coast of North America and Canada during the sixteenth, seventeenth, and eighteenth centuries, with an increasing influx of settlers from England, France, Italy, Holland, and Denmark from the seventeenth century onward. As the fleets of ships arrived, so too did the horses. The European breeds would go on to greatly influence the development of American horse breeds: in particular French horses that gave rise to the French Canadian horse, the early Thoroughbred, and running stock, Friesians, and heavier draft breeds from continental Europe. One of the overriding factors in the development of early American breeds was the requirement for versatile horses that could be equally at home working in harness and under saddle, and that were able to traverse difficult terrain smoothly, comfortably, and with intelligence. It is no coincidence that the majority of American horse breeds today reflect this great versatility.

The arrival of the horse in the Americas had a great impact on the native people, who had never seen these beasts before. At first, the horse was much feared or even revered as a god, but the American Indians quickly realized the importance and impact of this creature and rapidly began to absorb the horse into their own cultures. In South America, the people of the Pampas and Patagonian grasslands assimilated the horse into the very fabric of their society. Horses bred rapidly in these huge areas, benefiting from the nutritious grasses, and to such an extent that they became common property. With the ownership of horses and the ability to ride and cover distances, the structure of cultures shifted. People were now able to hunt over large distances and had much greater mobility, which allowed for a moving community. Horses soon infiltrated every aspect of society and were used in all capacities, including for meat and milk. They also formed part of ritualistic sacrifice, and it was common for horses to be slaughtered on the death of their owner,

in a manner not dissimilar to that evidenced by the ancient Scythian people from west of the Altai Mountains in Central Asia. As with the American Indians, the extent of their horse cultures was relatively short lived, falling in the face of European firearms.

In North America, the horse also had a resounding impact on native cultures, many of whose people became expert horsemen, breeders, and horseback warriors. It was also through the American Indian cultures of North America that the horse was widely dispersed, particularly from Mexico northward and across the Great Plains, through trading and requisitioning of stock from settlers.

Most significantly, the horse allowed American Indians to hunt buffalo with far greater effect, and this in turn meant that food was plentiful, as were the buffalo byproducts of skins and bone, none of which went to waste. It also meant that the tribes were more mobile, that women and dogs were relieved from the burden of carrying equipment, and, significantly, that they were better equipped during battles with the settlers.

Many tribes, such as the Nez Percé, who developed the Appaloosa and the Nez Percé Horse, and the Blackfoot selectively bred their horses for different purposes. The most highly prized were the buffalo horses: horses that were trained to aid the rider during the buffalo hunt. The riders had to be extremely agile, brave, and intelligent, as did their warhorses. There are ten recorded different types of horse that the Blackfoot bred. In many tribes, including the Blackfoot, wealth was measured according to the number of horses owned by a family. An average family would own upward of twelve horses, with these given various roles, from pulling the travois, packing provisions, and riding, to being the buffalo horse. Like the Blackfoot, the Cayuse and Umatilla tribes had at least twelve horses per family, and it was the Cayuse who developed the rarely heard of Cayuse Indian pony, much admired during the nineteenth century and thought to have derived from French-Canadian and Spanish stock. Equally, the Chickasaw pony, developed by the Chickasaw tribe in Florida and based on old Spanish and Barb stock, was much admired and spread into Virginia and the Carolinas through trading with the colonists. The Chickasaw, which shares similar heritage to the Florida Cracker (also referred to as the Florida Horse, the Cracker, or the Seminole), went on to influence the development of the American Quarter Horse, quite possibly one of the greatest horse breeding success stories of modern history. By around 1885, the wild buffalo of North America, around which so many tribes had based their existences, had been all but eradicated through the use of firearms and indiscriminate, disgraceful hunting, primarily by European settlers. This, in turn, led to a partial redundancy of the horse in this context.

For the white colonists, the horse was an essential part of everyday life, mirroring in many respects that same relationship between primitive cultures and their horses from the beginning of time. As new lands were explored and settlers traveled west from the east coast, crossing over the Appalachian Mountains and entering the great plains of the west, and also northward from the south, they relied entirely on their horses. Through necessity, these horses had to be incredibly tough and enduring, spartan in nature, and surefooted enough to traverse the often treacherous terrain in the days before roads were laid. They needed to be easy to ride and comfortable to sit on, strong enough to pull a heavy cart or a plow, and yet classy enough to take the family to church. Breeds such as the American Saddlebred, the Tennessee Walker, and the Missouri Fox Trotter—all with a comfortable gait and equable temperament—developed in their respective areas based on varying combinations of old Spanish stock, the little Narragansett Pacer, Canadian horses, Morgans, and early Thoroughbreds. The Morgan itself was another of the early American breeds noted for its great versatility. It was as comfortable in harness as being ridden and a talented livestock workhorse, yet also quiet enough for all the family to ride.

Nonetheless, the most successful (in terms of size of breed registry) of the American breeds is undoubtedly the American Quarter Horse, truly the horse for all people. These horses originally developed as racing stock that competed over a short distance—a quarter of a mile—and evolved primarily through crossbreeding between the Chickasaw pony, Spanish stock, and early English running horses. They excelled in this endeavor until longer distance races and the Thoroughbred became popular, but this was just the beginning of the story for the American Quarter Horse. They were widely used by early colonists for finding and settling new lands, and were used in all capacities, demonstrating a particular aptitude for working cattle. The Quarter Horse, as with many of the South American breeds—such as the Mangalarga Marchador and Argentinean Criollo—has an innate understanding of and ability to work livestock, naturally tracking cattle and often working from pure instinct. These traits can be traced back to the influence of the ubiquitous Spanish horse.

The Quarter Horse soon became the obvious horse of choice for the North American rancher and cowboy, particularly with the popular establishment of extremely large fenced ranches from the late nineteenth century.

It quickly became necessary to patrol the boundaries of each vast property and monitor the herds of cattle, an important job that fell to the cowboy and his trusty horses. Ranches would typically have enormous herds, or *remudas,* of working horses, which were highly trained and extremely agile, able to turn on a dime and accelerate with astonishing speed. The North American cowboy arose from the Spanish traditions of South and Central America, where cowboys, or *vaqueros*, looked after the livestock (as did the gauchos of the South American pampas). These traditions had in turn been brought over by the Spanish conquistadores and reflected the popular hacienda (large ranch) system of cattle rearing that had developed in medieval Spain. Slightly different equipment, techniques, and systems developed according to geographic location, and nowadays the American cowboy has its own identity and is greatly respected as an iconic part of the country's history.

Today, the United States boasts one of the world's largest horse industries and is home to an enormous, and growing, number of different horse breeds. Although in many instances life is very different in the twenty-first century for the country's horses, they have made the transition from predominantly working tools to the leisure industry with great alacrity, which is a reflection of the innate versatility of these horses. There are, as always, exceptions, and the American Quarter Horse (and many of the South American breeds) continues to play an important role within ranching communities, as well as being the country's most popular leisure horse.

No mention should be made of the United States's horses without including the Mustang, the wild (feral) horse on which so many films and books have been based. The Mustang in a sense is a faint living echo of the United States's history. These are the horses that originally escaped, were left, loosed, or forgotten during raids between settlers and native people, and made their way into the wild interior to forge a new life. The Mustang dates back to the first Spanish horses to arrive on the continent, and through their veins runs the tumultuous past of bloodletting, exploration, and exploitation. They are a splendid reminder that in a largely cultivated world there is still a little of the wild left.

NEW WORLD SPLENDOR

MUSTANG

HISTORIC — UNITED STATES — COMMON

HEIGHT	COLOR
14–15 h.h.	*Any color.*
APPEARANCE	**APTITUDE**
Varies greatly, but many Mustangs exhibit the influence of Spanish heritage, seen in their heads with either a straight or ram-like profile and a majestic bearing.	*Feral, but, once domesticated: riding, working livestock, dressage, jumping, competitive horse sports, Western riding horse sports*

TUCKED AWAY IN THE VAST, SPRAWLING interior landscape of the American West is the Mustang, an iconic part of American history and the fabric from which many romantic and thrilling tales have been woven. The American Mustang is indeed a national treasure, and one whose history goes hand in hand with that of the pioneers.

Although considered "wild," the Mustang derived from domesticated horses that escaped or were set loose and developed small self-sufficient herds; technically the Mustang is a "feral" animal. The first horses to arrive in America, and consequently the first to escape, were of Spanish origin, coming over with the conquistadores in the sixteenth century. These horses are reputed to have been the best stock that Spain had, though whether this is true is a matter of some debate: it is hard to imagine the Spanish sending their finest horses off on the treacherous journey to the New World, and yet the conquistadores would doubtlessly have wanted to be well horsed for their violent explorations. Only the toughest horses could have survived the transatlantic journey, however, and this toughness and stamina lie at the heart of all derivative stock.

The Mustang is an amalgamation of different breeds on a Spanish foundation; its Spanish roots are especially noticeable in the shape of the head, the compact, powerful conformation, and the majestic, Spanish spirit. In recent years, small herds have been discovered in remote areas that, through blood testing, have been proven to be of predominantly Spanish descent. The Kiger Mustangs discovered in Oregon in 1977 are just such a group and

bear a close physical resemblance to the old Spanish type, particularly in the shape of their heads, with their straight or ram-like profiles, as do the Cerbat Mustangs of Arizona.

Horses were spread throughout North America by the American Indian tribes, who adopted the horse into their culture with extraordinary rapidity. Horses were stolen, bought, bartered, and found, both between settlers and American Indians and between tribes. There were inevitable escapees, horses deliberately released, left behind, stolen, or lost. It was not unheard of for wild or feral stallions to break down a corral and "steal" the mares; equally, domestic mares would sometimes break out to join a wild herd.

These early domestic horses were of mixed blood that included that of the widespread Canadian Horse, majestic, predominantly black or bay horses that had French blood at their base, tracing back to the stock brought by the French during their exploration and colonization of "New France." European breeds like the superlative Friesian, which was imported in the late eighteenth and early nineteenth centuries for cavalry use as both remounts and artillery horses, also found their way into the Mustang herds. Many joined Mustang herds after their escape or abandonment during battle. Coaching breeds imported from England and continental Europe, as well as those developed in the United States, and even Thoroughbreds and draft horses, also joined Mustang herds over time. The influence of draft blood is quite apparent in many Mustangs, and some are even kept in separate herds managed by the U.S. Bureau of Land Management (BLM).

As with any wild animal, it is a case of survival of the fittest, and as such, Mustang horses represent some of the toughest, most enduring horses to be found. Although there are some instances of conformational problems caused primarily by inbreeding, the Mustang is overwhelmingly a horse of beauty and quality. They can make exceptionally good riding horses with the right training, and once tamed have a gentle, trusting nature.

Mustang herds are found across ten of the Western states, with the greatest numbers in Nevada, Oregon, and Wyoming. Although dearly beloved by many, the Mustang also has its share of human enemies who have hunted it mercilessly. Some ranchers resent the Mustang's living on public land, which they say might otherwise be used for grazing livestock; others charge the Mustang with destroying natural flora and grasslands. On the other hand, it is argued that the Mustang grazes in poor, dry areas that would not support cattle anyway, and that it is an important part of American heritage. Nonetheless, at the beginning of the twentieth century there were an estimated two million Mustangs; by 1935 this number had been reduced to 150,000, and today it is closer to 50,000.

The Mustang owes much of its current protected status to one woman: Velma B. Johnston, better known as Wild Horse Annie. A resident of Nevada, where the majority of the Mustang herds live, she became aware of the horrific manner in which Mustangs were being hunted down by motorized vehicles, shot, and harvested for the meat industry and for pet foods. She campaigned to raise awareness of this cruelty, and in 1959 a bill banning the use of vehicles in the slaughter of the horses was introduced. It became known as the Wild Horse Annie Act and came into full effect in September of that year.

By 1971, however, the number of Mustangs had again dropped because of hunting, and after dedicated lobbying an act of Congress was passed to protect the horses. The Wild Free-Roaming Horse and Burro Act (16 U.S.C. 1331–1340) declares that "wild, free-roaming horses . . . are living symbols of the historic and pioneer spirit of the West; they contribute to the diversity of life forms within the nation and enrich the lives of the American people." It is now a federal offense for anyone to maim or kill Mustangs in the wild.

The U.S. Forest Service, under the Department of Agriculture and the BLM, is responsible for administering the law, and the BLM is in charge of protecting and managing the herds that live on BLM land. Alternative ways of keeping herd numbers under control had to be introduced since the horses have very few predators. An adoption program was established in 1971, and suitable candidates are now allowed to take on a Mustang for a nominal fee; after a year, ownership of the horse is passed to the individual.

PERUVIAN PASO
HISTORIC — PERU — COMMON

HEIGHT	low-set tail. Exceptionally
14.1–15.2 h.h.	strong legs and tough hooves.
APPEARANCE	**COLOR**
A finely modeled head with	Bay, chestnut, dun, black, gray,
large, kind eyes and alert ears.	palomino, grullo, brown, or
Neck is muscular and well set.	roan; solid colors are preferred.
Deep, wide chest and long,	**APTITUDE**
muscular loin with a sloping	Riding, showing, competitive
croup. Luxurious mane and a	and Western riding horse sports

PERU IS A COUNTRY OF BREATHTAKING extremes, from the towering Andes that are Peru's vertiginous spine running from north to south through its midst to the swath of luxuriant Amazon rain forest in the east and the narrow, arid coastal plains to the west. By the early sixteenth century, Peru was at the heart of the Inca civilization, which stretched across a large portion of South America. Stories of Peru's great riches filtered up to Spanish conquistadores residing in the recently established Panama City, prompting a number of expeditions to discover the legendary, fabulous place. The first Spanish conquistadores arrived around 1531 under the leadership of Governor Don Francisco Pizarro (1471–1541), taking a number of horses with them. These were the first horses to set foot in Peru and formed the genetic base from which the mighty Peruvian Paso (also known as the Peruvian) would develop.

The first horses to land in South America arrived with Christopher Columbus (1451–1506) in 1493. These initial Spanish horses included the now-extinct Spanish Jennet, a gaited, ambling horse, as well as the Garrano, Sorraia, and other small breeds used for packing alongside larger Spanish riding horses. Stud farms, breeding facilities, and a healthy trade in fine horses were quickly established throughout the West Indies, the Dominican Republic, Puerto Rico, and Panama to provide horses for the increasing traffic of explorers and settlers. Once breeding farms had been established, some of the finest Andalusians from Spain were imported; there was also North African Barb blood in early and later importations.

The Peruvian Paso developed through careful and intensive breeding of these imported Spanish and Barb horses. It is one of very few breeds to have a naturally occurring gait, inherited from the Spanish Jennet and achieved without training. The gait has four beats and falls between a walk and a canter with two types, a slower one of four equal beats called the *paso llano*, and a faster one, the *sobreandando*, in which the lateral beats are closer together. This natural gait allows for an extremely smooth passage and was sought after by early settlers and explorers who needed to travel long distances. Peruvian Pasos also exhibit an unusual outward swing seen in their front leg movement, called *termino*, which originates from the shoulder area.

Horses were of crucial importance to the conquistadores both as a means for transportation and conquering new territory and for transporting essential goods. They were held in extremely high regard, and there are a number of early records of them written by the conquistadores, including names and numbers of horses, distances covered, and comments on their coloring, of which bay was a favorite. Pizarro, later founder of the capital, Lima, was said to be an expert horseman who rode only the highest class of Spanish horse, the Andalusian.

The Peruvian Paso was greatly prized in the country and was bred carefully, rigorously, and selectively to produce its particular characteristics—its gait, beauty, and exceptionally kind temperament. However, it also possesses an enormous energy and spirit (called *brio*) that gives it great charisma—though this energy should always be channeled toward performance and working in conjunction with riders and not against them. The breed suffered during the War of the Pacific (1879–84) when Chilean forces invaded the country from the south, and many of the beloved Peruvian Pasos were killed in the course of the conflicts. Many Peruvians let their horses loose in the hopes that they might survive better if living a feral existence and to save them from being killed by the soldiers. Added to this, by the early twentieth century, with increasing urbanization and the development of the Pan-American Highway, the demand for Peruvian horses decreased, particularly in the south of Peru, and the breed fell into decline. Many of the once fine horses now lived feral in the Andes or were reduced to the life of a workhorse in peasant families.

The restoration of the Peruvian horse in southern Peru owes much of its success to a horseman named Gustavo de la Borda, who kept and bred show horses in the early 1900s. At this time, the Peruvian horses in the north of the country were considered superior to those in the south, a situation that la Borda wished to redress. He began to travel through the remote mountain regions searching for high-quality horses that had been released or ended up in peasant homes during the Chilean conflicts. During his search he discovered a poor-looking stallion with a leg crippled from an earlier injury, but la Borda recognized some spirit within the horse and purchased him from his bewildered farmer owner. The horse, Sol de Oro (V) (f. c. 1945), was a prepotent sire and went on to produce a huge number of top-class horses throughout the southern region since la Borda allowed him to cover mares across a great area. Today Sol de Oro is considered one of the greatest of all Peruvian Paso stallions and has achieved a stupendous track record through his progeny, with innumerable National Champion of Champions in Peru tracing their lineage to him since 1961.

In the north of Peru, a similarly talented horseman, Federico de la Torre Ugarte, instigated a famous breeding program of Peruvian horses that stemmed essentially from the eminent mare La Zapata (n/d), who originally belonged to the horse breeder Don Andre Zapata. La Zapata, who was National Champion of Champions in Peru in 1946, gave birth to the stallion Limenito (f. 1942), one of the most important Peruvian foundation stallions in the north. The Peruvian horse in the north suffered a decline in numbers during the 1960s because of agrarian reforms that saw many of the major breeding farms and programs broken up and the stock dispersed. Many of the finest Peruvians ended up being sold in the United States or Central America. It is only within the last thirty years or so that the Peruvian Paso has been firmly reestablished in its own country and has been made an official part of Peruvian cultural heritage.

PASO FINO

HISTORIC – PUERTO RICO, COLOMBIA, PERU, CUBA, DOMINICAN REPUBLIC – COMMON

HEIGHT
13–15.2 h.h.

APPEARANCE
A finely modeled head with either a straight or slightly ram-like profile and a well-proportioned, muscular neck that is arched and set relatively high. Great depth through the chest, a well-sprung rib cage, and a short- to medium-length, muscular back. Fine but strong legs.

COLOR
Any color.

APTITUDE
Riding, showing, competitive and Western riding horse sports

THE MAJESTIC PASO FINO HORSE developed in Puerto Rico, Colombia, Peru, the Dominican Republic, and Cuba. Although these beautiful horses all share some similarities in type and characteristics, they also exhibit differences, depending on the bloodlines and breeding in their country of origin. The Colombian Paso Fino (also known as the Colombian Criollo), for example, has become a symbol of national pride in Colombia and is considered the purest of the Paso Fino horses by its homeland. The Peruvian Paso, meanwhile, shares the Paso name and exuberance but is very different in conformation and the way it moves.

The Paso Fino is a smallish horse of powerful build. It generally has a vivacious, charismatic nature but is also very obliging and kind. Like the Peruvian Paso, it also exhibits brio—a quality of fire and spirit—but only on demand. It is a compact horse, smaller than the Peruvian Paso and with a much shorter stride. Paso Finos tend to have an abundance of mane and tail hair, and the tail should be carried with grace when the horse is in motion. In contrast, the Peruvian Paso has a low-set tail that is carried close to the buttocks. Significantly, the Paso Fino's legs move true and straight, whereas the Peruvian Paso exhibits *termino*, an outward rolling motion of the front leg that originates in the shoulder.

All of these horses, however, share a similar original Spanish heritage and trace their history to the fifteenth century. Christopher Columbus (1451–1506) brought a number of Spanish horses to the New World on his second voyage, in 1493, and some of these were taken to what is now the Dominican Republic. These horses, and those left on subsequent trips, were a mixture of the now-extinct Spanish Jennet, ancient Sorraia, Asturian, Garrano, Barb, and Andalusian. The smaller Spanish stock, in particular the Sorraias and Garranos, would have been used as working horses, primarily for packing, whereas the Barbs, Andalusians, and other Spanish riding horses were of a different class and highly regarded as riding horses. The Spanish Jennet and also the Asturian had natural ambling gaits that made them very comfortable to ride, and more important in view of subsequent breed developments, they passed their ambling gaits on to their progeny, even when crossed to non-gaited breeds such as the Andalusian.

The horses on the Dominican Republic were used as foundation stock to implement horse-breeding programs to supply conquistadores on surrounding islands. Stock was spread throughout the Caribbean, with the first horses taken to Puerto Rico from the island of Hispaniola around 1509. By 1550, horse breeding was established and prolific across the Caribbean, with different types emerging in Puerto Rico, Peru, Hispaniola, Cuba, and Colombia.

In Puerto Rico, rigorous and careful breeding between base stock of ambling Spanish Jennets, Andalusians, Barbs, and other Spanish horses saw the emergence of a specific type of horse with a naturally occurring and extremely comfortable gait. Continued breeding for gait, conformation, and aptitude led to the development of the Puerto Rican Paso Fino (*paso fino* means "fine step"). These horses are born with a naturally occurring four-beat lateral gait that they perform smoothly and with great cadence; the gentleness with which they place their feet on the ground reduces jarring and makes them extremely comfortable to ride. The gait may be performed at three different speeds: the *paso fino* is the slowest, with a rapid footfall but small forward motion; the *paso corto* is similar in speed to a regular trot; and the fastest of the three, the *paso largo*, is akin to a fast canter.

NEW WORLD SPLENDOR

ARGENTINEAN CRIOLLO
HISTORIC – ARGENTINA – COMMON

HEIGHT	*short and muscular, frame*
13.3–15.1 h.h.	*sturdy, and croup sloping with*
APPEARANCE	*a low-set tail.*
Traditionally the head	**COLOR**
exhibited a slight ram-like	*Wide variety, but gateado, dun,*
profile indicative of its Spanish	*and grullo are most favored.*
heritage, but the modern	**APTITUDE**
Criollo has a straight or even	*Riding, working livestock,*
slightly concave profile. Neck is	*polo, endurance, horse sports*

ARGENTINA OCCUPIES A VAST SWATH OF LAND in South America, a huge, sublime landscape that bakes beneath an unforgiving sun during the summer and freezes in the winter. It is home to some of the highest peaks in South America, the glacial regions of Patagonia, extensive areas of pastoral steppes in the south, and Pampas grasslands in the northeast. It is here, against a background of great adversity, that one of the world's toughest horses developed: the indomitable Argentinean Criollo.

The first horses arrived in Argentina in 1535, shipped from Cádiz in Spain to the Rio de la Plata, the giant estuary formed by the Uruguay River and the Paraná River on the border of Argentina and Uruguay. One hundred horses of Spanish origin were brought to the area by the conquistador Pedro de Mendoza (c. 1487–1537), who founded the city of Buenos Aires in 1536 along the Argentinean banks of the estuary. The horses are thought to have been primarily Sorraias, but there were also Garranos, Barbs, and Spanish riding horses of either Andalusian or Andalusian-cross blood. Regardless of their breeding, those that survived the trip were undoubtedly the most resilient of their type. On arrival, these horses were drafted into immediate active duty with no time for recuperation.

The indigenous people of the area had initially been friendly toward the Spanish invaders, but the tides quickly turned and the Spanish began to meet heavy resistance. Skirmishes resulted in the loss of some valuable horses, and many escaped or were let loose when Buenos Aires was abandoned by settlers in 1541.

The horses had to fend for themselves in an inhospitable environment, roaming wild across the Pampas. Only the toughest survived, and the horses bred naturally, strengthening their inherent toughness. The wild horses were described as *baguals* by explorers, who reported their existence to be in the thousands. The indigenous people caught many of the horses, and when the colonists returned to Buenos Aires in 1580, they began to round up the horses, using them to work cattle and travel over huge distances. The Criollo was the essential mount for the gaucho, the Argentinean cowboy, and is still central to gaucho culture. The formative years spent fending for itself in the wild are what shaped the Criollo, and its extraordinary characteristics persist even when bred in captivity.

During the nineteenth century there was some infiltration of European blood to the breed, namely through the Thoroughbred and heavier riding types, as well as some horses from North America. This was disastrous for the breed and led to a rapid loss in quality. A group of concerned Criollo breeders created a purebred registry in 1918, and the Criollo Breeders Association was formed in 1923 with the objective of returning the Criollo to its original glory. The Argentinean Criollo has now been completely restored and continues to be an admirable working stock horse. Criollos crossed with Thoroughbreds also produce excellent and highly-sought-after polo ponies.

The Argentinean Criollo can thrive on the poorest rations and keep working. Its powers of endurance are legendary and unmatched—it could be argued that the Argentinean Criollo would give the Arabian a run for its money in staying power, if not speed. Although there are numerous accounts of its legendary stamina, perhaps the most famous is that of A. F. Tschiffely (1894–1954). Between 1925 and 1928, Tschiffely journeyed 13,350 miles (21,485 km) from Buenos Aires to Washington, D.C., with two Criollos, crossing some of the most difficult terrain imaginable and overcoming extraordinary adversity.

MANGALARGA MARCHADOR
HISTORIC – BRAZIL – COMMON

HEIGHT
Ideally 14.3 h.h.
APPEARANCE
A fine, light, triangular head set to an arched, well-set neck of medium length. Deep and long chest with a strong, proportionate back. Hindquarters are muscular and
powerful, with a medium-set tail and long, oblique shoulders. Exceptionally strong legs.
COLOR
Any color except albino.
APTITUDE
Riding, working livestock, showing, competitive and Western riding horse sports

THE MANGALARGA MARCHADOR is arguably Brazil's finest horse and one of the leading working stock horses in the world. The horses are common throughout Brazil and have recently become popular in the United States, but little is ever heard of the superlative Mangalarga Marchador beyond that.

The breed's history goes back to around 1740 to the southeastern state of Minas Gerais in Brazil and specifically to the area around the town of Baependi. In the eighteenth century, a Portuguese man by the name of João Francisco (later Junqueira) moved to the area and established Campo Alegre, a hacienda that he stocked with a number of Spanish and Barb horses. Exact details of the early horses at Campo Alegre are unclear, but it is generally considered that the majority of these horses were made up of Barbs and now-extinct Spanish Jennets, plus Criollos and Andalusians. João Francisco set in place a breeding program for his horses that was taken up by his son Gabriel, Baron of Alfenas. Gabriel Junqueira was friends with Dom Pedro I (1798–1834), Emperor of Brazil, who in turn was the son of João VI of Portugal (1767–1826) and acted as the representative to the Portuguese Crown for Minas. As a mark of their friendship, Dom Pedro presented Junqueira with a superb Alter Real stallion called Sublime.

Junqueira used Sublime for breeding with the horses at Campo Alegre. The foals quickly started to exhibit similar characteristics and developed into a specific type of horse of striking Spanish looks (although Portuguese, the Alter Real was founded on Andalusian stock) with a unique gait, derived from the Spanish Jennet foundation mares. These horses were referred to as Sublime horses and had extraordinarily docile and kind temperaments, but also great presence and spirit. They displayed two types of balanced, rhythmic gait, the *marcha batida* and the *marcha picada*. Both of these gaits exhibit moments of triple support—when three feet are on the ground at once—and are surprisingly swift and comfortable to sit to. The marcha picada is the smoother of the two and involves the horse moving its feet laterally and separately. *Picada* is Portuguese for "light touch," which is precisely how the gait feels. The marcha batida involves the legs moving in diagonals, again with moments of triple support. The breed's natural, inherited gaits undoubtedly came from the significant influence of Spanish Jennet blood, and the Mangalarga Marchador is often considered the Jennet's closest modern derivative.

Junqueira sold some of his Sublime horses to a friend who owned the hacienda Mangalarga in Paty do Alferes, in the state of Rio de Janeiro, and word of their great attributes soon spread to all the local ranchers and into the city of Rio de Janeiro. The horses became known as Mangalargas, and *Marchador* was added as a reflection of their very impressive marching ability. From that time on the Mangalarga Marchador's popularity has only increased. The horses provided the most comfortable means for traveling over long distances because of their gait, and they exhibited such kind temperaments that any member of the family, adult or child, could ride them. However, one of the greatest talents the Mangalarga Marchador has is for working cattle, an innate aptitude that, as with nearly all working stock horses, can be traced to their Spanish heritage. The Mangalarga Marchador is a tireless and highly intelligent working animal that possesses a built-in cow sense and ability to move and herd cattle. In 1949, the Brazilian breeders association was formed to preserve, protect, continue, and promote the horse.

APPALOOSA

HISTORIC – UNITED STATES – COMMON

HEIGHT
14.2–16 h.h.

APPEARANCE
A fine head well set to a neck of good length. Deep through the chest with a long, sloping shoulder, a short, muscular back, and a slightly sloping croup. Extremely sound legs and feet.

COLOR
Five main coat patterns (though others occur): snowflake, blanket, leopard, frost, and marbled.

APTITUDE
Riding, working livestock, jumping, competitive and Western riding horse sports

THE BEAUTIFUL APPALOOSA, with its distinctive coat coloring and appearance, is one of the best loved and most widely recognized of North American horse breeds. The American Appaloosa breed registry is one of the largest in the world, but today Appaloosas are also greatly prized internationally, particularly in the United Kingdom; they can make exceptional competition horses and are renowned for their toughness, stamina, and spirit.

The breed goes back to the late seventeenth century, to the northwestern corner of North America and specifically to the large area that covered what is now part of the states of Oregon, Washington, Idaho, and Montana. This was the land inhabited by the Nez Percé American Indians, and it is to their forward-thinking horsemanship and breeding practices that the Appaloosa owes its success.

Though the Nez Percé developed this spotted breed, the history of spotted horses is a long one, with images of spotted horses appearing in prehistoric European cave paintings from around 17,000 B.C.E. Spotted horses—in particular the Austrian Noriker and the Danish Knabstrup—were extremely popular in Europe and were in great demand from the sixteenth century to perform in the increasingly popular Riding Schools. Many of the hallowed Spanish horses, too, including the revered Andalusian, once exhibited spotted coat colorings.

Horses introduced to the Americas by the Spanish conquistadores carried the powerful spotted coat gene, which spread up into North America as the Spanish continued their explorations. The Shoshone tribe from southern Idaho became great horse traders, and it was largely from the Shoshone that the Nez Percé, whose territory was farther north and west, acquired their stock of horses. The Nez Percé's land, with its fertile plains and sheltered areas, was highly suitable for raising horses, and the tribe quickly established a substantial breeding stock. Unlike many of the American Indian tribes, the Nez Percé set about implementing breeding programs to specifically improve their horses. Only the best horses were kept as stallions, whereas those of inferior quality were gelded. The tribe kept the best of its breeding stock and got rid of the poorer horses through trading with other tribes. The numbers of their horses rose rapidly, and the Nez Percé became an affluent tribe based on their huge stock of horses. In the early 1800s, the American explorer Meriwether Lewis (1774–1809) described the Nez Percé's horses as "of an excellent race; they are elegantly formed, active, and durable."

Color was an important consideration for the Nez Percé, not just for ornamentation and decorative purposes but also for camouflage. However, their primary concern when breeding was to develop an all-around horse of great stamina, speed, and toughness, and one that was able to survive on sparse rations. Their horses became renowned for these qualities and were as capable of pulling a plow as they were of covering huge distances at speed with a rider. The most prized of their horses were used during warring campaigns and were swift, agile, and intelligent, and the most revered of these were the spotted ones.

The spotted horses belonging to the Nez Percé were described as Palouse horses by white settlers, who took the name from the Palouse River that ran through the Nez Percé territory. Later the horse became known as "a Palouse," then as an Appalousey. The name Appaloosa was not given to the breed until 1938 with the formation of the Appaloosa Horse Club, established to preserve the breed. Some fifty years before this, however, the plucky, spotted

breed was all but wiped out during the Nez Percé War fought between the American Indians and the U.S. government in 1877. The Nez Percé managed to outwit and outrun the U.S. cavalry for more than three months and across 1,300 miles (2,092 km) of treacherous terrain, solely because of the fortitude and endurance of their Appaloosa horses. The Nez Percé were undefeated in battle but eventually surrendered to prevent further hardships to the people trying to weather the frigid Montana winter. The conditions of their surrender stated that they be allowed to return to their lands in the spring with their horses, but instead they were sent to North Dakota and many of their beloved and prized animals slaughtered. Some escaped, and others were later rounded up by ranchers and used or sold.

After this, some of the horses that had survived were quickly dispersed at auction and acquired by a few private individuals and ranchers who recognized their innate qualities and began to breed them. In 1937, the magazine *Western Horseman* published an article on the Appaloosa written by Francis Haines, sparking public interest in the breed. The following year, Claude Thompson, a breeder of the spotted horses, joined with several others and established the Appaloosa Horse Club to preserve and promote the horses. By 1947, there were two hundred registered horses and a hundred members. Just three decades later, under the leadership of George Hatley, the club had a phenomenal figure of more than 300,000 horses registered, making it the third-largest light-horse breed registry. During this regeneration of the Appaloosa there was some introduction of Arabian blood and considerable influence from the Quarter Horse, which can be seen in the muscular frame of the modern Appaloosa.

In 1994 the Nez Percé tribe now based in Idaho began a breeding program to develop the Nez Percé horse. The aim of this program, which is based on breeding old Appaloosa stock with Akhal Teke stallions, is to produce an elegant, tough, versatile, and agile horse that is equal in its qualities to the original horses of the Nez Percé. Some, though not all, of these horses exhibit the spotted coat pattern of their Appaloosa heritage, though they generally adhere to the sleeker, finer frame of the Akhal Teke.

NEW WORLD SPLENDOR

PONY OF THE AMERICAS
MODERN – UNITED STATES – COMMON

HEIGHT
11.2–14 h.h.
APPEARANCE
Beautifully balanced ponies with excellent, athletic conformation. Attractive heads set to a well-arched neck. The shoulders are sloping, the back strong, and the hindquarters rounded and muscular. They exhibit mottled skin, sclera, and zebra-striped hooves.
COLOR
Spotted, occasionally roan.
APTITUDE
Riding, showing, competitive and Western riding horse sports

THE CHARISMATIC AND BEAUTIFUL Pony of the Americas (POA) is one of the country's most successful recent breeds, and also one of the most distinctly American. These gorgeous spotted ponies are the result of rigorous systematic breeding and exhibit the very best characteristics of a number of different breeds. Despite their pony size, they are distinctive in having the elegant conformation and appearance of a small horse.

The development of the breed can be attributed to a single person, the resourceful Leslie L. Boomhower and his tremendous vision to create an all-American pony breed in 1954. Boomhower, a lawyer in Mason City, Iowa, was a Shetland pony breeder who purchased an Arabian/ Appaloosa mare that had been bred to a Shetland stallion. The mare produced a beautiful, quality foal with the appearance of its spotted mother and the smaller size of its father; it was named Black Hand after a formation of dark spots on the pony's flank. This small, spotted stallion gave Boomhower the idea of creating a breed of similarly colored and sized ponies, and today Black Hand is recognized as one of the foundation stallions of the breed. Boomhower's intention was to create an intelligent, kind pony with quality, substance, and flashy good looks. He wanted an animal small and quiet enough to be enjoyed by children, yet also of sufficient size and spirit to be ridden by small adults.

Boomhower arranged a meeting with several other Shetland pony breeders at his ranch to discuss his ideas for the formation of a new breed. The enthusiastic breeders set up rigorous guidelines to ensure that a distinctive type could be produced within a relatively short time frame. At first, these included a definitive height range of between 44 and 52 inches (11–13 h.h.), but this has since been increased to 46 and 56 inches (11.2–14 h.h.). Early breeding was based on predominantly Appaloosa and Shetland crosses, though the breed was later greatly influenced by Quarter Horse, Arabian, Indian pony, and Welsh blood. Today the early Shetland influence is barely discernible in the POA, and instead it has all the characteristics of a small spotted horse of Quarter Horse/Appaloosa conformation, bearing the quality and slightly dished head of the Arabian. They can have a number of different coat patterns, one of the most common of which is the blanket pattern, in which the loins and hips are white with darker colored spots; others may have spots all over their body like a leopard. Some POA ponies may have a roan coat, but any indication of parti-colored markings as seen in the Paint or Pinto are not recognized by the breed standards and the horse may not be registered. A further distinctive feature of the POA is its mottled skin, also seen in the Appaloosa, which appears as a mixture of pigmented and nonpigmented skin most commonly around the eyes, muzzle, and genital areas. The POA, like the Appaloosa, also exhibits sclera, which is when the iris of the eye is visibly encircled by white. Finally, the POA may also have zebra-striped hooves, in which the hoof is made up of dark and pale vertical stripes of horn.

Above all, the POA has a wonderful temperament. Combined with its high-quality, balanced, and muscular frame, this makes it highly sought after as a children's pony. POAs are extremely versatile and can compete in virtually all Western and English riding disciplines; they are also talented in harness. The Pony of the Americas Club was founded by Boomhower in 1954 and has gone from strength to strength, boasting a large and growing membership. It is also particularly active with its youth programs and activities and promotes a great ethos of sportsmanship and encouragement.

NEW WORLD SPLENDOR

AMERICAN PAINT

HISTORIC – UNITED STATES – COMMON

HEIGHT	*well-defined withers.*
15–16 h.h.	COLOR
APPEARANCE	*Any color and white, or*
Generally solidly built,	*occasionally, solid colors.*
muscular horses predisposed	APTITUDE
to athletic endeavors.	*Riding, working livestock,*
Powerful hindquarters and	*showing, dressage, jumping,*
shoulders, a well-sprung rib	*showing, competitive and*
cage, deep chest, and	*Western riding horse sports*

THE HIGHLY ATTRACTIVE MARKINGS of Paint horses (and Pintos) are, like the spotted coat patterns, of ancient origin and evolved to aid primitive horses' survival through camouflage. Horses with coats marked in this way have appeared frequently in the ancient arts of Eurasia, and were, much like the spotted horses, highly prized for their great attractiveness. The tough little horses that streamed across the central and west Asian steppes of prehistoric times carried these different-colored coat genes, passing them into the desert horse breeds of Eurasia and spreading through Europe and North Africa. The North African Barb carried the colored coat pattern into the Spanish and Iberian breeds, which by around 700 C.E. frequently exhibited these different colors. During the sixteenth century, Spanish horses, some of which were spotted and parti-colored, introduced this coat pattern to the New World. According to the Spanish historian Diaz del Castillo (1492–1585), who accompanied Hernán Cortéz (1485–1547) on a 1519 expedition, one of the horses on board was a "pinto," with white markings on his front legs, and another was a dark roan horse with white patches.

Horses with parti-colored coats were particularly prized by various American Indian cultures, including the Sioux and the Crow, for their beauty and ability to camouflage. The Comanche were famed for their horsemanship and revered their parti-colored horses. These horses were the most prized within the herds, and their representation appears on many Comanche buffalo robes. Some cultures considered the loudly marked horses magical, and because of their considerable riding qualities they were regarded as among the best warhorses.

The American cowboy also favored the parti-colored horses for their flashy appearance and because the unique markings made it easy to distinguish them. These markings fall into two main categories, *overo* and *tobiano*, which are defined according to the distribution of white across the horse. *Overo* is a word of Spanish derivation originally meaning "like an egg," in which the white on the horse is splashy (or egg-like) and irregular. White rarely crosses the back and normally an overo horse has at least one solid-colored leg, though frequently all four are solid; often there is also white on the face. Tobiano horses, conversely, often have white legs, and white often crosses over the back. The white patches on a tobiano horse are normally regular and smooth in shape, unlike the overo.

The American Paint Horse Association (APHA) formed in 1965, bringing together two earlier organizations, the American Paint Stock Horse Association and the American Paint Quarter Horse Association. The APHA operates a rigorous registry based on bloodlines, and only horses of Quarter Horse, Thoroughbred, and Paint lines may be registered. Although the majority of Paint horses exhibit the parti-colored coat pattern, not all do, and it is possible for a solid-colored Paint to be registered. Paints are extremely attractive working animals whose conformation is heavily reflective of the working stock type, typified by the Quarter Horse. They tend to be extremely muscular and athletic and excel in all working cattle competitions as well as English riding disciplines.

Alongside the American Paint horse is the Pinto. The Pinto is a similarly parti-colored horse (or pony), but unlike the Paint, Pintos may be of any bloodline or breed, and therefore exhibit a huge range of physical characteristics. Any Paint horse may be registered with the Pinto Horse Association of America, but not every Pinto can be registered with the APHA.

AMERICAN QUARTER HORSE
HISTORIC – UNITED STATES – COMMON

HEIGHT
14.3–16 h.h.

APPEARANCE
A fine head, small, alert ears, and a muscular neck of medium length. Short through the back with a long, rounded croup and particularly muscular thighs. Shoulder is long and sloping and the chest deep and wide.

COLOR
Any of 17 recognized colors, of which sorrel is the most common.

APTITUDE
Riding, working livestock, racing, showing, jumping, Western riding horse sports

THE UBIQUITOUS QUARTER HORSE is an iconic part of American history and culture. These horses and their early ancestors transported the settlers westward, pulling wagons, working the land and livestock, and being ridden long distances, as well as being raced. The Quarter Horse is one of the most versatile and obliging of horse breeds, which when combined with its intelligence and impressive appearance, accounts for its enormous popularity.

The Quarter Horse is one of America's oldest horse breeds; it has its roots in the Spanish stock brought over in the sixteenth century, and in particular in horses bred in Florida. St. Augustine, the first European settlement there, was named by Spanish explorer Pedro Menéndez de Avilés (1519–74), who brought around a hundred horses with him from Spain; these, along with subsequent imports, were used as foundation breeding stock. His horses are reputed to have come from the province of Cádiz, noted for its superlative Spanish horses bred at Jerez de la Frontera, as well as from the royal Spanish ranches on Hispaniola.

The first ranches were established by Jesuit and Franciscan friars who set up a series of missions across north and central Florida. The Friars implemented serious livestock breeding programs, particularly for cattle and horses, both of which thrived on the vast grasslands there.

Many horses were obtained by the Chickasaw American Indians and taken north from Florida, where they were traded extensively with early plantation settlers. These stout, muscular, and thrifty horses were known as Chickasaws and were noted for their quick turn of speed over a short distance. The Chickasaw is today recognized as a breed in its own right but exists only in very small numbers; the horses do, however, bear a striking resemblance to the Quarter Horse and are widely believed to have been instrumental in its early foundation.

As these Chickasaw horses spread through the southern states above Florida, a group of enthusiasts in Virginia began importing English horses, particularly those of early running stock. Seventeen English horses were imported for the first time in 1611, probably a mixture of the now-extinct Irish Hobby and lightning-quick Galloway, Connemara ponies, and small but fast English stock. These horses were bred to Chickasaws and to the existing American/Spanish stock, primarily to produce horses for racing.

Informal racing became popular in the United States almost as soon as the horses arrived. However, there were few stretches of straight track suitable for racing, and the earliest races took place over a short stretch, not more than a quarter mile (0.4 km), and were most often held between only two horses. Often the races took place along town streets, and betting quickly became a fixture of such events. These short races required a horse capable of catapulting into a flat gallop from a standing start, and the modern Quarter Horse, taking its name from the quarter-mile races, is still renowned for its fast acceleration. They were also referred to as "short horses" because of the race length and were particularly popular in Colonial areas before the Revolutionary War (1775–83).

By the mid-eighteenth century, a distinct type of horse had been firmly established, and although bred along different lines in different areas, the horses exhibited a similar robust and muscular conformation and a great turn of speed. An early influence on the developing breed was the English Thoroughbred Janus (f. 1746, also known as Little Janus or Flying Dick), who was imported to Virginia in 1752 by Mordecai Booth, a plantation owner. Janus was a grandson of the Godolphin Arabian, one of the three foundation sires of the Thoroughbred breed. He was a small, compact, sorrel horse who passed his speed over short distances on to his progeny. He lived to the age of thirty-four and during his long life greatly influenced the development of running horses.

NEW WORLD SPLENDOR

By the beginning of the nineteenth century, however, longer distance racing on an oval track was becoming more widespread thanks to the increasing popularity of the English Thoroughbred. The Thoroughbred could sustain a fast pace for a much greater distance, and gradually the gap between the short- and long-distance horses widened. As the fashion for distance horses grew, the short horses fell out of favor with the racing crowd.

This was not, however, the end of the Quarter Horse. Just as the short horse had been bred to race in the southeastern states, it was also being bred for speed and agility in the southwestern states. These horses, which shared very similar bloodlines, were prized by the early cattlemen, ranchers, and cowboys for their athleticism and uncanny ability to work livestock. As more pioneers headed west, the short horses grew in demand. They were able to pull buggies and wagons, carry people safely across difficult terrain, and accelerate quickly when needed. Furthermore, despite their speed and spirited attitude, they have an extraordinarily calm and tractable character.

Much of the early genetic history of the Quarter Horse is unrecorded, but it is clear that it developed from a diverse range of influences, primarily Spanish, but also including North African Barb, Arabian, Mustang, Morgan, English Thoroughbred, and even some European draft blood. One of the great early influences in the breed was the stallion Sir Archy (f. 1805), son of the stallion Diomed (f. 1777). Two of the foundation stallions of the modern Quarter Horse— Steel Dust (f. 1843) and Shiloh (f. 1844)—were both descended from Sir Archy. Steel Dust was brought to Texas in 1844, where he quickly earned a reputation for his speed and skills. Such was his following that Quarter Horses from the area were described as Steel Dust Horses. Shiloh was born in Tennessee and taken to Texas in 1849. The stallion was greatly respected and gave rise to a number of bloodlines still seen in the Quarter Horse, as well as earning a formidable reputation on the racetrack. Another of the great early influences on the Quarter Horse was the horse Peter McCue (f. 1895). He was such a prolific sire that of the first nineteen stallions registered with the American Quarter Horse Association (AQHA), twelve were descended from him. Currently the AQHA is the largest breed registry in the world, with several million horses registered, and the Quarter Horse itself is one of the most international breeds.

MORGAN

HISTORIC – UNITED STATES – COMMON

HEIGHT
14.1–15.2 h.h.
APPEARANCE
A beautiful, quality head, broad between the eyes. Neck is finely modeled, muscular, and well arched. Defined withers and compact, muscular frame with a short

back and well-sprung rib cage. Deep, wide chest and a good, sloping shoulder.
COLOR
Any color; often bay or chestnut.
APTITUDE
Riding, light draft, dressage, jumping, showing, competitive and Western riding horse sports

RARELY HAVE THE ORIGINS OF A HORSE BREED been subject to such controversy as those surrounding the elegant Morgan horse, America's oldest registered breed. There are no definitive accounts for the Morgan's early history, though many challenge this, but there are a number of theories. What is set in stone is the extraordinary influence of a single stallion—a small bay with a heart the size of a lion, known as Justin Morgan—in the development of the breed.

First called Figure, Justin Morgan was born in New England in 1789. He was an undersized bay, standing around 14 hands high, but he quickly proved to have the strength, courage, and stamina of an animal twice his size. Figure is said to have been given to a man named Justin Morgan as payment for a debt when the horse was around two years old. Unable to sell him, Morgan leased him to a local farmer. The small horse proved his merit on the farm, outworking every other horse in the area and demonstrating incredible strength and endurance. Word began to spread about the horse's fantastic abilities, and he was sold a number of times.

Figure was used for plowing, hauling timber, clearing woodland, pulling carts, riding, and racing in harness and under saddle—he was apparently never beaten. One story tells that Figure's owner won a bet when, after working in the fields all day, the horse managed to pull a tree that no other horse had been able to budge. Figure did it with just two short breathers, and with three men sitting on the tree.

Figure was a very compact horse with a fine head and arched neck, a short, strong back, and rounded muscular quarters. He had a long, flowing mane and tail and was

very attractive, but most compelling was the way his progeny universally reflected their father's appearance and character. After Justin Morgan died, Figure became known as the Justin Morgan horse, later shortened to Morgan.

That the elegant and gifted horse Justin Morgan gave rise to the Morgan breed is undisputed, but of great debate is Justin Morgan's own heritage. It is speculated that he was sired by the horse True Briton, an early Thoroughbred type with Arabian and Barb links, by a mare of Wildair breeding. However, with the exception of its high quality, the Morgan bears little in common with either the Thoroughbred or the Arabian. Others suggest that Justin Morgan must have had Friesian and/or Welsh Cob blood, which would seem more plausible in light of those breeds' appearance, conformation, pulling power, stamina, and tractable temperament. Leading U.S. breed authority Bonnie Hendricks has suggested that the Morgan may owe much of its heritage to the little-known Canadian horse, which itself was influenced by Andalusian, Friesian, and French stock. Canadian horses were widespread in New England at the time, and there are striking similarities in the two breeds' appearances.

Many of Justin Morgan's progeny gained great fame for their pulling and working abilities, and the horses were bred and used for transportation, freight, and agriculture. They were used as cavalry remounts and for pulling artillery during the Civil War (1861–65), and they also became extremely popular for harness racing. Two famous Morgans were Black Hawk (f. 1833) and his son Ethan Allen (f. 1849), who were influential in the development of the American Standardbred and the Saddlebred. Morgans also contributed to the Tennessee Walker.

However, their popularity waned as larger, taller horses became fashionable, and Morgans were bred to larger, non-Morgan types, leading to a loss of original type. In the 1890s, new breeding programs were established to regain the qualities of the original breed, and in 1894 the first volume of the studbook was published.

TENNESSEE WALKING HORSE

HISTORIC – UNITED STATES – COMMON

HEIGHT	barrel. The back is compact and
14.3–17 h.h.	*the hindquarters are muscular.*
APPEARANCE	**COLOR**
Solid and muscular, but carries	*Any color, though most often*
itself with enormous cadence	*black and shades of chestnut.*
and elegance. An attractive	**APTITUDE**
head well set to an elegant,	*Riding, light draft, showing,*
arched neck, with sloping	*competitive and Western*
shoulders and a rounded	*riding horse sports*

THE TENNESSEE WALKING HORSE, or Tennessee Walker, originally developed as an all-around utility horse with a remarkable ability to traverse difficult terrain at a consistent, medium speed, providing a smooth and comfortable ride.

The breed evolved early in the nineteenth century when pioneers traveled west over the Appalachians to settle in Tennessee, Kentucky, and Missouri. Middle Tennessee, at the heart of the state, was a major destination for these early travelers, many of whom came from Virginia. The wealthiest established sprawling plantations that reaped the rewards of the area's natural fertile soils. Plantation owners required horses that could not only work the land but could also pull their buggies and make attractive, useful riding horses, classy enough to take the family to church yet tough enough to work all day. These horses, originally referred to as Tennessee Pacers, Southern Plantation Horses, or Turn Row horses, were extremely agile and able to turn between the plantation rows without damaging the crops and to pick their way across the often treacherous countryside.

The Tennessee Walker is one of America's gaited breeds, which makes it comfortable to ride and accounts for its great demand early in its history. It developed from a base of Spanish influence, primarily Spanish Mustangs. Many of these horses retained the gait passed to them through the ancient Asturian and now-extinct Spanish Jennet. The most influential breed early in the Tennessee Walker's history, however, was the now-extinct Narragansett Pacer,

also a gaited breed. The Narragansett Pacer was one of the leading riding horses of its day and was an exceptionally fast trotter, prized for its smooth gaits and speed and frequently raced. It is at the foundation of all of the American gaited breeds and was most associated with Rhode Island and Massachusetts, where racing was very popular. The Pacer's heritage is unclear but is often attributed to the now-extinct British and Irish Hobby and Galloway, Spanish Jennet, and Canadian horse.

Other breeds that contributed substantially to the development of the Tennessee Walker were the Canadian Pacer, Morgan, Standardbred, Saddlebred, and Thoroughbred. The Canadian Pacer also contributed to the breed's gait, and both Canadians and Narragansetts were popular in North Carolina from the eighteenth century. Many pioneers crossed the Appalachians from North Carolina, bringing their smooth-gaited horses with them. These horses also moved back and forth between North Carolina and Middle Tennessee, including a Canadian Pacer/Thoroughbred stallion called Copperbottom, who was used extensively for breeding and established the Copperbottom line of Tennessee horses.

The most significant horse in the Tennessee's development was Allan F-1 (f. 1886), now classed as the foundation sire of the Tennessee Walking Horse breed. Allan F-1 was by the stallion Allandorf (f. 1882), a Standardbred horse of the Hambletonian line, and out of the mare Maggie Marshall (f. 1869), a Morgan. Allan F-1 was an elegant black horse who exhibited an unusual walking pace. When he was bred to Tennessee Pacer mares, he passed this gait on to his progeny, and the Tennessee Walking Horse was born. A further important stallion in the breed's development was the Saddlebred Giovanni (f. 1910), who sired multiple show winners. He was brought from Kentucky in 1914 and is credited with endowing the Tennessee Walker with its flashy good looks and elegance.

MISSOURI FOX TROTTER

HISTORIC – UNITED STATES – COMMON

HEIGHT
14–16 h.h.
APPEARANCE
Proportionate head set to an elegant, muscular neck. Deep and wide through the chest with shoulders sloped to an angle of 45–50°. Strong back, with strong, clean, sound

limbs. Tail is set and carried quite high.
COLOR
Any, though shades of chestnut predominate.
APTITUDE
Riding, light draft, showing, competitive and Western riding horse sports

THE MISSOURI FOX TROTTER'S HISTORY goes back to the early 1820s and the westward migration of settlers seeking their piece of American soil. By 1820–21, pioneers were crossing the Mississippi River, leaving the fertile plantations of Tennessee and grasslands of Kentucky and Virginia behind them and striking out toward the magnificent Ozark highlands of southern Missouri. This huge area, part dense woodland, part pasture, became an important center for cattle ranching and mining.

Horses were vital to the early pioneers: the passage of people and livestock across this as-yet-undeveloped landscape was a treacherous one, and a sure-footed horse was an essential for everyday life, as was one that could work or travel all day and be suitable for all members of the family to handle and ride. The horses brought into the Ozarks from Tennessee, Kentucky, and Virginia were of mixed heritage and included the Tennessee, Narragansett, and Canadian pacers, as well as the Kentucky Saddler (American Saddlebred), Morgan, Arabian, and early Thoroughbred types. Speed and comfort were prerequisites for early horse breeders in the area, and it quickly became apparent that gaited horses such as the Pacers, Tennessee Walkers, and Saddlebreds filled these needs most effectively.

A number of early bloodlines, still of mixed heritage, were developed by these early settlers—such as the Brimmer horses bred by Moses Locke Alsup in the Ozark Hills and descended from the Thoroughbred Jolly Roger—and the Old Skip line descended from the Morgan/

Thoroughbred stallion of the same name. The stallion Cotham Dare (f. 1941) was also significant in the development of the Fox Trotter; he was the first stallion to be registered with the Missouri Fox Trotting Horse Breed Association, established in 1948, despite also being a registered Saddlebred.

During the nineteenth century, a fixed type of horse gradually began to emerge: a gaited animal that afforded an incredibly smooth, gliding ride. The horses have three gaits: the flat-footed walk, the famous fox trot, and an expressive canter. The flat-footed walk is a rapid, four-beat pace. The fox trot is a broken gait, in which the horse walks rapidly with its front legs and trots with its rear legs, sliding its back feet and thus preventing rider (and horse) from being jarred. As a result of the sliding the rider is able to sit without any interference of movement, and this pace can be sustained at between 5 and 8 miles per hour for long periods without tiring either horse or rider. While performing the fox trot, the horse nods its head and tail in time to the pace, not unlike the Tennessee Walker.

With the advent of motorized vehicles, there was a brief decrease in demand for many of America's versatile breeds before a resurgence as part of the leisure industry. The Missouri Fox Trotter, however, remained a favorite in its area, primarily because of the size of the cattle industry. The Fox Trotter was (and to a lesser extent still is) used widely on the Missouri cattle outfits for moving and working livestock, a capacity in which it excelled thanks to its sure-footedness and stamina. Today the Fox Trotter is a popular breed for both trail riding and showing. Like the Tennessee Walker, the Fox Trotter has an excellent temperament, making it suitable for children and nervous riders as well as the more experienced. The Missouri Fox Trotting Horse Breed Association oversees the protection and promotion of the breed and holds the breed registry; since 1982 only horses with a dam and sire registered may be entered into the registry.

AMERICAN SADDLEBRED
HISTORIC — UNITED STATES — COMMON

HEIGHT	and the pastern long
15–16 h.h.	*and flexible.*
APPEARANCE	**COLOR**
A fine and quality head well	*Any color.*
set to a long, well-arched neck.	**APTITUDE**
Deep, wide chest; good, sloping	*Riding, light draft, light*
shoulder; well-defined withers;	*agricultural work, packing,*
and a short, strong back. Legs	*showing, dressage, jumping,*
should be clean and strong	*competitive horse sports*

THE AMERICAN SADDLEBRED, or Kentucky Saddler, is perhaps the best known and flashiest of the American gaited horses and is the perfect combination of spirit and fire with a tractable temperament. The horses are extraordinarily beautiful to watch when moving—they possess a natural cadence and elegance rarely matched by other breeds.

The foundations for the American Saddlebred were laid in the seventeenth century when British colonists arrived in North America with their Galloways and British and Irish Hobbies. The ambling Spanish Jennet probably also had an influence, but the major contributor to the Saddlebred was the naturally gaited Narragansett Pacer. The Pacer was not a particularly grand horse, and as flashier horses became popular, it began to be crossbred out, primarily to the newly imported early Thoroughbreds. Pacers were also bred to good Canadian trotting mares to produce the Canadian Pacer, a similarly popular smooth-gaited breed that also contributed toward the Saddlebred, particularly through the stallion Tom Hal (f. 1806). Tom Hal was also influential in the development of the Tennessee Walker and the American Standardbred.

These early mixes of Narragansett and Canadian Pacer with primarily Thoroughbred blood gave rise to a type called the American Horse, a general purpose, versatile animal with a smooth gait and plenty of substance and quality. Along with Morgans and Spanish horses, these are the horses from which the American Saddlebred ultimately evolved. In Kentucky breeders continued to breed their tough, gaited horses to Thoroughbreds and Morgans, and gradually a definitive type emerged, which was first called the Kentucky Saddler. These horses were used to plow the land, haul crops, and pull wagons and traps, but they were also extravagant riding horses with a majestic self-carriage. These Saddlers were in great demand during the American Revolutionary War (1775–83) and were especially popular as officers' horses during the Civil War (1861–65).

The most influential stallion early in the American Saddlebred's history was the Kentucky-born Denmark (f. 1839), son of the imported Thoroughbred Hedgeford (f. 1825). Denmark was bred to a gaited mare and produced Gaines Denmark (f. 1851), a stunning black stallion who produced four famous sons: Washington Denmark (f. 1855), Diamond Denmark (f. 1858), Star Denmark (f. 1856), and Sumpter Denmark (f. 1865). In 1908, Denmark was listed as the foundation sire of the American Saddlebred breed, and more than 60 percent of horses in the first three volumes of the American Saddlebred Horse Association studbook trace to Gaines Denmark. In 1991, Harrison Chief (f. 1872) was recognized as the second foundation sire of the breed. Harrison Chief's bloodlines trace to the Thoroughbred Messenger (f. 1780), who was imported in 1788 and is recognized as one of the foundation stallions of the Standardbred breed.

Saddlebreds are naturally gaited horses, although their gaits can be emphasized through training; they are shown in three- or five-gaited classes. In the three-gaited classes, the horse must exhibit an animated walk, a high-stepping park trot, and a slow, rhythmic canter. The horses have their manes roached and tails trimmed for these classes to accentuate their overall look. In the five-gaited classes, they must exhibit speed and animation and perform a classy walk; a bold, high-stepping trot; a slow gait involving high knee action and great precision and deliberation; a rack with rapid footfalls; and a slow, smooth canter. In five-gaited classes the mane and tail are left naturally long. Saddlebreds also excel in nearly all spheres of equestrian competition, including driving, dressage, jumping, reining, and endurance.

BANKER HORSE

HISTORIC – UNITED STATES – RARE

HEIGHT
13–14.3 h.h.

APPEARANCE
Spanish ancestry is evident in the horse's appearance, particularly seen in the head, with its straight or ram-like profile, and in its majestic bearing.

COLOR
Predominantly dun, buckskin, chestnut, and brown; occasionally parti-colored.

APTITUDE
Feral, but if domesticated: riding, light draft, competitive and Western riding horse sports

THE OUTER BANKS, a long chain of sandy islands off the North Carolina coast, are home to the rare and threatened Banker horse. Its dramatic history includes danger and marauding, and there are few breeds that would have survived the incredible hardships to which these horses were subjected. Now, however, their amazing survival is threatened by human encroachment on their habitat.

The Algonquin American Indians who inhabited the string of islands described them as *hattersail*, which loosely means "there is less vegetation." It is an apt description, for these sandy islands were one of the most isolated and underpopulated areas of the United States for many years. The islands protect the coast from the Atlantic Ocean and are battered by ferocious eroding seas and subject to major storms and hurricanes. They sit along a treacherous passage renowned for shipwrecks to such an extent that the area has become known as the Graveyard of the Atlantic.

The history of the horses began with the first explorations of the North Carolina coastline, made between 1500 and 1526 under the Spaniard Lucas Vázquez de Ayllón (c. 1475–1526), a plantation owner from Hispaniola. By this time Hispaniola and other islands of the West Indies were supporting large horse-breeding operations based on Spanish stock, and it was these horses that Ayllón brought on his expeditions. In 1526, six vessels under his command landed near present-day Georgetown, South Carolina, to establish a colony. Ayllón died several months later, and the ill-fated colony was sacked during an American Indian uprising; the Spanish fled, abandoning their horses.

The next documented introduction of horses to the Outer Banks area was during the 1580s when the Englishman Sir Walter Raleigh (c. 1552–1618) attempted to colonize Roanoke Island. For four years Raleigh's ships sailed between England and the Outer Banks, but the settlers would not remain. In 1585 an expedition of Raleigh's ships stopped to trade at Puerto Rico en route to Roanoke, and the fleet acquired a number of horses from Hispaniola. Disaster struck as they entered an inlet into the Outer Banks, however, and the lead ship was beached. Supplies and livestock were off-loaded in an attempt to save the ship, and those horses that made it ashore became known as Bankers.

Despite the inhospitable nature of the islands—their coarse grasses, extensive sand, and lack of fresh water—they provided a habitat free from predators and protected on all sides by large bodies of water. The horses learned to paw the sand away until they got deep enough to locate fresh water, and today the Banker still has an amazing ability to find fresh water. From their first arrival on the islands the horse population grew rapidly and the Banker existed relatively undisturbed by human activity. Their isolation has kept the breed extremely genetically pure.

Those that were captured proved to make excellent riding horses because of their natural gait—a throwback to their Spanish Jennet and Asturian heritage—that many of them exhibit. They were used for hauling produce, moving the heavy fishing nets, and working the land, and they were regularly rounded up and sold to the mainland, where they were prized for their notable attributes.

In the past sixty years or so, there has been a massive growth in the tourist industry on the islands of the Outer Banks, and this has had a devastating effect on the Banker horses. Their habitat has been increasingly diminished, and they are now also victims of human-related incidents, particularly traffic fatalities. The Banker is now seriously threatened, and it is only because of the efforts of a number of dedicated people that they continue to survive.

ASSATEAGUE + CHINCOTEAGUE

HISTORIC — UNITED STATES — RARE

HEIGHT	COLOR
12–14 h.h.	*Any color, with a*
APPEARANCE	*predominance of*
A high-quality head that can	*parti-colored.*
reflect Spanish or Arabian	**APTITUDE**
qualities. They can be	*Feral, but if domesticated,*
reasonably long in the leg in	*riding, competitive*
proportion to their body size,	*and Western riding*
and are extremely tough.	*horse sports*

ASSATEAGUE AND CHINCOTEAGUE are a pair of islands just off the coast of Maryland and Virginia. Assateague is the larger of the two and is famous for its wild, idyllic beauty; long, beautiful beaches; secret coves and bays; and untamed marshland. It is a national park, and also home to the Assateague and Chincoteague ponies. Assateague Island falls partly under the state of Maryland and partly under Virginia, with a fence line marking the border between the two states. The ponies on the Maryland side are called Assateague, and those on the Virginia side are commonly referred to as Chincoteague.

Several romantic myths surround the appearance of these plucky, attractive animals on the island of Assateague: one claims that they swam ashore from a shipwrecked Spanish galleon; another, that they are descended from stock left there by pirates. In fact, the ponies' presence there dates to 1669, when settlers on the mainland let their livestock loose on the island to avoid paying taxes and to reduce the need to spend money on building fences on their homesteads. The animals were branded or marked and set free on the salty marshes to roam at will. The early foundations of the ponies were colonial horses: a mixture of Spanish, Barb, and Arabian blood.

Although the Assateagues and Chincoteagues are recognized and referred to as ponies, they bear more similarity to undersized horses, particularly in their conformation and the aspect of their heads. It is conjectured that the colonial horses, which were small at this time anyway, might have suffered a reduction in growth over time because of the spartan living conditions on the island. The diet of salt-marsh grass and coarse fodder, combined with extreme temperatures and constant battering from mosquitoes, could have led to the continued small size of the animals. Through the years, concentrated inbreeding in the herds led to a massive decline in the quality of the ponies and certain conformational issues. These were addressed by the introduction of some Welsh and Shetland blood, as well as that of Pinto origin, which has resulted in the predominance of parti-colored ponies. There has been a huge improvement in the ponies, and today they are beautiful, tough, and useful children's ponies.

A traditional part of the ponies' history is "penning"—a practice thought to date back to the 1700s on Assateague and somewhat later on Chincoteague—which allowed the ponies to be captured, sold, branded, and checked. By 1885, penning was held on one island one day and on the other the next, and by 1909 the penning days had become huge festivals held on the last Wednesday and Thursday of July. In the 1920s the tradition changed when a rich landowner restricted the locals' access to the oyster-rich area of Tom's Cove, and many people moved across the water to Chincoteague. By 1925, the now-famous event of swimming the ponies from Assateague to Chincoteague for the penning had begun. The ponies of Assateague were herded by saltwater cowboys to the narrowest part of the channel between the islands, then herded across. That same year, the Chincoteague Volunteer Fire Department held a carnival during the pony penning to raise much-needed funds. The event was a great success, and the fire department later began to build up its own herd of ponies. Today the annual pony penning and auction on Chincoteague, which inspired the famous novel *Misty of Chincoteague* by Marguerite Henry, is a hugely popular event attended by thousands and allows the herd of ponies to be regulated to prevent overstocking.

ROCKY MOUNTAIN HORSE

HISTORIC – UNITED STATES – UNCOMMON

HEIGHT
14.2–16 h.h.

APPEARANCE
A fine head well set to a slightly arched neck of good length. Shoulders have a good slope and a deep, wide chest. A natural four-beat ambling gait allows horse and rider to travel

long distances without tiring.

COLOR
Range of brown coat colors, flaxen mane and tail. Solid body with no white marks above knee or hock.

APTITUDE
Riding, working livestock, showing, dressage, jumping, Western riding horse sports

THE ROCKY MOUNTAIN HORSE is one of Kentucky's less-well-known treasures. The breed's early development was little documented, but since the formation of the Rocky Mountain Horse Association in 1986 there has been a sustained effort to preserve and promote it. Despite its short recorded history, the Rocky Mountain Horse exhibits true definitive characteristics through all its progeny.

The Rocky Mountain Horse evolved in the eastern parts of Kentucky at the foot of the Appalachian Mountains, probably at the same time as the American Saddlebred (Kentucky Saddler). This was in the days when pioneers set off from eastern states such as Virginia and the Carolinas and trekked over the Appalachians in search of new land. These settlers needed horses that were versatile, full of stamina, and sure-footed enough to cover the treacherous landscape smoothly and with some speed. Money was often tight, and a single horse was required to perform a multitude of tasks, from working the land to hauling produce and carrying riders. The horses also had to have an excellent temperament, one that was calm, biddable, and easily trained. It is no coincidence that the breeds of Missouri, Kentucky, and Tennessee—the American Saddlebred, the Missouri Fox Trotter, the Tennessee Walker, and the less widespread Rocky Mountain Horse— are remarkable for their gentle temperaments.

Like its neighbor the Saddlebred, the Rocky Mountain Horse may be traced both to Spanish stock and to the ubiquitous little Narragansett Pacer, which was so formative in the American gaited breeds. Its characteristics were reinforced by its geographic environment. Living in the foothills of the Appalachian Mountains, these horses had to be tough to withstand extreme winter weather, often without shelter. Feed was not always in good supply, and the horses had to be thrifty, eating coarse grasses and even tree bark to survive.

Although never formally documented, there is a story of a gaited colt who was brought into eastern Kentucky in the 1890s called the Rocky Mountain Stud Colt (of 1890). He was by all accounts a beautiful, dark chocolate brown with a flaxen mane and tail. Bred to him, the local mares produced offspring in his likeness to which the term "Rocky Mountain Horse" began to be ascribed. However, many horses at this time would have exhibited a natural gait, and both the gaited Narragansett Pacer and the Canadian Pacer were then widespread. Nonetheless, it is possible—and has been seen in other breeds, most notably the Morgan—for a single prepotent stallion to reproduce progeny in his own image, and the uncorroborated story of the "birth" of the Rocky Mountain Horse is not perhaps as outlandish as it sounds.

The most important, and best documented, period of the breed's development was at the hands of breeder Sam Tuttle. One of the Rocky Mountain Stud Colt's offspring had been a colt foal named Old Tobe (f. 1928), who sired the colt foal Tobe (f. 1942) on Tuttle's farm. Tobe was much loved for his character and was sought after as a stallion because of the quality of foals he sired. Tuttle used him for ten years while managing the trail-riding concession at the Natural Bridge State Park in Powell County, Kentucky. Tobe was the most popular trail horse there, and he was also used prolifically as a stallion until he was retired at age thirty-four. He lived to thirty-seven, and longevity remains a predominant feature of the Rocky Mountain Horse. Tobe is recognized as the foundation stallion of the breed, and the five main stallions of the breed, registered in 1986 (when the registry opened), were all his sons.

NEW WORLD SPLENDOR

AMERICAN BASHKIR CURLY

HISTORIC — UNITED STATES — COMMON

HEIGHT
13.3–16 h.h. (average 15 h.h.)
APPEARANCE
An attractive head with a strong jaw and wide-spaced Oriental eyes. Muscular, well-set neck, defined withers, and muscular, sloping shoulders. Short to medium-length back and a sloping, rounded croup. The front legs should have long forearms and strong, dense cannon bones.
COLOR
Any color, coat invariably curly.
APTITUDE
Riding, light draft, jumping, working livestock, competitive and Western riding horse sports

THE SPLENDID AMERICAN BASHKIR CURLY horses (also known as American Curly Horses or simply Curlies) have an enigmatic history that has been greatly colored by stories of little substance and further confused by their misleading name. "Bashkir" implies a direct relationship to the ancient Russian Bashkir horses bred by the Bashkiri people in the region of the Urals and Volga, but there are no actual accounts to substantiate this, and recent genetic testing has been inconclusive. In truth, there is as yet no concrete explanation for the arrival of these gorgeous, talented, curly-coated horses in North America.

The popular story of their Russian origin has its roots in the Russian occupation of Alaska from the late eighteenth to mid-nineteenth century. Russians trekked through Siberia with their packhorses before crossing over the Bering Strait and into Alaska, where they tried to establish farms. Their agricultural endeavors were unsuccessful, however; livestock and crops perished, and few horses survived either the trip across Siberia or life in Alaska. What's more, it is likely that the horses that did survive were those of the (straight-coated) Yakut breed, one of the hardiest breeds in existence, which lives farther north than any other breed in Siberia. In any case, only sixteen horses were recorded as living in Russian Alaska in 1817. Finally, Bashkir horses are not universally curly coated—it is instead the Russian Lokai that exhibits the most predominant curly coat, and neither the Bashkir nor the Lokai are thought to have been taken into Alaska. Even had Lokai horses been in Alaska, it is highly implausible that they could have made

their way several thousand miles south through treacherous terrain to arrive in Nevada, where the curly-coated American horses were later discovered.

There is evidence of curly-coated horses being sighted in South America in the late 1700s, which would suggest that they had derived from Spanish and other European stock introduced by the conquistadores. The next evidence of curly-coated horses was during the winter of 1801–2 when the Sioux American Indians of South Dakota are said to have procured the horses from the Crow tribe. Several decades later, in 1848, showman and circus owner P. T. Barnum (1810–91) wrote in his autobiography about purchasing a curly-coated horse for use in his shows.

These few tenuous pieces of the Curly's history shed little light on their origins, and it was not until 1898 that the modern history of the breed can be traced with any certainty. This was the year that Italian-born rancher John Damele and his son came across three stunning curly-coated horses among a herd of wild horses high in the Nevada mountains while the men were checking on their cattle. The Damele family owned the Three Bar Ranch, northwest of the desolate mining town Eureka, a place of brutal winters and scorching summers in the high-altitude Nevada desert. The area was home to huge herds of Mustangs, and several years later, in 1931, the Dameles caught one of the curly-coated horses from the Mustang herd, trained it, and sold it on. According to the family, this was their first close dealing with the horses, but in the following year, they began to truly realize the qualities of the Curlies.

The winter of 1932 was one of the worst, with temperatures plummeting and the severe weather lasting for many months. In the spring, when the snow had cleared and the family went to search for their own herds of horses, they discovered that they had all perished except for the curly-coated horses. The Dameles realized that these tough horses would make excellent working stock for use on the ranch if they could be captured and trained.

After two more horrific winters in 1951 and 1952, where again only the Curlies survived, the Dameles began to breed the horses in earnest to build up a Curly herd. They caught their first stallion from the Mustang herd and named him Copper D, training him as a two-year-old. They registered their 3D brand and began an intensive and calculated breeding program to improve the quality and appearance of the Curly horses while maintaining their extraordinary characteristics of endurance, intelligence, and tractable temperament. The Dameles introduced substantial outside blood, including the Morgan stallion Red Ruby King and the Arabian stallion Nevada King, along with Quarter Horse blood and a Saddlebred stallion called Idaho. Copper D became one of the most sought-after Curly horse stallions, and many Curlies can trace their ancestry to him. The Dameles are still respected breeders of the Curly horse, and it is thanks to them that this breed has survived and developed into the talented, beautiful horses that they are. Different early lines of Curly horse were also found in other states, including Wyoming, where they are found in the feral herds in Rock Springs and are thought to go back to the Laramie Stud, where Curly horses were bred during the 1940s.

Of significant interest is the recent genetic testing that has been carried out on Curly horses to look at their heritage and determine unifying characteristics of the breed. The results indicate that the modern Curly is not a genetically distinct breed because of massive crossbreeding to primarily but not exclusively Quarter Horses and Morgans. Further, there was no single blood marker found that is present in all Curly horses, indicating that "pure" Curlies do not exist; instead, there are specific Curly types of horse with similar characteristics that have been fixed through recent selective breeding. As such, there is huge diversity in the appearance of the Curly that extends to their height and body frame. Typically they have an excellent, kind, and intelligent temperament and move well; they can also sometimes exhibit a natural gait similar to a running walk.

The American Bashkir Curly Registry was formed in 1971 to try to preserve and promote the horses, and to define and collate the characteristics particular to the horses. The International Curly Horse Organization and the Curly Sporthorse International registry were both formed in 2003, also to continue promoting and improving the Curly.

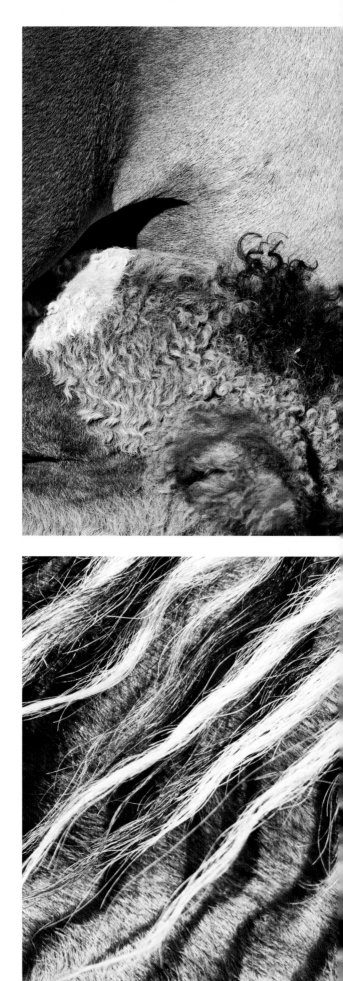

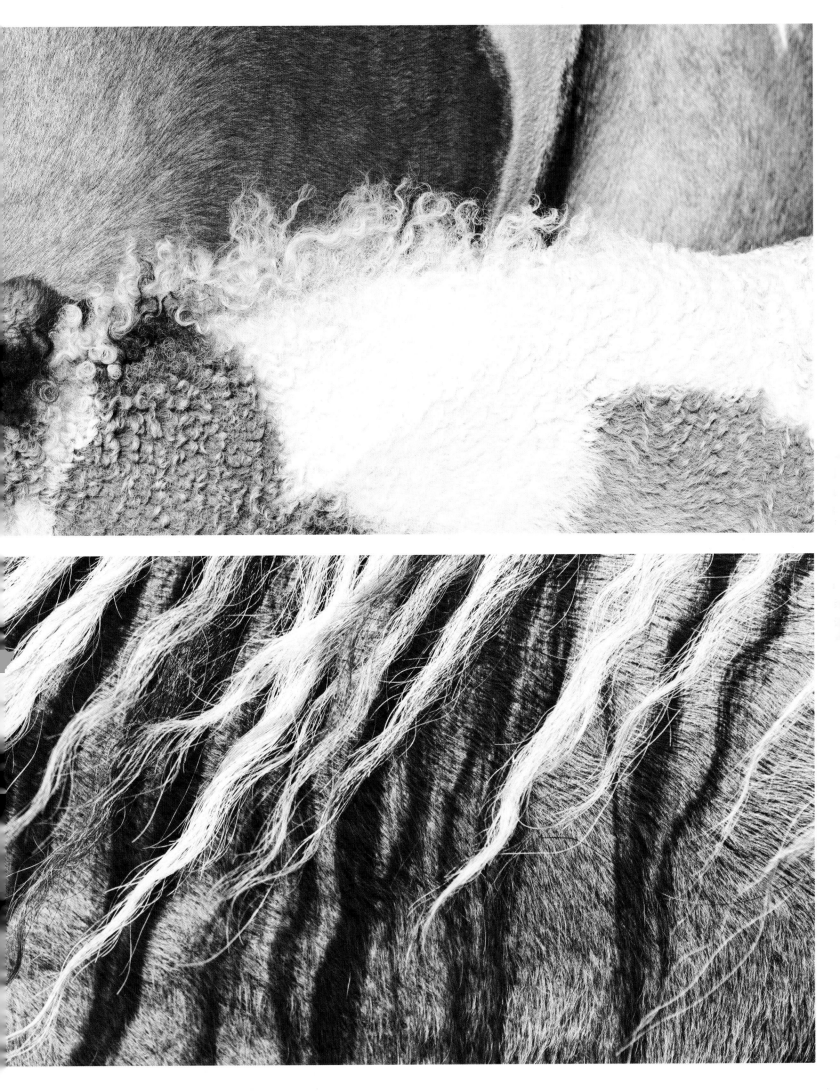

5 | ENERGETIC GRANDEUR

The pursuit of speed with a competitive edge is inherent in humankind, and there is little doubt that the very earliest horse people indulged in impromptu races. Entertainment aside, the requirement for speed and sustained energy in early cultures was born out of need—primarily the need to be faster than one's enemy, or one's prey. Those individuals with the best equestrian skills and the best horses were destined to be the most successful.

The first formal races were chariot races that evolved from the art of early warfare. Evidence of these races can be seen on pottery that dates to the Mycenaean period of Ancient Greece (1600–1100 B.C.E.), and it was the Ancient Greeks who organized the sport of chariot racing and were the first known people to build tracks called hippodromes. They devised a special lightweight chariot for war and for racing that was the forerunner of the sulky—reintroduced to harness racing in the early nineteenth century. Chariot or harness racing for two horses preceded that for four horses and was seen at the first Olympiad in 776 B.C.E. The first organized ridden races, which were bareback, were introduced to the Olympiad in c. 644 B.C.E. At this time, horses were still rather small, as evidenced in ancient artworks, and it would be many centuries before there was an appreciable increase in their size.

Chariot racing was adopted by the Romans who called their tracks "circuses." The largest of these was the Circus Maximus, which could seat a staggering two hundred thousand people, and race days were treated as festivals. It was the Romans who made the significant introduction of monetary prizes, and today prize money and monetary gain through gambling are central to all major forms of horse racing. Charioteers were at first slaves or lower class citizens eager for the opportunity to win riches and honor, but the system was later changed and the prize money awarded to the owner of the chariot, not the driver. Contestants were frequently killed during the high speed races, and the horses were also prone to devastating injuries.

The Romans raced using different sized teams, including two, three, four, and even ten horse hitches, established by the Emperor Nero (37–68 C.E.). They also introduced spring-loaded starting gates that ensured a fairer start to the race and introduced rules, although it appears corruption and race tampering were rife. To increase the speed of their horses, the Romans imported faster types from North Africa, and desert-bred horses were highly valued. However, despite the enormous emphasis on these races and the acquisition of fast, enduring horses, it is generally considered that there was a decline in actual equestrian skills throughout the Roman era, particularly in comparison with the prowess of the early Greeks.

Great Britain has one of the longest historic traditions of ridden horse racing, and today racing remains one of the country's leading sports. Interestingly, the earliest native British stock was generally of poorer quality than that of continental Europe, being smaller in stature and less elegant in appearance. In spite of this, British stock has always demonstrated a predisposition toward speed and an inherent toughness. The earliest formal flat races are thought to date to the reign of Emperor Lucius Septimus Severus (145–211 C.E.), who held his Imperial Court in York. It is of some significance that the earliest races trace to Yorkshire, a place that still retains a tremendous racing following, and that has also historically been a center of excellence in horse breeding. It was here that the magnificent coaching horse, the Cleveland Bay, developed, along with the splendid Hackney (associated with Norfolk as well), Hackney pony, and Yorkshire Roadster (now extinct). It was also in Yorkshire that much of the formative development of the Thoroughbred occurred.

The first written account of flat races dates to 1174 when William Fitzstephen described races at Smithfield Market in his *Description of the City of London*. However, by this time, the Age of Chivalry was in full swing and sports such as jousting became more popular than simple horse races.

Racing gained in popularity during the reign of Henry VIII (1491–1547), and great importance was attached to the improvement of British horses, chiefly to increase their size and their speed. There was extensive importation of horses to England from North Africa and mainland Europe, including Barb, Neapolitan, Iberian, Friesian, and desert-bred types, all of which were bred to native English stock. However, it was only royalty and those of considerable wealth who had the means to import expensive foreign horses, and the breeding of bloodstock therefore remained very much the domain of the upper classes.

James I (1566–1625) continued the royal tradition and established racing in Yorkshire, Croydon, and Enfield Chase, and regularly attended race meets at Epsom. Charles II (1630–85) also patronized racing, and in 1634 he financed the first Gold Cup. He increased the prize money, laid the foundations for rules and guidelines, and was the first king to openly run horses under his own name. It was during his reign that Newmarket, along with Yorkshire, was established as the center of British racing, and it has remained so to the present day.

Ridden races were also popular throughout Europe by this period. In Italy, the famous Palio di Siena began in 1656, which continues to the present, although horses had been racing here since the fourteenth century. While racing was taking off in Europe, in the United States it was just beginning, with some of the earliest races thought to date to the 1620s in Virginia. Racing was legalized in the 1630s in this area, and, with increasing imports of blood horses from England and from North and South Africa, the quality and speed of horses in North America began to improve. Horse breeding was not, of course, unilaterally focused on the production of fast horses for the track. Hunting on horseback with hounds (primarily for deer) had been popular since the times of William the Conqueror (c. 1028–87), with the first recorded instance of fox hunting dating to 1534 in Norfolk. The nature of hunting changed with the introduction of the Enclosure Acts (1450–1640 and 1750–1860), which required a horse that could jump obstacles, be fast and nimble, and maintain its speed for sustained periods of time. From this and from flat racing, the sport of steeplechasing developed in the eighteenth century. The first specific steeplechases were so called because they were generally run between two significant landmarks, such as church steeples. Today steeplechase races in England are run for professional jockeys under National Hunt rules, but there are also similar races called point to points. These are open to amateur jockeys, but the horse must have been hunted for at least four days before it is allowed to compete, reflecting the early origins of the development of this type of racing.

While horses of tremendous energy and stamina were needed to fill the role of racehorse, hunter, and steeplechaser, horses of similar qualities were also required in the transportation sector. The greatest obstacle for early horse-drawn vehicles was the terrain, which was often deeply rutted and treacherous in the days before proper roadways. While the heavier draft breeds were in extensive use for hauling large loads at a steady pace, there was a need for a lighter weight and faster horse capable of transporting smaller loads more quickly. These included private vehicles and coaches, with one of the first in England dating to around 1555 and built by Walter Rippon for the Earl of Rutland. The first coaches to be built are believed to date to the fourteenth century in Hungary, where the *kocsi*, or coach, was developed. The British golden age of coaching did not take off until the eighteenth century, and this was guided by two overriding factors: the improvement of roadways, allowing for lighter weight and faster coaches, and an overall increase in horse breeding activities. Most particularly, this coincided with the development of the Thoroughbred and a sustained program of breeding blood horses. Among the best of the coaching horses were those especially destined for the job, and in British stock there was a long tradition of solid trotting horses. The trot as a pace is one that can be both fast and maintained for long periods making it the most suitable gait for long distances. With the rise of coaching and private driving during the eighteenth century, there was a demand for horses that were elegant, that covered the ground smoothly and efficiently, and that had tremendous stamina.

Inevitably, private drivers engaged in informal races and competitions, and from this the sport of harness racing reemerged, along with competitive driving. One of the world leaders in harness racing is North America, although the sport has a large following in Australia, France, Russia, and across continental Europe. In these countries, specific breeds such as the American Standardbred, French Trotter, Orlov Trotter, Russian Trotter, Finnish Universal, Coldblooded Trotter, and North Swedish Trotter have developed to meet the needs of a huge sporting industry. Harness racing is conducted at the trot, with races for conventional diagonal trotters and also for pacers. Pacing is inherent in the American Standardbred and is a gait that is slightly faster than the diagonal trot and involves the legs moving in lateral pairs. The first trotting races in the United States were ridden races that became popular in colonial New England during the eighteenth century, by which time Thoroughbred racing was also established. The biggest impact of early American trotting horses was the English Thoroughbred Messenger (f. 1780), who was imported to the United States in 1788. It was through Messenger—with his strong trotting blood from Norfolk Roadster influence and crosses with American Morgans, Narragansett Pacers, and Canadian horses—that the world's fastest trotter, the American Standardbred, developed.

Harness racing with a vehicle took off in the United States from the 1830s, when both vehicles and roads had improved significantly. The lightweight sulky was introduced during the 1850s, and in 1892 the sulky was replaced by the bike, which made an enormous difference to trotting speeds because of the lightness of its frame. Racing had also become popular in Australia, with the earliest races held outside Sydney in 1810. These were for trotters and for flat racehorses, and both these industries have grown exponentially in Australia. The country's most famous race, the Melbourne Cup, was first run in 1861 and continues to bring the country to a standstill on race day.

A sport that is gaining increasing momentum is that of competitive driving, which also requires horses of tremendous energy, durability, and intelligence. By the nineteenth century, driving competitions in a number of different forms were popular across much of Europe, particularly in Germany, Hungary, and Austria; continental Europe is most famous for its driving horses, many of which are also now used in other competitive forums such as dressage, show jumping, and eventing. Among the most popular of the driving competitions are the driving trials, which are loosely modeled on the format of a three-day event. The trials can be held for four horses, pairs, tandems, and single horses and involve a dressage competition that tests the skill, obedience, and finesse of the horse (and driver); a marathon that tests a combination of endurance and speed; and an obstacle course that requires accuracy, speed, and skill.

ENERGETIC GRANDEUR

ARABIAN

ANCIENT – MIDDLE EAST – COMMON

HEIGHT	*Croup is broad and quite flat*
14.1–15.1 h.h.	*and the tail set and carried high.*
APPEARANCE	**COLOR**
A delicate head, with large eyes	*Gray, bay, black, chestnut,*
and alert ears that curve inward	*and occasionally roan.*
at the tip. An elegant neck is	**APTITUDE**
well-set to a long, sloping	*Riding, endurance, showing,*
shoulder. Defined withers, short	*dressage, jumping, competitive*
back, and deep, wide chest.	*and Western riding horse sports*

THERE ARE FEW BREEDS WHOSE HISTORY is so enigmatic and laced with myth and romance as the Arabian horse. With its inner fire and exquisite countenance, it is the horse to inspire such stories above all others. For the romantic, the Arabian horse was forged in the hearts of gods, powered by the furnace of the world, and shaped in the image of perfection. The truth, however, is fragmented at best, and a little less exotic, but what is irrefutable is the enormous, predominantly positive, impact this small desert horse has had on almost all other modern horse breeds.

The Arabian's place of origin is hotly contested, and, like all of its early history, the subject of much contention. Traditional explanations describe the Arabian magically appearing fully evolved from the wind-whipped sands of Saudi Arabia, whereas some regard the Arabian as a completely separate subspecies of horse, though neither version is true. The Arabian does exhibit some conformational differences from other breeds, including having one less vertebra and a pronounced forehead, but these differences can also occur in other horses; the Arabian also has the same number of chromosomes as all other domestic horses.

It is more commonly believed today that the Arabian probably evolved farther north of the Arabian Peninsula across part of the large area known as the Fertile Crescent. This swath of land, often referred to as "the cradle of civilization," includes parts of what are now Syria, Turkey, Iraq, Iran, and Egypt. The region has a more moderate climate than the area to the south and enough rain to sustain a habitat suitable for horses. Along with the area to the east that includes Turkmenistan and Kazakhstan and stretches away into the Central Asian steppes, it gave rise to the desert breeds of horse—such as the Akhal Teke and the Caspian—that evolved from the postulated prehistoric Horse Types 3 and 4. Though these desert-bred horses developed slightly differently in their different geographic locations, they display overwhelmingly similar characteristics: a fine coat and thin skin, resistance to extreme heat and cold, ability to survive on minimal water and limited forage, great stamina, intelligence, and a light frame. It has been suggested that the Caspian, which bears many similarities to the Arabian in appearance, could have been extremely influential in its development.

Whatever the breed's actual origins, even today the Arabian inspires a strong, almost spiritual reverence from those who breed it. To the ancient people of Islam and the nomadic Bedouin tribes of the desert regions who were instrumental in the Arabian's early history, the horse was a gift from Allah and to be treated as such. The horse's bulging forehead, or *jibbah*, was believed to hold the blessings of Allah: the larger the jibbah, the greater the blessings carried by the horse. The arched neck—and in particular the area where the head and the neck join, the *mitbah*—was a sign of courage, and the high tail carriage indicative of spirit. These attributes, bound up with religious symbolism and romantic associations, were specifically bred for, and because of the enormous reverence the horses were treated with, they were kept in near isolation, perpetuating the purity of the breed. Maintaining purity was and continues to be of the utmost importance, resulting in a horse of indelibly fixed characteristics. Whereas an English Thoroughbred might not always be distinguishable from a French Selle Français of racing type, or a Dutch Warmblood from a Danish Warmblood, it is rare to find an Arabian that is not immediately identifiable.

The Bedouins' history is closely bound to that of the Arabian horse. The camel was originally a fundamental part of the Bedouins' culture, but by around 2500 B.C.E. they had assimilated the Arabian horse into their hearts and lives and had taken it with them into the vast interior of Saudi Arabia, where people and horses lived a completely symbiotic relationship. Their horses were fiercely guarded and highly treasured, a symbol of wealth and prestige, and essential for warfare. The mares were most highly valued and were used as warhorses since they did not vocalize like stallions and could be ridden silently on the enemy to launch surprise attacks. The mares would carry warriors into and out of battle with utter loyalty and bravery and formed unshakable bonds with their owners—a trait still apparent in many Arabians. It was not unheard of for mares to be ushered into the Bedouins' tents and to be treated with the same care and respect as the rest of the family group.

The mare breeding lines were of the utmost importance, and it was the mare's characteristics that would predominate in the progeny, particularly their physical appearance. This again is commonly seen in the modern Arabian horse. The greatest gift a Bedouin could bestow was that of a fine mare, and this tradition perpetuated, with Arabian horses eventually being offered as gifts by the Turkish rulers of the Ottoman Empire to European leaders.

The Bedouins were not the only people to use the Arabian horse; images of horses of Arabian-like appearance can be found in Egyptian hieroglyphs dating to around the sixteenth century B.C.E., and descriptions of just such a horse are found in the Old Testament and in the writings of the Greek writer Xenophon (c. 430–354 B.C.E.). The ancient Hurrians, Hittites, Kassites, Assyrians, Babylonians, and Persians used small, swift desert-bred horses, which could quite possibly have been the Arabian or its ancestor, but it is the Bedouins who are widely credited with being the first to selectively breed and maintain this most precious horse breed.

Although they kept no written records, the Bedouins had a strong verbal tradition of memorizing breeding stock and lines, and they were absolute in their adherence to breed purity. Breeding stock was bought and sold between tribes, but rarely did their prized war mares change hands. Significantly, the Bedouins placed enormous importance on the breeding of specific strains of Arabians that have been largely lost in the West. These types were bred for purpose and exhibited slightly different physical aspects.

There is great debate over the different strains and many names for these and sub-strains, but five primary ancient ones said to derive from the prophet Muhammad's (570–632) mares are the Kuhaylan, Ubayyah, Saglaviyah, Dahmah, and Shuwaymah. Strain breeding is very much still practiced in the Middle East, with three chief modern strains being the Kuhaylan, Saglawi, and the Muniqi, though these are largely unseen in the West.

It was with the rise of Islam that the Arabian horse left its isolated desert homelands and spread across the world. Muhammad encouraged the ownership and breeding of horses, which were then used for conveying the message of Islam across countries and continents stretching from the Middle East into North Africa, Europe, the Mediterranean, and as far east as China. As these horses came into contact with those of innumerable other countries and cultures, they had a universally positive effect. The small, sleek, and swift Arabian horses were the opposite of the sturdy, heavier European breeds and were highly sought after. The possible exception to this universally improving aspect is the Andalusian horse, which was arguably already perfect and ill-suited to Arabian influence.

During the late seventeenth and early eighteenth centuries, the Arabian greatly influenced the development of British breeds, most notably the Thoroughbred, and during the eighteenth and nineteenth centuries the Arabian increased in popularity across Europe. Important stud farms were established by royalty in Poland and Germany and in Hungary, Austria, Great Britain, Russia, Australia, and the United States. Today the Arabian horse is one of the most international and widely dispersed breeds around the world, yet it has unquestionably maintained its most evident quality and characteristics. The Arabian is one of the most beautiful of creatures and combines an effortless grace with extraordinary spirit and energy. Its ravishing appearance belies its steely strength and endurance, and it is one of the leading endurance horses in the world today.

Typically, Arabian horses are highly intelligent and easily trained. They have excellent memories and will remember kindness as much as they do the opposite. Unlike many breeds, the Arabian also exhibits a tangible sense of loyalty and affection to their owner. They make first-class athletes and excel in virtually any competitive arena, from racing to dressage, in both English and Western disciplines.

ENGLISH THOROUGHBRED
HISTORIC — ENGLAND — COMMON

HEIGHT	*Long, clean, and strong legs.*
15–17 h.h.	**COLOR**
APPEARANCE	*Mostly bay, chestnut, black, or*
A fine, well-proportioned head	*gray, but can be roan, palomino,*
with large, alert ears and a long,	*or brown; white markings common.*
arched neck. Defined withers,	**APTITUDE**
well-sloped, muscular shoulder,	*Riding, racing, showing,*
and long back. Wide, high chest,	*dressage, jumping, eventing,*
sloping croup, and high-set tail.	*competitive horse sports*

THERE ARE A HANDFUL OF HORSE BREEDS that may be considered omnipotent, breeds that have stamped their mark across the world and through the centuries, positively contributing to the development of innumerable others. The Andalusian is one such breed, the North African Barb another, and the Arabian a third of these superbreeds. The fourth is the Thoroughbred, perhaps all the more remarkable given its relatively brief modern history.

The Thoroughbred is an athlete of unrivaled ability and the pinnacle of modern breeding. There is simply no other horse in the world that can match the Thoroughbred in terms of speed and stamina. Some horses may be faster over a short distance and others may be able to continue a moderate speed for longer, but nothing comes close to the Thoroughbred in terms of a speed/distance combination. Added to this, the Thoroughbred is renowned for its spirit, that esoteric quality that sets a horse apart from its rivals, and is defined by its bravery, tenacity, and effort.

The modern history of this giant of a breed traces to the late seventeenth and eighteenth centuries, but the foundations for the Thoroughbred began many centuries before. For centuries, British stock was largely small in stature and stocky in frame, and certainly inferior in size and elegance compared to many of the horses of Europe, North Africa, and Asia. This did not, however, affect their speed and usefulness; the Galloway of Scotland and northern England was noted for its quick, smooth (often pacing) action, and the Irish Hobby exhibited great energy and vigor. Both of these breeds are sadly now extinct, but

they contributed to the Fell and Connemara respectively, and both contributed to the base stock from which the Thoroughbred would emerge much later.

Historically, racing is strongly tied to royalty, and still today the British royal family are great supporters. It was largely through the royal stables, and those belonging to nobility, that efforts were made to improve the home stock through the importation of foreign horses and subsequent crossing of these with native British stock. Andalusian stallions were imported during the reign of William the Conqueror (c. 1028–87), and some years later Andalusians were used to breed horses suitable for knights and squires. King Stephen (c. 1096–1154) imported "royal mares and stallions" to the royal stables, and Richard II (1367–1400) spent considerable money on "coursers," horses also used for racing. He was given two horses by the King of Navarre, which were described as Spanish but were possibly light French breeds. These accounts reflect how early in British history there was an interest in improving the country's horses, not just for war, but also for hunting and racing.

The majority of horses imported were of Spanish (Andalusian), North African (Barb), and Middle Eastern (Turkmenian) origin, with some also coming from Italy. Some confusion has arisen over the extent of Arabian imports because of the tendency for all horses from Arab countries to be referred to as Arabians, when clearly this was not the case; Arabian horses were closely guarded by their owners, and the best mares rarely sold. Although Arabians did have a significant effect later on in the development of the Thoroughbred, they were not so extensively used early in its history.

Henry VIII (1491–1597) laid down a number of statutes regarding horse breeding, including limiting the minimum height of stallions pastured on common land in an effort to increase the average height of "common" horses. He also established the Royal Paddocks at Hampton Court, importing Spanish and Barb horses as well as Oriental

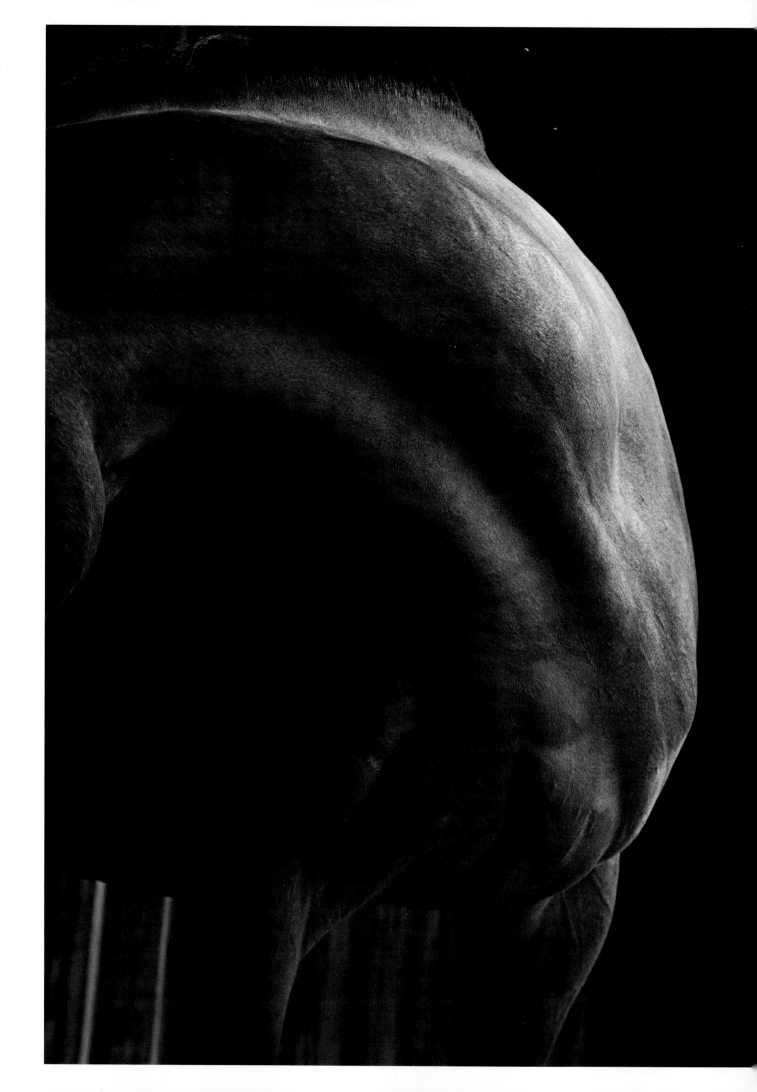

horses from Padua in northern Italy from the esteemed horse-breeding dynasty the Gonzagas. It was during his reign that the first recorded formal horse races took place at Chester, in 1511, and York, in 1530. By this time, the crossbreeding of the swift British stock with foreign imports had resulted in a type of fast "running horse." These running horses, which carried considerable Oriental and Spanish blood, were the precursors of the Thoroughbred.

The modern history of the Thoroughbred is typically attributed to three stallions—the Byerley Turk (f. c. 1684), the Darley Arabian (f. c. 1700), and the Godolphin Barb (f. c. 1724)—though this is an oversimplification that ignores the wide range of Eastern influences and the quality of the mares. It is interesting to note that British horses were already capable of considerable speed by this point, and the introduction of hot-blooded horses (Turkmenian, Arabian, and Barb) while enhancing their speed and elegance was also significant in fixing a type within the breed. All three of these breeds are exceptionally prepotent and breed true to type, which helped the Thoroughbred establish definitive breed characteristics.

The Byerley Turk, although often referred to as an Arabian, is now widely believed to have been an Akhal Teke. The horse was imported to England in 1689. Among the Byerley Turk's offspring was the stallion Jigg (f. 1701), whose progeny gave rise to the stallion Herod (f. 1758), who established one of the great Thoroughbred bloodlines, and also to the giant of twentieth-century racing, the Tetrarch (f. 1911). The Tetrarch was never beaten on the racetrack.

The Darley Arabian was bought at the Syrian horse market at Aleppo before being shipped to England in 1704. The horse was from the Muniqi racing strain of Arabians, among the most prized in its homeland, but this strain of Arabian is also said to have been influenced by Turkmenians. The Darley Arabian was the most stunning of the three stallions, with a beautifully balanced conformation; at 15 hands high he was also the tallest. He was sent to stud in Yorkshire, a primary center of racehorse breeding, and while there was bred to a mare called Betty Leedes (f. 1704), whose own heritage included the famous Leedes Arabian line as well as heavy Barb and Turkmenian influence.

There is some dispute surrounding the Godolphin stallion, thought to be either a Barb from Morocco or Tunisia, or an Arabian from Yemen. Whatever the case,

by around 1730 the Godolphin Barb was being used as a teaser stallion at Lord Godolphin's Gog Magog Stud in Cambridgeshire. His enormous worth as a sire was not realized until he was mated with the mare Roxana (f. 1718), producing several outstanding offspring.

The massive and rapid success of the Thoroughbred horse had a profound effect on the development and improvement of other breeds in England and internationally from the eighteenth century onward. Once the definitive characteristics of the Thoroughbred were recognized, most significantly its ability to improve other stock through crossbreeding leading to "half-bloods," it was widely used to produce coach horses, cavalry horses, hunters, trotters, and later competition horses. The Norfolk Roadster, now extinct, was one of the preeminent horse breeds in England during the eighteenth and nineteenth centuries, and its history parallels that of the Thoroughbred at this time, with crossover between the two. The Norfolk Roadster traced to the Thoroughbred stallion Original Shales (f. 1755), son of Blaze (f. 1733), who was also the great-great-grandfather of the stallion Messenger. Messenger went on to found the fastest trotting breed in the world, the American Standardbred. Through crossing the Thoroughbred in England and Ireland with the native stock, breeds such as the now-extinct Yorkshire Coach Horse and the Hackney emerged, with the Norfolk Roadster also influencing the Hackney. There was considerable overlap at this time between these extraordinary trotting horses and the Thoroughbred.

Thoroughbreds were exported in large numbers to the Continent. The leading Hanoverian stud of Celle was established in 1735, with breeding stock based on many English Thoroughbred foundation sires. Thoroughbred stallions found their way to East Friesland and to Germany, where they influenced the Oldenburg and Holstein breeds; to Prussia, where they influenced the Trakehner; to Hungary, where the Thoroughbred stallions Furioso (f. 1836) and North-Star (f. 1844) produced the Furioso breed; and to France, where they gave rise to the Anglo-Norman. There are in fact, few modern European warmblood breeds that have not been directly influenced at some time during their history by the Thoroughbred, whose presence can be seen and felt throughout almost every country in the world.

AUSTRALIAN THOROUGHBRED
HISTORIC – AUSTRALIA – COMMON

HEIGHT
15–17 h.h.
APPEARANCE
A fine, well-proportioned head with large, alert ears. Long, arched neck well-set to the body. Defined withers, well-sloped, muscular shoulder, and long back. Wide, high chest,
sloping croup, and high-set tail. Long, clean, and strong legs.
COLOR
Mostly bay, chestnut, black, or gray; white markings common.
APTITUDE
Riding, racing, showing, dressage, jumping, eventing, competitive horse sports

HORSES DID NOT ARRIVE IN AUSTRALIA until 1788, and the first to do so were not Thoroughbreds but horses of mixed heritage purchased in South Africa. In this short time, however, Australia has developed one of the world's leading Thoroughbred industries and is the second-highest producer of Thoroughbred foals after the United States, a feat that is all the more remarkable given the extreme hardships and difficulty of shipping early English Thoroughbreds there.

The most significant imports in the early history of the Australian Thoroughbred were the stallions Rockingham, Washington, and Northumberland, and for many years Australian blood stock was described in terms of relationships to these horses. Rockingham arrived around 1797/99 from Cape Town and is thought to have carried Thoroughbred and/or Eastern blood. Washington (n/d) was of American origin and would have been part Thoroughbred; he arrived in Sydney around 1800. Northumberland (n/d), a fine British coaching horse, arrived

from England around 1802. An influential Arabian stallion called Shark was shipped in from India around this time along with a number of other Arabian or Oriental horses, and they had a rapid improving effect on the colony stock.

The Australian Thoroughbred emerged from a foundation stock of tough, intelligent horses who had learned to survive in difficult conditions. As wealthy military officers and traders matched their increasingly high-quality saddle horses against each other, imports of Thoroughbred stock to improve speed increased and more organized selective breeding began. These horses were still chiefly saddle horses, however, and were raced as a diversion from their normal working life.

Rockingham, Washington, and Northumberland featured heavily in the early breeding of running horses, as did the Arabians Shark and (Old) Hector (f. c. 1800), and from the 1830s onward there was a sustained importation of Thoroughbred stallions from England. That any of them survived the grueling five-month trip by ship is extraordinary and thanks to the careful handling of the precious cargo and specially constructed onboard stables.

The English Thoroughbred Steeltrap (f. 1815), a respected sire whose offspring won on the track and were significant in the early Australian Thoroughbred history, was imported in 1824. He fathered the stallion Chancellor (f. c. 1826), who is credited as being the first colonial-born pure Thoroughbred stallion. Sadly, he died young before he had an impact on Thoroughbred breeding, but by the 1840s there were a number of prepotent, talented, and pure Thoroughbred stallions born on Australian soil. By this time, racing had taken off, and with the establishment of each new state, local race clubs developed, in turn fueling the Thoroughbred breeding industry. Racetracks were built across the country, and at one point there were an estimated five hundred local race clubs in operation.

Today the Australian Thoroughbred is extremely impressive and its bloodlines are seen across the racing world. With modern transportation, the shipment of leading stallions for breeding and racing purposes between Australia, Britain, and the United States is common, and many stallions serve half the year in the Southern Hemisphere and half in the Northern Hemisphere.

AMERICAN
THOROUGHBRED

HISTORIC — NORTH AMERICA — COMMON

HEIGHT	sloping croup, and high-set tail.
15–17 h.h.	Long, clean, and strong legs.
APPEARANCE	**COLOR**
A fine, well-proportioned head	*Mostly bay, chestnut, black, or*
with large, alert ears. Long,	*gray; white markings common.*
arched neck well-set to the	**APTITUDE**
body. Defined withers,	*Riding, racing, showing,*
well-sloped, muscular shoulder,	*dressage, jumping, eventing,*
and long back. Wide, high chest,	*competitive horse sports*

THE AMERICAN THOROUGHBRED developed from early English Thoroughbred imports with some inevitable crossbreeding to local stock. The first imports from England began in the eighteenth century, and Thoroughbred racing swiftly gained in popularity, leading in turn to concentrated breeding efforts to produce homegrown racehorses. The relatively rapid emergence of the Thoroughbred in America, just as in England, and its overwhelmingly positive influence on other horses, led to Thoroughbreds being used in the development of many of the American breeds. Significantly, the Thoroughbred has been shown to exert a positive effect on gaited breeds when crossbred, without losing the particular gait.

America's first racetrack was built in 1665, many years before Thoroughbred breeding was established. The track was 2 miles (3.2 km) long and built on the Salisbury Plains (later Hempstead Plains) on Long Island, New York. The first race meet was overseen by Governor Nicolls, a keen horseman who hoped the track would encourage the breeding of quality horses. The first English Thoroughbred to arrive in North America was Bulle Rock (f. 1709), imported by James Patton around 1730 and then owned by Samuel Gist of Hanover County, Virginia. Bulle Rock was a son of one of the foundation stallions of the breed, the Darley Arabian (f. c. 1700), and had had a fairly successful career on the racetrack before he left England at the age of twenty-one. In 1755, Edward Fenwick emigrated to America, settling in South Carolina. His family was well respected in horse circles and owned the British champion

Thoroughbred Matchem (f. 1748), who sired 354 winners in England. When the young Edward moved to the United States, he brought ten of Matchem's descendants with him, as well as the roan Thoroughbred Brutus (f. 1748), who sired a number of champions on the racetrack in South Carolina. South Carolina, Virginia, New York, and Maryland quickly became important areas of Thoroughbred breeding, and from 1730 to 1775 a large number of English Thoroughbreds were imported, including the horses Monkey (f. 1725), Fearnought (f. 1755), and Janus (f. 1746). Janus, imported in 1756 by Mordecai Booth, a plantation owner and horse breeder, was important in the development of the American Quarter Horse; Monkey sired more than three hundred foals in Virginia; and Fearnought commanded one of the highest stud fees on record.

The onset of the American Revolution in 1775 brought the importation of good British stock to a halt, but after the war the trade in horses resumed, and by 1800 an estimated 340 Thoroughbreds had been brought to North America. Kentucky and Tennessee became the center of Thoroughbred breeding after the war, with their rich grasses, fertile limestone soils, and a manageable climate.

Two important post-Revolution stallions to arrive on U.S. soil were Messenger (f. 1780) and Diomed (f. 1777). Messenger was imported in 1788 and produced several notable offspring, particularly the mare Miller's Damsel (f. 1802), who was almost undefeated on the track and then retired to stud where she produced American Eclipse (f. 1814). Messenger's greatest legacy, however, was his influence on the development of the American Standardbred breed, one of the fastest trotting horses in the world, both directly and through his descendant Rysdyk's Hambletonian (f. 1849).

Diomed had won the British Epsom Derby in 1780 and was one of the top racehorses in England for a short time during his youth. After his early successes, however, he lost

ENERGETIC GRANDEUR

his enthusiasm and fell from favor. On top of this, he was not a potent stallion and produced few offspring. He was sold cheaply to two Americans who shipped him to the United States and tried breeding him there. Diomed turned a corner in his new country and became a valued sire of outstanding stock. At the time of his death in 1808 he was something of a national hero and his death was greatly mourned. Among others, Diomed sired Potomac (f. 1803), Duroc (f. 1806), Ball's Florizel (f. 1801), and the superlative Sir Archy (f. 1805). Sir Archy went on to become one of the greatest early American Thoroughbreds and was eventually retired from racing because there was no suitable opposition for him. He was a prolific sire, and it is said that Sir Archy "filled the hemisphere with his blood."

As racing became more popular on a national level, the purses increased, adding to the excitement generated by the sport. Gambling, too, became an important factor in the spread of racing and the interest in Thoroughbred breeding. One famous early race took place on Long Island in 1823 between several horses, including Sir Henry (f. 1819) and American Eclipse (f. 1814), the latter of which was related to both Diomed and Messenger, and the former to Sir Archy. The race was run in three heats; Sir Henry won the first, and American Eclipse took the second two. The race is said to have been watched by both Andrew Jackson, governor of Florida at the time, and Daniel Tompkins, vice president of the United States. Other famous early races include one that took place in 1838 between Boston (f. 1833), a descendant of Sir Archy, and Fashion (n/d), with a reputed $20,000 bet from both sides, and two races between Lexington (f. 1850) and Lecompte (f. 1850), both of whom were sons of Boston. Lecompte won the first race in 1854, but Lexington's owner challenged him to a rematch the following year and won. He went on to have great success as a sire, breeding 236 winners, including three winners of the prestigious Preakness Stakes.

After the American Civil War (1861–65), there was a change in the format of racing that affected the breeders' strategies. Races were shortened from around 4 miles (6.4 km) to a maximum of around 1.5 miles (2.4 km), and instead of being run in heats they were run as straight, one-off races. These changes meant that the horses needed to be faster over a shorter distance, and staying power and stamina became less important. Sprinters are typically smaller and lighter in frame than the larger "stamina" horses, and a fashion developed for starting to race the horses much younger. Today, there are races for sprinters, held over a short distance, and for "stayers," run over a longer distance, including flat races and those over jumps.

The first volume of the American Studbook was published in 1868 by Sanders Bruce and his brother. Sanders spent his life working on the studbook and published several more volumes before his offices were damaged by fire and he fell into financial difficulties. In 1896, after a legal fight, the Jockey Club (formed in 1894) bought the American Studbook from Sanders, and the Jockey Club has since maintained it.

In the same postwar period, American Thoroughbreds began to be shipped back to England because of the introduction of a gambling ban in many U.S. states. The ban greatly affected the racing industry, and American breeders turned elsewhere to run their horses. However, the British racing fraternity was deeply unhappy about the infiltration of American-bred horses, which were thought not to be purebred and therefore detrimental to English Thoroughbred breeding stock; they were also afraid of American horses flooding the English market and bringing prices of English horses down. In 1913, the Jersey Act was introduced by the British Jockey Club to prevent American Thoroughbreds from being registered in the British General Stud Book. It effectively prevented any American horses from being registered unless all of their ancestors had been registered; the act remained strictly in effect until 1949. At this point, the ruling was relaxed to allow any horse that could prove eight or nine crosses of pure blood to be registered.

The Jersey Act was not entirely beneficial to the English Thoroughbred, since by this time the American Thoroughbred was of an equal (if not greater) class and speed to its English relative, and many American-bred horses were winning on English tracks. The ruling also limited the use of French-bred Thoroughbreds on British stock, since many French Thoroughbreds also contained American blood and were therefore not eligible for registration. Before the act, French blood had often been introduced to prevent the English Thoroughbred gene pool from becoming too small. Today, the American Thoroughbred is a superlative horse and has had an enriching influence on many other American breeds.

AMERICAN STANDARDBRED
HISTORIC – NORTH AMERICA – COMMON

<table>
<tr><td>HEIGHT</td><td>and extremely powerful.</td></tr>
<tr><td>15–16 h.h.</td><td>Luxuriant mane and tail.</td></tr>
<tr><td>APPEARANCE</td><td>COLOR</td></tr>
<tr><td>A large, attractive head that may have a straight or convex profile. Long through the body with a flat rib cage; can be higher in the croup than the wither. Quarters are sloping</td><td>Mostly bay, chestnut, black, or brown; occasionally gray.
APTITUDE
Harness racing, riding, dressage, jumping, competitive horse sports</td></tr>
</table>

THE STANDARDBRED IS AN INTEGRAL PART of American history and culture, and though the breed is only just more than two hundred years old, it has proved itself to be a world leader of trotting horses. No other horse can match the American Standardbred's trotting speed, yet it is notable for its quiet, kind, and docile temperament, which is quite at odds with the great energy and speed it is able to exhibit. Given its enormous talents, the Standardbred has often been used to improve and develop other trotting breeds.

The sport of harness racing, at which the Standardbred excels, is not a new phenomenon. The ancient Mesopotamians, Greeks, and Romans all used horses in harness for war chariots, holding sideline races to determine the swiftest horses for pulling chariots. However, the change in military requirements around the time of the fall of the Roman Empire (476 C.E.) led to the demise of the sport; as the advantages of riding horses into battle became clear, emphasis was placed on training ridden horses and harness racing dropped by the wayside.

In the United States, racing trotting horses began during the eighteenth century and became formalized at the beginning of the nineteenth. The first races were ridden, since the horse-drawn vehicles at that time were not suitable for racing and thoroughfares were still extremely rough. Ridden trotting races became particularly popular in New England—especially in Rhode Island, where the Narragansett Pacer developed, and Massachusetts—which remained a center of trotting-horse breeding. In 1802,

horse racing was temporarily banned on the grounds of immorality, but because of a loophole in the wording of the law, trotting races were allowed, increasing the popularity of the still largely rural pursuit. The earliest races no doubt took place along tracks, country roads, and even through village main streets. Gradually an assortment of vehicles was introduced and harness races began to be held on public tracks in New York, Boston, Philadelphia, Trenton, and Baltimore between 1818 and 1830.

By 1830, harness racing had gained in popularity, coinciding with an overall improvement in the design of vehicles and the emergence of specific trotting horses. Most significant in the Standardbred (and some other trotting breeds) is the horse's ability to pace. In pacing, the horse's legs on the left and right sides move forward together in lateral pairs, as opposed to the slightly slower trot, in which the legs move forward in diagonal pairs. The Standardbred exhibits a natural tendency to pace without training but is then trained and raced with a type of hobble to help it maintain the pacing gait.

The Standardbred can trace its history to the English Thoroughbred Messenger (f. 1780), who was imported to the United States in 1788. Messenger did not race in harness, but his father, Mambrino (f. 1768), a leading racehorse in England, is said to have also been an excellent trotter. Messenger was also the great-great-grandson of the Thoroughbred Blaze (f. 1733), a fast trotting horse whose son, Original Shales (f. 1755), founded the Norfolk Roadster trotting horse. The Norfolk Roadster, which is now extinct, contributed its considerable trotting ability to the Standardbred as well as the Hackney. Messenger spent twenty years standing at stud in Pennsylvania, where he was bred to a mixture of mares that included Morgans, Narragansett Pacers from Rhode Island, and Canadian mares, many of which were traded back and forth across the border. Both the Narragansett and the Canadian often exhibited a natural ambling gait introduced to the

Americas through the importation of the ambling Spanish Jennet in the sixteenth and seventeenth centuries. Messenger's progeny displayed a great talent for trotting and began to breed true to certain characteristics such as a muscular frame, speed, ability to pace, courage, and tractable temperament. Such was Messenger's success as a sire of trotting horses that by the time of his death in 1808 he had become a national treasure and was buried with much pomp on Long Island.

In 1849, an unlikely pairing between an old crippled mare (the Charles Kent mare), daughter of the Hackney stallion Bellfounder (f. 1816) and a line-bred descendant of Messenger, and a bad-tempered, unattractive horse called Abdullah (f. 1823), also a line-bred descendant of Messenger, resulted in a colt foal named Hambletonian (f. 1849). The foal and its mother were sold cheaply to Bill Rysdyk of Orange County, New York, and after several years the colt began to prove himself as an unsurpassed sire of trotting horses. By then he was known as Rysdyk's Hambletonian, and today he is regarded as the foundation sire of the modern Standardbred. Every Standardbred can trace its heritage to Hambletonian, and in particular to his sons, George Wilkes (f. 1856), Happy Medium (f. 1863), Dictator (f. 1863), and Electioneer (f. 1868).

The United States Trotting Association was formed in 1870 to organize and regulate the industry, and the studbook was founded for the Standardbred in 1871. In order for horses to be registered, they had to meet a standard requirement of completing a mile (1.6 km) in two minutes thirty seconds for trotters and two minutes twenty-five seconds for pacers, giving rise to the breed's name. Today, with selective breeding, the speed of the Standardbred has increased, and it is not uncommon for horses to complete the mile in less than two minutes.

Whereas Thoroughbred racing is commonly referred to as the "sport of kings" and developed initially through royal or wealthy channels, Standardbred racing is referred to as the "sport of the people." It has a large following, and, despite suffering briefly during the early twentieth century with the arrival of the automobile, enthusiasm for harness racing was reignited during the 1940s, aided by the approval of pari-mutuel betting in New York State, the development of mobile starting gates, and the introduction of evening races under floodlights.

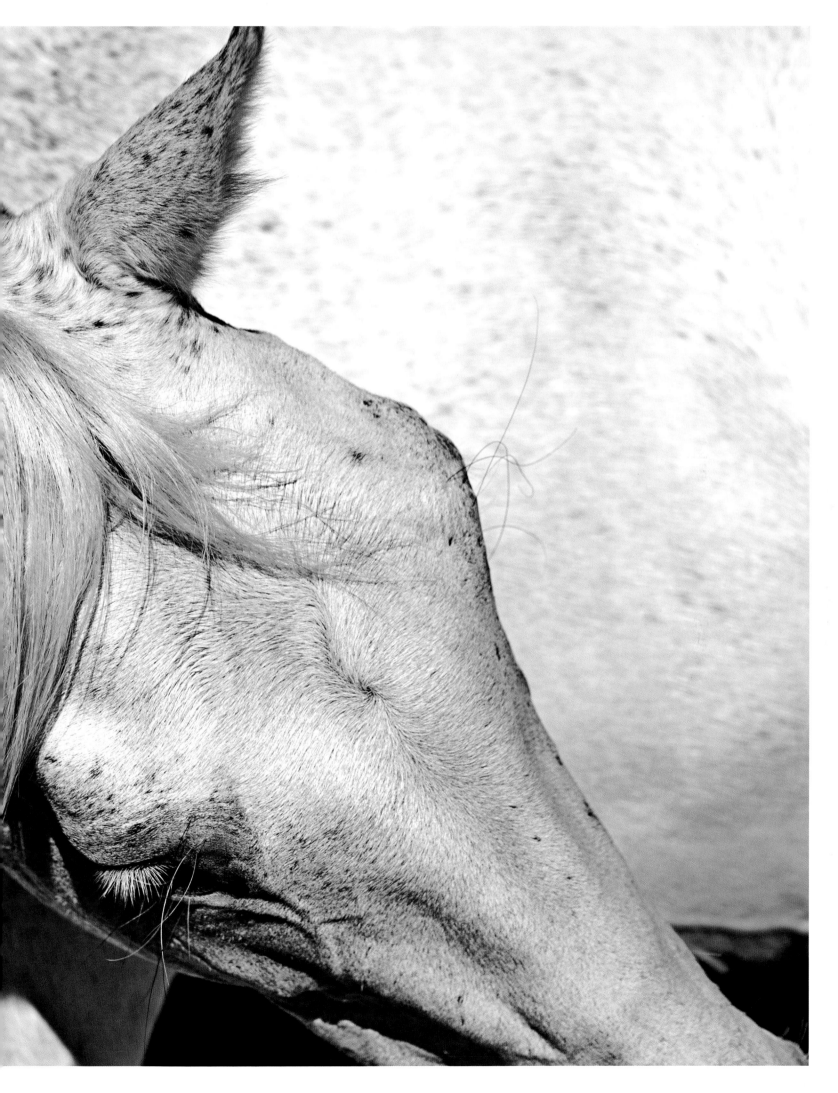

ENERGETIC GRANDEUR

NORMAN COB
ANCIENT — FRANCE — UNCOMMON

HEIGHT
15.3–16.3 h.h.
APPEARANCE
A compact, muscular horse of good proportions with a very attractive, though quite large, head. Extremely athletic, with tremendous paces. In France they traditionally had their | *tails docked to prevent them from becoming trapped in the harness reins, but this is less common now.*
COLOR
Bay or chestnut, though occasionally roan or gray.
APTITUDE
Light draft, trotting, riding

MANCHE IS THE WESTERNMOST department of Normandy, one of the centers of French horse breeding and home to the French national stud at Saint-Lô. Farther to the south but still in Normandy is a second national stud, the Haras du Pin. These two studs, and the area of Manche as a whole, are most associated with the development of the majestic Norman Cob.

These powerful yet agile horses are thought to have developed from horses that originally came from the steppes of Central Asia, brought west by nomadic cultures such as the Cimmerians. These early horses would have been largely based on tough Mongolian stock and were then greatly refined through crossbreeding with Eastern desert-bred types and traded across much of Europe. The Romans became aware of these useful, small horses, which were then referred to as *bidets*, and found throughout Normandy and Brittany. The word *bidet* is believed to have been coined by the Romans as an affectionate term for a small horse or pony, reaffirming that these horses must still have been small in stature and were likely to have been reasonably fine in build because of the influence of Eastern desert-bred types.

The bidets were crossed to the coarser and heavier Roman base stock to produce a small but muscular and high-quality general utility horse, and this was the base from which the Norman horse and later the Cob evolved. By the tenth century, Normandy had already become famous for its horses, and for the Norman farmer's ability to produce superlative horses to fulfill the changing needs of the market. Some of the best warhorses in Europe were bred there, benefiting from the superb environment, and were of medium size, still not particularly tall, but with a very muscular and dense frame.

The first of two major developments for these horses occurred in the sixteenth and seventeenth centuries when they were crossbred to Arabians and North African Barbs. The reintroduction of this desert blood to the Norman horse had a greatly refining effect, increasing the horse's speed and agility and lightening the body frame. The second major influence came about in the nineteenth century when Norfolk Roadster, Thoroughbred, and part-bred blood were introduced, again improving the quality of the breed; of these, the influence of the Norfolk Roadster remains most apparent in the Norman Cob in its extremely energetic trot. At this time a type known as the Anglo-Norman emerged, which went on to be significant in the development of the Selle Français and French Trotter.

In 1806, the stud at Saint-Lô was opened, establishing a large and productive stallion bank. By the beginning of the twentieth century, there was a clear distinction in the Norman-bred horses between those lighter-weight riding horses used as cavalry horses and the heavier, muscular type more suitable for harness work. The latter became known as the Norman Cob, a supremely versatile horse that excels in harness, with an eye-catching trot and an exuberant presence but also suitable for riding and even light agricultural work. Within the Cob, there are a further two types, a lighter-weight type that is more suitable for riding, and a heavier type more suitable for draft, though both types can be used in either capacity.

Despite its very distinctive characteristics and history, and the fact that it is still bred at the national studs, no studbook exists for the Norman Cob. Any foal born whose father was a Cob is considered a Cob, regardless of the dam, though they do still breed very true to type.

ENERGETIC GRANDEUR

FRENCH TROTTER
MODERN – FRANCE – COMMON

HEIGHT	
15.1–16.2 h.h.	*shoulder and a long croup.*
APPEARANCE	*Hindquarters are powerful*
A large but attractive	*and the legs strong and*
head with a straight	*sound. A robust frame*
profile set to a medium	*and plenty of bone.*
to long neck. Reasonably	**COLOR**
long in the back, with	*Mostly bay or chestnut.*
a moderately sloped	**APTITUDE**
	Harness racing, riding

THE MAGNIFICENT FRENCH TROTTER is yet another product of intelligent horse breeding in Normandy and is bred extensively by private individuals, as well as at the large studs. Individual owners will typically keep and breed two to three horses that they then train and race themselves.

In the first half of the nineteenth century, horse breeders in Normandy were supported in their endeavors by the Administration of National Studs, which helped to import English Thoroughbreds, Norfolk Roadsters, and part-bred hunter-type horses. These finer, quality horses were then crossed to the old Norman stock, which was generally heavier in frame and slightly smaller in height. The now extinct Norfolk Roadster was among the most important of these breeds, and it was from the Roadster that the Norman horse developed its very great trotting ability.

One stallion that was significant early in the development of the French Trotter was the part-Thoroughbred Young Rattler (f. 1811), who also had substantial Roadster blood. Rattler is given the same recognition in France as the Thoroughbred Messenger (f. 1780), who influenced the American Standardbred, is in the United States. Ultimately, it was through Rattler that some of the important breeding lines of the French Trotter were established, including those of Conquerant (f. 1858), whose son Reynolds (f. 1873) and grandson Fuchsia (f. 1883) were of great significance to early Trotter breeding. The stallion Lavater (f. 1867) was another important early trotting sire, and other early influence came from the Norfolk Roadster Norfolk Phenomenon (f. 1824) and the Thoroughbreds Sir Quid Pigtail (f. 1874)

and Heir of Linne (f. 1853). This Thoroughbred/Roadster combination on the old Norman stock rapidly gave rise to a new type, a refined version of the Norman horse with improved conformation of the shoulders that allowed for better movement. It became known as the French Trotter and has become increasingly refined over the past hundred years with substantial influence of Thoroughbred and later Standardbred blood.

Today, French Trotters are high-quality, fairly substantial horses. They are balanced through their frame with powerful hindquarters and an excellent length of stride. Although there has been a substantial influence of Standardbred blood to the breed, they have retained their diagonal trotting gait and do not pace like their American rivals. The French Trotter is renowned for its extremely obliging temperament and is often used in crossbreeding to produce saddle horses and competition horses; invariably, it will pass on its lovely nature and impressive muscular frame.

In order to maintain the quality of the breed, French Trotter stallions have to meet certain criteria before they can be used for public breeding. They are required to have achieved certain results on the racetrack according to their age and whether they are being raced under saddle or in harness. Mares can be put forward for selection premiums or conformation premiums. The studbook was closed to non-French horses in 1937 to preserve the unique and admirable qualities of the breed, though more recently French/Standardbred crosses have been allowed.

The earliest trotting races in France date to 1806, coinciding roughly with the emergence of the sport in the United States. The first formal race was held on the Champs de Mars in Paris and was for ridden horses. Ridden trotting races are still held in France, though they are not quite as popular as harness races. Ridden and driven horses do not generally overlap, though there are a few instances in which both races have been won by the same horse.

ENERGETIC GRANDEUR

ORLOV TROTTER
HISTORIC – RUSSIA – RARE

HEIGHT
Average height 16 h.h.

APPEARANCE
A large but attractive head with an intelligent eye. Neck is long, elegant, and well-arched; withers are defined. Long and flat through the back with a deep, wide chest and strong, muscular quarters. Long in the leg, which may have some feathering.

COLOR
Gray and black; occasionally chestnut or bay.

APTITUDE
Harness racing, competitive driving, light draft, riding

A PRODUCT OF CAREFUL SELECTIVE BREEDING, the magnificent Orlov Trotter is an elegant, muscular horse of great durability, tough enough to withstand often-frigid winters, sure-footed in snow, beautiful in appearance, and possessed of a long stride.

Count Alexius Girgorievich Orlov (1737–1808) is the person solely responsible for the development of the breed, which was established very rapidly through intense breeding initiatives. Orlov was rewarded for services to Catherine the Great (1729–96) with an enormous estate in the region of Voronezh, where he built the Khrenov Stud. The Russian count was an intelligent horseman and wished to breed a hardy but elegant horse suitable for the Russian nobility for both riding and driving. The horse needed to have good stamina, decent speed, and a smooth, ground-covering trot to make short work of long distances and difficult terrain.

Orlov set about importing some of the finest horses he could, acquiring desert types from the Middle East, including the important Arabian Smetanka, and some of the majestic European breeds like the Danish mare Isabelline (f. 1768) from the Royal Frederiksborg stud. She produced the colt foal Polkan I when bred to Smetanka, and Polkan I, bred to Friesian mares, produced outstanding trotters, including the stallion Bars I (f. 1784), who is considered one of the foundation sires of the breed. The Arabian Sultan I (f. c. 1763) was also highly influential.

Breeding was rigorously selective and only those with the best ability and conformation were used. Orlov closely guarded his horses and controlled all breeding through his stud by never selling any of his stallions. He was also responsible for introducing harness racing to Russia, and for a short time the Orlov Trotter was the fastest trotting horse in Europe, beating even the American Standardbred. The Orlov became one of the most popular trotting horses around and was favored as a carriage horse as well as for racing. It was also used to improve other breeds, including the Russian Trotter, Don, Tersk, and Russian Heavy Draft.

After Orlov's death, breeding at the Khrenov Stud was continued by his assistant, Vasily Shishkin, but in 1831 Shiskin left and the management of Khrenov passed to Orlov's daughter Anna. The stud no longer maintained control of the Orlov Trotter, and the horses started to be bred throughout the region. Simultaneously, there was a decline in the quality of the Khrenov horses. By this time, the American Standardbred, which was rapidly gaining popularity in the United States, had become a faster trotter than the Orlov, leading to widespread crosses between Orlovs and Standardbreds to increase the Russian horse's speed. This led to a deterioration in the purebred Orlov and also eventually led to a separate breed, the Russian Trotter. The Russian Trotter is a faster trotting horse than the Orlov but lacks its quality, elegance, stamina, and refinement.

The Orlov breed was severely affected by both world wars and the intervening civil war, during which time breeding programs collapsed, horses were killed in battle or for food, and money for breeding was unavailable. Because of the Orlov's versatility, however, it was used widely in agriculture between the wars. Its use in a light draft capacity caused a brief resurgence of numbers, and during this time crossbreeding Orlovs was banned to try to increase purebred numbers. However, by the second half of the twentieth century, and with harness racing again popular, the Orlov had been firmly overtaken by the Russian Trotter in terms of speed, and it again fell from favor. A concerted effort has been made by Orlov enthusiasts to protect and save the breed, and today numbers are slightly on the increase.

HACKNEY

HISTORIC — ENGLAND — ENDANGERED

HEIGHT
14–15.3 h.h.
APPEARANCE
A small, elegant head with an intelligent aspect. Very compact through the body, with a long, graceful neck, powerful, sloping shoulders, and a deep, wide chest. Quarters are muscular, the croup is level, and the tail is set and carried high. Limbs are clean and sound.
COLOR
Generally bay, black, chestnut, or brown.
APTITUDE
Carriage driving, competitive driving, riding, showing

THERE ARE FEW SIGHTS AS SPECTACULAR as the Hackney horse or pony trotting in harness. These beautiful horses have a wonderful trotting action that combines energy and extravagance in equal measure, with a distinctive, vivacious high-knee-action trot. They did not, however, develop initially as harness horses but were favored for riding, and today, though most associated with driving, they can also make talented riding horses.

The name Hackney comes from the French word *haquenée*, commonly used to describe a light riding horse with a notably comfortable trot. Before the construction of roadways or proper tracks, it was essential to have a horse that could cover difficult ground smoothly and at a decent pace. By the Middle Ages, a type of horse had developed in England that was widely acclaimed for its trot and versatility; it was commonly referred to as a "hackney."

There were two main areas in England famous for trotting horses: Yorkshire, with the Yorkshire Roadster, Coach Horse, or Hackney; and Norfolk, with the Norfolk Roadster or Trotter. In the early 1700s these trotting horses were refined through the introduction of some Arabian blood, and as roadways improved there was a move toward producing flashy, fast, and enduring horses for use primarily in harness. A major influence in the modern development of these trotting horses was the stallion Original Shales (f. c. 1755). Original Shales was the son of the early Thoroughbred Blaze (f. 1733), who was in turn grandson to the Darley Arabian (f. c. 1700); the dam of Original Shales is listed as a Hackney mare.

Original Shales's two sons, Driver (f. 1765) and Scot Shales (f. 1762), and the stallion Marshland (f. 1802), who had Scot Shales blood on both sides, were predominant influences on the Norfolk Roadster during the eighteenth century. By this time, the Norfolk Roadster was slightly heavier in frame than its Yorkshire cousin, which had developed from Cleveland Bay/Thoroughbred crosses, but both had an enormous trotting ability and great stamina. The Hackney of today emerged largely through the crossing of Norfolk Roadster horses with Yorkshire Trotters, implemented by Robert and Philip Ramsdales, who took the Norfolk stallions Wroot's Pretender (f. 1788) and Norfolk Phenomenon (f. 1824) to Market Weighton, Yorkshire, where they bred them to local stock. Gradually the regional differences in the trotters vanished and a distinctive type emerged.

In the latter half of the nineteenth century, the Hackney Pony was developed by Christopher Wilson in Cumbria. He wanted to create a distinct type that bore the qualities of the Hackney but retained pony characteristics. Wilson bred the best Fell mares he could find to trotting stallions, occasionally also breeding to Welsh mares. His crosses brought about the Hackney Pony Sir George (f. 1866), who Wilson then rigorously bred to produce an excellent line of ponies referred to as Wilson (or Hackney) Ponies.

During the first half of the twentieth century the Hackney horse was immensely popular and was exported all over the world, but World War II (1939–45) changed the fortunes of this beautiful animal. Breed shows were greatly reduced, and, with economic hardship, the breeding of what was by then essentially a luxury horse was not easy. Motorized vehicles had largely replaced the need for elegant harness horses, and the Hackney was for a short time in real danger of disappearing altogether. However, enthusiasts continued to breed the lovely Hackney horse, and in the postwar years it emerged as an even more showy and extravagant animal, full of spirit and energy and a great show-ring spectacle.

CLEVELAND BAY
HISTORIC — ENGLAND — CRITICAL

HEIGHT
16–16.2 h.h.
APPEARANCE
A lovely, sensible head; large, kind eyes; and long, fine ears. Long, muscular, and arched neck well-set to broad shoulders with a good slope. Deep and wide through the

chest and frame. Limbs are strong and muscular with no feathering on the legs.
COLOR
Bay with black points.
APTITUDE
Carriage and competitive driving, light draft, riding, dressage, jumping, hunting

THE MAGNIFICENT, EMINENTLY DISTINCTIVE Cleveland Bay is the oldest British breed of horse with the exception of the native pony breeds. They are first mentioned in the Middle Ages as being bred in the area of northeast North Riding in Yorkshire and Cleveland, from where the breed takes its name. Centuries of freezing winters have contributed to the Cleveland's hardy constitution and innate intelligence. The sweeping, open landscape offers little in the way of protection and is largely made up of clay soils; as a result, the Cleveland developed with clean, feather-free legs.

Farmers in this northern area had developed a hugely strong and versatile horse, small in height but reasonably heavy in frame, that was used for riding, packing, light draft, and agricultural purposes. Although not massive, these horses were renowned for their strength, and today the Cleveland remains exceptionally robust, far stronger than its refined aspect would suggest. The powerful Yorkshire horse was first known as the Chapman Horse, named after the traveling salesmen who covered the large area with their distinctive bay horses laden with goods. The Chapman was also widely used in the area's thriving mining industry and was admired for being able to pack incredibly heavy loads from the remote mines to the coast.

It is believed that the Cleveland owes many of its characteristics to the influence of North African Barb blood introduced to local stock in the seventeenth century. The prized Barb's influence can be seen in the Cleveland's distinctive ram-like profile and effortless majesty. After the end of the English Civil War (1642–51), there were also

a number of Spanish, mostly Andalusian, horses in the area that had belonged to high-ranking military officials. The Spanish influence in the Cleveland is discernible in the shape of its head and self-carriage, as well as its equable temperament.

Early in the eighteenth century, the breed was again upgraded through the introduction of Eastern blood and early Thoroughbred types. By then, the Cleveland Bay had increased in size and was a supremely high-quality coaching horse that also made an admirable riding horse and hunter. By the end of the eighteenth century the breed had fixed characteristics and was breeding true to type; there is no evidence of outside influence on it after the end of the eighteenth century. It was recognized at the time as the leading coach horse in England, if not Europe, and was used widely to improve other breeds.

With the improvement of roads came a demand for a faster carriage horse, and Cleveland Bays were crossed with Thoroughbreds to produce the excellent (but now extinct) trotting horse the Yorkshire Roadster. The success of the Yorkshire Roadster nearly led to the demise of the Cleveland, and by the 1880s the breed was in crisis. The Cleveland Bay Horse Society (CBHS) was formed in 1884, and shortly after, there was a revival in interest, particularly from overseas.

Cleveland Bays were used extensively during World War I (1914–18), but their success in the military again contributed to their downfall since so many of the horses were lost in battle. By the 1960s, the breed was in real danger of extinction, with only four stallions left in the United Kingdom. In 1961, Queen Elizabeth II purchased the young stallion Mulgrave Supreme (f. 1961) to prevent him from being sold overseas; she later became patron of the CBHS. Mulgrave Supreme was used extensively for breeding on both pure- and part-bred mares, and by the 1970s the British stallion count had risen to thirty-six. Today Cleveland Bays can be found in the Royal Mews and are bred under royal patronage.

KLADRUBY

HISTORIC – CZECH REPUBLIC – RARE

HEIGHT
16.2–17 h.h.
APPEARANCE
An attractive head with a ram-like profile, a broad forehead and a large, kind eye. Neck is arched, set high, and carried majestically. Frame is balanced, with powerful shoulders and hindquarters. Typically has a high-knee-action at the trot.
COLOR
Gray or black.
APTITUDE
Carriage driving, competition driving, light draft, riding, dressage, classical dressage

THE TUMULTUOUS HISTORY of the magnificent Kladruby horse stretches back over 400 years and has been one of great highs and tremendous lows. These horses, grand in every sense of the word, are among the rarest breeds today. They are the Czech Republic's only indigenous horse breed and are an iconic part of the country's history to such an extent that in 1995 they were recognized as being a "national cultural monument."

In 1562, an enormous estate that included a horse-breeding farm was given to Maximilian II (1527–76), Holy Roman Emperor and part of the House of Hapsburg. There, he established his own horse-breeding activities based primarily on horses of Spanish descent. Around 1579, Emperor Rudolf II (1552–1612), Maximilian's son, founded a stud at Kladrub, one of the world's oldest studs in existence and still central to the breeding of the Kladruby horse. Rudolf was a great admirer of Spanish horses, and he continued to stock the stud with horses of mostly Spanish and Neapolitan origin with the goal of producing an elegant but weighty carriage horse for use in teams of six or eight to pull ceremonial vehicles. The following year the stud at Lipizza in Slovenia was founded by Maximilian's brother, Archduke Charles II (1540–90), to produce majestic riding horses and cavalry mounts for the Hapsburg nobility, and became famous for its production of the Lipizzaner, with which the Kladruby shares a very similar heritage.

The Kladruby has been bred to be either gray (white) or black since the eighteenth century, and these are the only two colors seen in the breed today. Originally there were occurrences of palominos and even spotted coats, but with the importance placed on matching horses for use in carriage teams, irregular coat colors were undesirable. Based on the Kladruby's Spanish and Neapolitan beginnings, the horses exhibit many characteristics associated with these breeds, including a distinctive and very attractive head with a straight or ram-like profile, a majestic bearing, active trot, and luxurious mane and tail. The breed was also influenced through the introduction of Danish, Irish, and Oldenburg blood, as well as some of the heavier Czech working horses.

All of the records for the Kladruby were destroyed in a fire during the Seven Years War (1756–63), but today there are four bloodlines for the gray horses—Generale, Generalissimus, Favory, and Rudolfo—and four for the black horses—Sacramoso, Solo, Siglavi Pakra, and Romke. Of these, the Generale and Sacramoso lines are considered the most important.

In the 1930s, the herd of black Kladrubys was broken up and many of the horses were slaughtered for meat, though a few of the black mares survived, as did the stallion Sacramoso Solo XXXI (renamed Solo), who gave rise to the modern Sacramoso line. The black Kladruby horse was saved through the efforts of Professor Prantisek Bilek and the Research Institute for Horse Breeding, which introduced Lipizzaner and Friesian stallions to the surviving black Kladruby mares to build the herd back up. The gray horses are still bred at the national stud at Kladruby.

The gray and black Kladruby horses exhibit some differences based on their specific breeding. The gray horses are generally finer, taller, and lighter, with very Spanish movement, whereas the black Kladrubys that were bred specifically as carriage horses for clerical dignitaries are heavier and more reflective of their Neapolitan heritage. Kladrubys excel at competitive driving and are splendidly baroque in appearance; they also make excellent recreational riding horses and particularly excel at dressage.

DØLE GUDBRANDSDAL + COLDBLOODED TROTTER

ANCIENT – NORWAY – COMMON

HEIGHT
14.1–15.3 h.h.

APPEARANCE
A small, square head with a straight profile. Neck is short, muscular, and well-set to broad shoulders. Reasonably long in the back and deep through the chest with
exceptionally powerful hindquarters. Legs are short, strong, and feathered.

COLOR
Brown or bay; occasionally black, chestnut, dun, and gray.

APTITUDE
Agricultural work, light draft, harness racing, packing, riding

NORWAY'S BREATHTAKING GUDBRANDSDAL VALLEY is a place of lakes and fertile pasture overlooked by mountainous ridges. It forms a central channel through the country and was traditionally a major trade route, particularly in providing passage from Oslo to the North Sea. It is also the home of the Døle Gudbrandsdal, or Døle Horse, and closely related Coldblooded Trotter, or Døle Trotter.

There is little doubt as to the antiquity of the Døle Horse's origins, which are similar to those of the ancient British Fell and Dales ponies. All three of these breeds were greatly influenced by the indomitable Friesian, to which the Døle still bears a resemblance, but the Døle's particular habitat also played a large role in its development. The horses are extremely tough, hardy, sound in wind and limb, and able to subsist on sparse rations. To this day, they are bred and raised on open mountain pastures where they must fend for themselves.

Døle horses are tremendously strong for their size and were originally used extensively in forestry and as pack animals. They were also used in agriculture in a light draft capacity, as harness horses, and for riding. In size and stamp, they were small draft horses, heavy through their frames and with great pulling power. As times changed, so too did the Døle's uses, and the breed began to separate into two types: a heavier draft animal and a lighter, faster trotting type. By the mid-nineteenth century, the heavy Døle Gudbrandsdal was still used for draft work, but with racing and equestrian sports gaining in popularity, the lighter Trotter, with its active paces, became a favorite

for trotting races. To increase its speed, there was some influence of Thoroughbred blood, namely through the stallion Odin (f. 1830), imported to Norway in 1834 and to whom all modern Døle Trotters can trace their pedigree, and the stallion Balder 4 (f. 1849), who influenced the heavier Døle Horse. Despite the influence of light breeds, some Thoroughbreds, and trotting breeds, the Trotter has retained its essential characteristics: a solid frame; a quiet, calm temperament; and tremendous power.

With increasing emphasis on the production of a hugely energetic trotting horse and decreasing demand for working horses, the original, heavier Døle Gudbrandsdal started to disappear. Breeders noticed this decline and set about restoring the small draft horse that had served them so well for centuries. Today the gap between the heavier Døle and the agile, lighter trotting horse has narrowed, though it is still discernible.

Horse breeding in Norway is monitored by the state and there are laws regarding the quality of stallions used. The Døles are graded at horse shows, and all stallions must be inspected and graded in order for their offspring to be entered into the studbook. This rigorous system of grading largely accounts for the Døle's continued quality. The heavier type must pass certain tests to prove its pulling power, and both types must complete a trotting test. X-rays are taken of the horses' knees and lower legs, and any stallion with defects is not allowed to breed, in an effort to eliminate certain leg weaknesses that occurred in the late twentieth century when breeding efforts to sustain the heavier type included extensive line breeding. Mares are also tested, and those mares of the trotting type who do not meet the minimum speed may be entered as heavy horses if their conformation is sufficient. Coldblooded or Døle Trotter stallions must also achieve a certain standard on the racetrack before being allowed to breed. Harness racing for these coldblood trotting horses remains very popular in Norway.

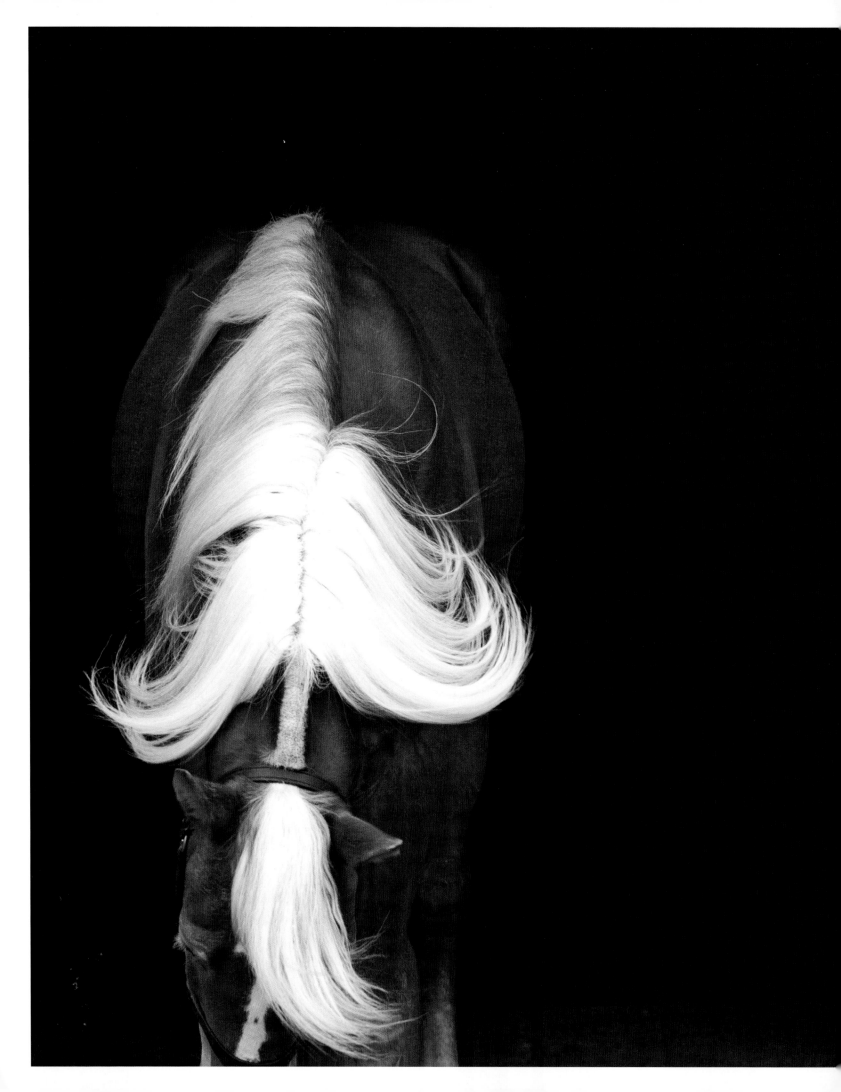

FINNISH UNIVERSAL

MODERN – FINLAND – COMMON

HEIGHT
Average 15.3 h.h.

APPEARANCE
Variation among the four types, but all are supremely athletic and balanced animals with high-quality, attractive heads, an intelligent aspect, and a muscular frame.

COLOR
Chestnut; occasionally black, brown, or roan.

APTITUDE
Harness racing, competition driving, light draft, agricultural work, riding, dressage, jumping, racing, competitive horse sports

THE MODERN FINNISH UNIVERSAL, or Finnhorse, has been recognized since the establishment of the Finnhorse studbook in 1907. However, the history of these truly impressive horses goes back over millennia. They are among the most versatile in the world, a true reflection of their name, but perhaps the most striking thing about them is their superb temperament, which is evident throughout the breed and has greatly contributed to their ability and willingness to fill any role required.

Finns have historically relied heavily on their horses and developed a particularly close relationship with them, born out of mutual necessity in a country whose winters are so severe. People relied on horses to transport them safely and quickly over treacherous terrain, haul goods, and work in agriculture, forestry, and, much later, urban situations, such as pulling fire trucks and taxis and providing transportation. Many ancient finds reveal Finnish horses buried alongside their owners, and horses were often ushered into the home in the harshest weather. By the nineteenth and early twentieth centuries, there were hundreds of thousands of Finnhorses working across the country.

Finland has a long tradition of equestrian sports, and in particular harness racing. Documented harness races exist from the early 1800s, though they were probably established long before. Some of the earliest were held on ice, a testament to the Finnhorse's sure-footedness. The first publicly organized and timed races date to the 1860s with state-run races held in Hämeenlinna on a horseshoe-shaped track. By the nineteenth century, the Finnhorse's incredible stamina was also being put to the test in long-distance endurance races.

Both the Tarpan and its descendants and the Mongolian Horse have been posited as ancestors of the Finnhorse. More likely, it was a combination of the two, with additional influence from the horse's dramatic environment. The horses are extremely tough and durable, and notably sure-footed. Initially, they were quite small— so much so that when large numbers of Finnhorses were taken to central Europe in the 1630s by Finland's light cavalry, they were criticized for their stature. However, during the Thirty Years' War (1618–48) the pint-sized horses astonished everyone with their tenacity, speed, bravery, and endurance. The horses' height has been increased through the years, and today, with the exception of the "pony-sized Finnhorse," they stand around 15.3 hands high. The main influences in this respect came from Friesians introduced during the sixteenth and seventeenth centuries, with later influences from Arabian stallions and from heavy draft types from southern Sweden.

Early in its history, the Finnhorse developed into two types, a heavier draft type that was used extensively in agriculture and forestry as well as for haulage, and a lighter type used for transportation. Both types exhibited a natural energetic trot, but this was emphasized by breeders of the lighter type. Throughout the nineteenth century there was a move toward greater selection in breeding. The state kept the stallion studbook from 1907 and in 1918 the mare studbook was moved under state control. In 1970 both studbooks came under the control of the National Horse Breeding and Trotting Association, and it was at this point that the Finnhorse was divided into four distinct and separate types that are still adhered to today: the workhorse, the trotter, the riding horse, and the pony-sized horse. All four types are required to undergo testing before registration, and this system of testing has been responsible for a continued improvement in the breed.

6 | OUTSTANDING AGILITY

There are no better examples of the superb athleticism and agility of horses than those seen in competitive horse sports. This area has given rise to the greatest explosion of different breeds, primarily during the nineteenth and twentieth centuries when the horse's role in cavalry and agriculture diminished and the leisure industry expanded. Many horse sports have their origins in the military and training for the battlefield, and also in hunting, and it is in the East that the story of these athletes begins.

The earliest horse sports developed in Central and Eastern Asia and they were fast, furious, and extremely dangerous. The precise dates and details are unrecorded although the accounts that exist indicate that early sports followed a loose general theme—a battle between two teams over possession of an object—and varied greatly in format from region to region. There is evidence of a form of polo being played in the sixth century B.C.E. in Persia, which is commonly cited as the birthplace of the game. However, Indian sources indicate that a form of stick-and-ball game played on horseback existed during the reign of King Kangba, ruler of the Manipur region from 1405 to 1359 B.C.E. The ferocious game of buzkashi dates to a similar time and originated in Afghanistan, where it is still played today. Buzkashi is one of the world's most dangerous sports and can result in injury or death to both horse and rider. It is played by teams that vary in size from tens to many hundreds, all of whom battle for possession of a calf or goat carcass. The horses used in this event are extraordinarily tough, quick, and agile; only male horses participate, and the best horses are extremely valuable.

Games such as this clearly have their roots in early warfare, and the practice and playing of these games served to increase the players' equestrian skills, which were then transferred to the battlefield. A form of early polo originated during the reign of Persian king Darius I (550–486 B.C.E.), and was less fierce than buzkashi but still served to hone and show off the competitors'

horsemanship. The Persians boasted some of the finest horse stock of the time, and the great Persian horse, known as the Nisean, was much sought after for its size and speed. In Persia, polo was called *chaugan* (also *chougan*), and the game soon spread throughout the Middle East and into China, Japan, Tibet, India (specifically Manipur between Assam and Burma), and Pakistan. It was from Tibet that the modern name "polo" derived, taken from the Tibetan word *pulu*, which means "ball." Polo became extremely popular in China during the Tang dynasty (618–907 C.E.), coinciding with a golden age of horse breeding in the country. Evidence from artifacts and tombs shows that horses during this period were typically heavy bodied but fine limbed, suggesting the influence of breeds such as the Persian Nisean and desert-bred types (the Turkmenian, ancestor to the Akhal Teke) crossed with Mongolian horses.

Mongolian horses were second to none in terms of stamina and endurance and were central to the lives of the nomadic Mongolian people. The Mongolians were also fierce proponents of early horse sports with speed, danger, and a combative edge at their core. Genghis Khan (c. 1162–1227) and his hordes are reputed to have played a form of polo using the severed heads of their enemies. Other early Asian and primitive games involving multiplayer teams and few rules were played using the heads of goats or sheep. The barbarity of the games notwithstanding, the underlying element was the agility of the small, tough, tireless horses.

Polo was played extensively in India and Pakistan, and in Gilgit, Pakistan, they still play a form of high-octane polo that reflects the original, ancient game. It is played on a narrow field enclosed by stone walls on the high altitude Shandur Pass, described as being "halfway to heaven and halfway to hell." The journey to Shandur Pass, along precipitous tracks, takes a four-wheel-drive vehicle between nine and thirteen hours and takes the horses,

which are ridden, up to five days. Each rider has only one horse, which is ridden throughout the one-hour polo match—modern Western polo requires a pony change for every chukka (seven minutes)—having already made the five-day trek to the field. During the game, the horses demonstrate great bravery, dexterity, and legendary stamina. The best of these horses are reputedly those bred in the Punjab hills or the northern parts of Afghanistan.

The founder of the Mughal Empire, Muhammad Babur (1483–1581), was a great supporter of polo and made it popular in India in the sixteenth century among the wealthy set. His grandson, Akbar the Great (1542–1605), introduced a set of rules for the game and established vast stables outside Agra where he bred small, agile ponies for the sport. With the decline of the Mughal dynasty in the mid-eighteenth century, polo began to disappear from much of India, although it remained popular in remote country areas, including Assam and Manipur. The game was not restricted to the wealthy but was played by

everyone and with its own rules, using the small Manipuri pony. It was here that the British first came across polo during the nineteenth century.

Lieutenant Joseph Sherer of the Bengal Army was posted to the Cacher district of Assam in 1857, and saw the game being played. Sherer became hooked, and helped establish the first European polo club (the Silchar Polo Club) in 1859 in Manipur. It was through Sherer, known as the "father" of modern polo, that the Calcutta Polo Club was established in 1863, the oldest polo club still in existence. The first game of polo in the United Kingdom took place in 1869, played on British native ponies, which were crossed to small Thoroughbreds, Arabians, and Barbs. From Britain, polo spread to Australia and North and South America during the 1870s, and these remain centers for specialized polo pony breeding.

Another of the ancient horse sports to originate in Central and Eastern Asia is pig sticking, a sport that developed from hunting wild boar with spears, around three thousand years ago. This practice is very dangerous and involves chasing a wild boar at high speed, often across treacherous terrain. The sport requires horses that are incredibly brave but also extremely agile and able to both follow the prey and get out of its way during an attack. British officers came across pig sticking in India during the late eighteenth century and engaged in it until the sport's demise during World War II. The sport continues to be practiced in Spain and Argentina today, and the Spanish and Portuguese horses that are so prized for their use in the bullfighting arena also excel at pig sticking.

Hunting in England and Ireland contributed toward the development of the modern sports of show jumping and eventing (as well as steeplechasing), which also have strong historical links to the military. With increasing urbanization in England, there was a gradual decrease in the amount of open land, as forests were felled to make way for settlements and to create farmland and pasture. The numbers of wild game decreased, and the proliferation of foxes that preyed on livestock became the main quarry of the hunt. Meanwhile, land was increasingly divided up and fenced off, creating obstacles that the horses had to jump. With the exception of steeplechasing, the first official jumping competition was staged in 1865, when the Royal Dublin Society's annual show had a class for "high and wide" jumps. These were based on the cross-country jumps seen on the hunting field, but the competition took place in an arena. Show jumping classes were primarily held for military riders, because at this time horses still formed an integral part of the military across much of the world, although some civilians also participated. The following year, a show jumping competition was held in Paris.

One of the most influential figures in the nineteenth-century equestrian world was the Italian cavalry instructor Federico Caprilli (1868–1907). He introduced the "forward seat," or cross-country, style of riding, before which riding styles in the West had barely changed since classical times. Caprilli recognized the advantages of riding with shorter stirrups, which allowed riders to come forward out of the saddle and balance their weight over the horse's moving center of gravity when riding at speed. It took some time for Caprilli's methods to filter overseas, but this was helped by the Italian cavalry schools accepting foreign military students. A young American cavalry officer trained at one of the Italian schools and introduced the forward seat to the United States on his return. The very first Nations Cup competition—in which teams of military riders from different countries participated in a jumping competition—was held at the National Horse Show in the United States in 1909. Today, the Nations Cup is the oldest and most prestigious team show jumping event in the world and is open to civilian riders.

The Paris Olympics in 1900 was the first to hold a show jumping competition, and all three disciplines—show jumping, dressage, and eventing—were included in the Olympics in Stockholm in 1912. However, show jumping competitions remained predominantly, although not exclusively, the domain of cavalry riders until after World War II. The Fédération Equestre Internationale was formed in 1921 to regulate international equestrian competitions. Two years later, the governing body for show jumping in England, the British Show Jumping Association (now British Showjumping) was formed, in 1923, and the American Horse Shows Association was founded in 1918, becoming the United States Equestrian Federation in 1933.

The French cavalry is credited with the development of eventing as we know it today and staged a four-part event called the Championnnat du Cheval d'Armes outside Paris in 1902. The event was for army horses and comprised a dressage test, a steeplechase, a 30-mile (48 km) roads and tracks, and a round of show jumping. Early events such as this were first called "Military," later known as combined training. These events tested every aspect of the horse, from its endurance and obedience to its agility and speed. Eventing in the Stockholm Olympics of 1912 took place over five days, although it was still only for military men, who were only allowed to ride their own horse or a horse belonging to their military division. The first day was an endurance test of 33 miles (53 km) to be completed in four hours, followed by the cross-country course. Day two was a rest day, and on the third day the horses were tested for their speed over a steeplechase course. On the fourth day, they completed their show jumping, and on the final day was the dressage test. Only male cavalry officers were eligible to ride at the Olympics until 1952, when the event was made open to both male and female civilian riders. Because of the great stamina, speed, and agility required for eventing, the best horses are originally Thoroughbreds or contain predominantly Thoroughbred blood. There is, however, an increasing number of other breeds that are taking on the eventing leader boards, notably warmblood breeds such as the Holstein, Selle Français, Belgian Warmblood, Dutch Warmblood, and Irish Sport Horse.

The biggest change in the horse market came about after World War II, which saw the demand for cavalry horses drop away steeply, matching a similar drop in the use of working horses. This was paralleled by the growing popularity of horses in the leisure industry, which includes competitive horse sports for civilians and pleasure riding. Horse breeders internationally reacted to changing market needs, and this has seen the exponential growth in the number and type of warmblood breeds. In general, these horses are based on older stock of military or working origin and have been redefined through sustained, intelligent breeding into top-rate competition animals.

The term "warmblood" refers to sports horses of Thoroughbred or Arabian heritage crossed with other breeds. They are mostly recognized as the Continental sporting horses, which generally exhibit outstanding jumping or dressage abilities. Dressage is one of the fastest growing sports. Its origins trace back to the Ancient Greeks, and throughout subsequent centuries the movements of dressage have been used as training exercises for military horses. The dressage competition that was included at the Olympics in 1912 comprised three phases: a dressage test, a jumping course, and an obedience test.

Another branch of equestrian sports developed through working life, rather than through hunting or the cavalry. It is best represented in some of the sporting traditions of North and South America and Australia that evolved through working livestock on horseback. These events, of which there are a great many, reflect the skills of the person working the cattle and the agility and sense of their horses. The most famous of these is the Australian sport of campdrafting, largely conducted on the Australian Stock Horse or the Waler, and the American and Canadian competitions of cutting, roping, steer wrestling, and penning, at which the American Quarter Horse and Canadian Cutting Horse excel.

OUTSTANDING AGILITY

MANIPURI

ANCIENT – INDIA – RARE

HEIGHT
11–13 h.h.

APPEARANCE
A quality head with a straight profile; large, almond-shaped eyes; and very mobile ears, often slightly curved. Neck has some arch, withers are defined, the shoulder is sloping, and the
chest is deep. Muscular back, sloping croup, and high-set tail. Legs are sound and very tough.

COLOR
Mostly bay, but can be gray, chestnut, brown, or parti-colored.

APTITUDE
Riding, polo, competitive horse sports

THE STATE OF MANIPUR sits in the northeastern reaches of India bordered by Burma to the east, Assam to the west, Nagaland to the north, and Mizoram to the south. It is a small but beautiful pocket of India—Manipur translates as "jeweled land"—with lush river valleys, undulating hills, and wide open plains. This is the home of the world's oldest polo pony, the Manipuri, or Meitei Sagol.

There is no specific record of the Manipuri's early beginnings, though the ponies are mentioned in some of the area's exotic myths and are connected with the Lai Haraoba festival, which honors deities associated with creation, fertility, and evolution. It is said that the Manipuri is a descendant of Shamadom Ayangba, a flying horse created by the deity Ashiba, son of the supreme deity Atiya Shidaba. One ancient legend relates that Ashiba became jealous of his brother Apanba, who had created humans and given them agriculture. Ashiba sent his winged horse, Shamadom Ayangba, to destroy the industrious who were planting the earth, but the horse was captured by Apanba and his wife. Shamadom Ayangba's wings were clipped in punishment, and he was domesticated and given to the humans. Though this story exists chiefly through the oral tradition of local Meitei storytellers, there is also a small statuette of Shamadom Ayangba, with wings, in the temple of Lord Marjing, a sylvan deity connected to horses, in Heingang.

The history of the Manipuri, of polo, and the region of Manipur are all closely interwoven and heavily based on local legends. Although polo is popularly believed to have

developed in Persia during the sixth century B.C.E., Manipur legend, with its roots in an ancient treaty the *Kangjeirol* (*Art of Polo*), recounts that King Kangba of Manipur created the game. King Kangba ruled the region from 1405 to 1359 B.C.E. and is said to have demonstrated his skill in dribbling a bamboo root using his walking stick during a local festival. Kangba requested that the following day his subjects practice this skill from the backs of their small ponies, and the game developed from this. It was called *sagol kangjei*, with *sagol* translating as "pony" and *kangjei* as "Kangba's stick." There is a mention of a game of polo centuries later in 33 C.E. to mark the marriage of Ngonda Lairen Pakhangba and Laisana, and the game appears to have remained popular throughout the ages, particularly from the sixteenth to the nineteenth century under the Mughal dynasty.

The fast-moving game required ponies of great dexterity and skill, also essential qualities for cavalry, and the Manipuri formed the core of the Manipur cavalry. The pony was greatly respected for its speed and tenacity, and its diminutive height was of no apparent hindrance. Warfare indirectly affected the development of the Manipuri through the exchange of horses brought back to Manipur as booty or abandoned after skirmishes, including breeds such as its close neighbor the Shan of Burma and the Mongolian. Mongolian horses were brought into the Manipur area sporadically by Tatar invaders, and Manipuri ponies and Mongolian horses were frequently bartered and swapped. The Manipuri also shares much in common with the Shan, with which there was considerable exchange of blood throughout history, though the Shan is typically larger than the Manipuri.

Arabian blood was introduced to the Manipuri when the British government sent an Arabian stallion and eight mares to Manipur in 1859. After this, Arabian horses continued to be imported in small numbers, including at the beginning of the twentieth century when Maharaja

Churachand Singh (1891–1941), a keen sportsman and polo player who did much to promote horse sports during his reign, imported two Arabians. During World War II, the Manipuri was further influenced by Australian Walers brought into the region by the Army Remount Department, but it is the Arabian influence that is most prominent.

Manipuri ponies are small in stature but very elegant through their frame. They are compact and sturdy through the body and extremely muscular, much stronger than their small size would suggest. Typically their color is a bay that ranges from light to dark, but they can be one of fourteen colors, including gray, chestnut, brown, roan, and black. There is some variation in the shape of the Manipuri's head, which can either exhibit a concave profile that reflects the Arabian influence or a ram-like profile that is more indicative of its Mongolian heritage. Possibly the most distinctive characteristic of the Manipuri, however, is the tremendous endurance and agility that serve it so well during polo. In polo at the highest levels, a pony will be changed for each chukker (seven minutes of play) because the pace of the game is so fast; in Manipur, the little ponies are only infrequently changed, testament to their stamina.

The Manipuri pony and the game of polo were unknown in the West until the mid-nineteenth century, when British soldiers and civilians came across the game while establishing tea plantations in Manipur's Cacher Valley. By this time polo was the regional pastime and was played widely throughout the villages, with each village having its own team. In 1859, the first European Polo Club was formed in Cacher by Captain Robert Stewart and Lieutenant Joseph Sherer of the Bengal Army. The maximum height of the polo pony was restricted to 13 hands, which was the upper height limit of the Manipuri's range, though this was later raised and then abolished altogether. As a result, the pony became highly sought after for the game; such large numbers were exported and the native stock dwindled so rapidly that export of the ponies eventually had to be banned.

Today, unfortunately, the Manipuri pony has suffered a steep decline in numbers, primarily because of the increased urbanization of the region and the impact this has had on its habitat.

OUTSTANDING AGILITY

OUTSTANDING AGILITY

OUTSTANDING AGILITY

POLO PONY

HISTORIC — UNITED KINGDOM, AUSTRALIA, UNITED STATES, ARGENTINA — COMMON

HEIGHT
Up to 15.3 h.h. (no height restriction)
APPEARANCE
In general, polo ponies are small and elegant and supremely tough. They are balanced and athletic through the frame

with exceptionally strong leg bones and hooves. They are highly intelligent and attractive horses.
COLOR
Any color.
APTITUDE
Riding, polo, showing, competitive horse sports

THE POLO PONY IS A TYPE, NOT A BREED, and is bred along different lines and using different combinations of breeds, depending on the country of origin. The major centers of polo-pony breeding are Argentina, North America, Australia, and the United Kingdom, but despite the wide geographic and cultural differences, all polo ponies exhibit certain characteristics that predispose them to playing this energetic and demanding game.

Polo ponies are universally tough, intelligent, and agile horses of medium size that possess tremendous speed, athleticism, and endurance. They should be well built with good, muscular shoulders, a deep chest, strong back, and powerful hindquarters. Polo ponies must have sound feet and strong, well-articulated joints and bones. They will typically have their manes shaved off and their tails plaited up and bandaged out of the way to prevent them from becoming entangled with equipment during play.

British cavalry officers and tea planters first came across polo being played in the Indian state of Manipur during the 1850s, and they were immediately taken with the sport. The first game in the United Kingdom was played in 1869 by officers of the 10th Hussars at Aldershot, and the first polo club was the Monmouthshire established in 1872. In 1874 polo was established at the Hurlingham Club, Hurlingham, which was the headquarters for polo in the British Empire until 1939. In 1875 the first English rules for the game were drawn up by the Hurlingham Polo Committee, and the following year the first British height restriction of 14 hands was established. In 1925

the committee was renamed the Hurlingham Polo Association, the governing body for polo in the United Kingdom, Ireland, and twenty-five other countries.

The British were the first westerners to start breeding ponies specifically for polo, based on native British pony breeds, particularly the Dartmoor, Welsh, New Forest, and Connemara, which were crossed to small Thoroughbreds, Arabians, or Barbs. These crosses quickly began to produce a type of pony that combined the elegance and speed of the Thoroughbred with the stamina, spirit, and agility of the native pony breeds.

The Polo Pony Stud Book Society was formed in 1893 to improve the breeding of "riding ponies." Barb and Thoroughbred stallions were among those used on native ponies, and crosses with small Thoroughbreds produced some of the best early polo ponies. In 1894, the first studbook was published, listing 57 stallions and 316 mares. Significantly, the first stallion in the studbook was an American-bred Arabian, indicating that within just a year of its formation the society had earned international recognition. The polo pony seemed on track to become an established British breed.

Horse shows for polo ponies were held at the beginning of the twentieth century to raise the profile of the ponies and improve breeding initiatives. Around this time, the society also began to push the breeding of a more general riding type of pony and to incorporate the British native breeds, since these were particularly useful in keeping the height of polo ponies below the limit of 14.2 hands, which had been raised in 1895. In 1913, the society's name was changed to the National Pony Society, and in 1919 the height restriction on British polo ponies was removed, after which increasing amounts of Thoroughbred blood was used to create larger animals. This change in breeding policy led to polo "ponies" with decreasing amounts of actual pony blood in their heritage, and the modern polo pony is a pony in name only. By this time the National

Pony Society had moved emphasis away from specific polo-pony breeding to champion the British native breeds, with the goal of preserving and improving the native breeds and producing versatile riding ponies. These ponies are greatly sought after today for show classes and for competitive driving.

In the 1870s, polo spread around the world like wildfire. There are conflicting accounts of precisely when the first game of polo was played in Australia, but it was sometime in the mid-1870s. By the 1880s, games were being played between the clubs of the Western district of Victoria and the Southern Australia clubs, causing a lively state rivalry that still exists today. Initially, the Australian Waler was used, as well as crosses between Walers and Arabians or Thoroughbreds. Many Walers were also exported to India from the 1840s to the 1940s for the British Indian Army, which led to some crossbreeding with native horses, particularly the Manipuri, to produce polo ponies. The Australian Stock horse also provided a foundation breed to which Thoroughbreds were bred to produce homegrown Australian polo ponies. Today the Australian polo pony is largely influenced by Thoroughbred blood.

The American newspaper tycoon James Gordon Bennett saw polo being played at the British Hurlingham Club in 1876, and full of enthusiasm for it, brought it back to the United States. He was responsible for the first American polo match, which took place in New York at Dickel's Riding Academy at 39th Street and 5th Avenue. The first American polo club, the Westchester Polo Club, was formed the same year and is now based in Newport, Rhode Island. In 1886 the Westchester Polo Club challenged the British to compete in the world's first international match—the Westchester Cup, one of the most prestigious polo events.

The earliest North American polo ponies were based on crossing small Thoroughbreds to the working stock and ranch horses from which the Quarter Horse emerged. This cross produced a small, fast, and intelligent animal capable of great speed and endurance. Horses of South American origin were also greatly favored for crossing with Thoroughbreds to produce polo ponies, particularly horses from Argentina. The Americans stopped playing by the British pony height rule in 1916, which led to the British abolishing the rule in 1919 and paved the way for their polo ponies to increase in size.

Polo was introduced to Argentina by British engineers and ranchers; the first mention of the game appeared in an Argentinean newspaper in 1874 in a report covering an event held by the Azul English Race Meeting that included a number of races, a steeplechase, and three polo matches. The following year, the same newspaper reported the "first" game of polo to be played in South America, which took place at a ranch belonging to the Englishman David Anderson Shennan in the province of Buenos Aires. The Buenos Aires Hurlingham Club was opened in 1888, and in 1889 the club held its first polo tournament. The Argentine Polo Open Championship, one of the most prestigious polo events in the world, was first held in 1893 in Palermo barrio in Buenos Aires, and takes place annually—the stadium at Palermo is commonly referred to as the "Cathedral of Polo."

Since the game first arrived in Argentina, the people have taken it to their hearts, and the country produces some of the top players and ponies. Argentina has a long tradition of highly skilled horsemen, and its horses are also impressive on virtually every front, particularly the Argentinean Criollo, one of the toughest working stock horses in existence. The Criollo formed the base for the early polo ponies in the area, and native Criollo blood is at the foundation of the superlative modern Argentinean polo pony. Argentinean breeders began to cross the Criollo to Thoroughbred stallions to increase the speed of their native stock, and the result is a polo pony of great quality and speed but with the soundness, strength, and endurance of the Criollo. The Argentinean Association of Polo Pony Breeders was formed in 1984 to establish the Polo Argentino breed through rigorous bloodline documentation and inspections.

The breeding of top-level polo ponies is extremely difficult and requires enormous skill and knowledge. Furthermore, many of the top-level ponies are actually mares, so breeding them used to mean having to interrupt their successful careers. This has since changed with the introduction of embryo transfers, which allow the top mares to continue playing while surrogate mares carry their embryos. Meanwhile, in both Argentina and the United States, detailed registers with breeding bloodlines and performance records have been created in the hopes that significant patterns of excellent breeding stock will emerge, allowing breeders to become even more selective.

AUSTRALIAN PONY
MODERN – AUSTRALIA – COMMON

HEIGHT	
Up to 14 h.h.	*Defined withers, strong back, and muscular croup.*
APPEARANCE	**COLOR**
An attractive head, broad across the forehead, with large eyes and small alert ears. Neck is well proportioned with some crest and arch and well-set to shoulders with a good slope.	*Typically gray, though any color is accepted.*
	APTITUDE
	Riding, showing, dressage, polo, jumping, eventing, competitive and Western horse sports

AUSTRALIA PRODUCES SOME OF THE BEST horses in the world and yet horses were not indigenous to this enormous landmass. The first horses to set hoof on Australian soil arrived in 1788 with the First Fleet, which had set sail from Cape Town, South Africa, bearing provisions and equipment for the establishment of a new colony in New South Wales. The initial development of horses in Australia was entirely reliant on the successive passage of imported horses, many of which came from India, South Africa, continental Europe, and the Indonesian islands north of Australia, including Timor, Sumba, and Sumbawa. For many of these horses, particularly those coming from Europe and South Africa, the journey was long, grueling, and incredibly dangerous—only the toughest survived. Those horses from the Northern Hemisphere that did survive suddenly found themselves living in totally alien climatic conditions to which they had to rapidly adapt, and though the kinds of horses and ponies arriving in Australia differed widely, the survivors had one thing in common: tenacity.

The first ponies to be shipped over, just like the horses, were brought primarily to work. They were tough, resourceful, and sound in body and limb, providing a very solid foundation stock from which the Australian Pony would emerge. Some of the earliest ponies to arrive in Australia were of Indonesian origin, chiefly the tough little ponies from Timor and the more refined Sandalwood ponies from Sumba and Sumbawa. Both of these pony breeds, as with all the Indonesian breeds, originally

evolved from the Mongolian Horse, Asiatic Wild Horse, and Tarpan, with Arabian and Barb influence coming much later in their development. Imports of these Indonesian ponies began in 1803, when the first Timor ponies landed in Sydney Cove. The first Timor ponies to arrive in the northern territories landed in the 1840s at Port Essington. This ill-fated site on the Cobourg Peninsula, originally settled in 1831, was intended to be a major trading link to Asia, but it was abandoned in 1849 and all that remains today are some ruins. It is quite possible that during the course of the settlement's abandonment some of the ponies were let loose and bred in the wild, eventually joining feral herds known as "Brumbies." During this time there was also a steady traffic of Arabian horses being shipped from India and many native British pony breeds coming from England. These included the Shetland, Welsh Mountain, Welsh Section C, Exmoor, Hackney horse and pony, and Hungarian pony. These, along with small Thoroughbreds and Indonesian ponies, formed the basis from which the beautiful Australian Pony would develop. The specific breeding of ponies primarily as working tools was well established by the turn of the nineteenth century, with breeding aims focused on the production of strong, sound, enduring, and obliging working animals.

The Australian Pony Stud Book Society (APSB) was formed in 1931 to register the bloodlines and pedigrees of ponies in Australia. Initially the society established three breed sections for Shetland, Hackney, and Australian ponies. At this time, the Australian section covered all other imported native British breeds as well as homegrown ponies that had been crossbred in Australia. In 1950, an additional section was created for the Welsh Mountain Pony, with Welsh B, C, and D added; following this, other sections were opened for the New Forest, Highland, Dartmoor, Connemara, and, most recently, the Fjord in 1995. Today the APSB registers nine separate pony breeds, including the Australian, and also holds a register for APSB riding ponies and for part-breds.

The first volume of the APSB studbook, published in 1936, also included a reference section that listed the influential pony breeding stock established before the foundation of the society. This reference section is particularly interesting because it reveals that some of the earliest significant pony stock in the country that would contribute to the Australian Pony was predominantly of Welsh Mountain or Welsh C origin. Seven of the eight listed stallions and the one listed mare in the reference section were imported to Australia in the late nineteenth and early twentieth centuries, and of these the Welsh Mountain stallion Dyoll Graylight (f. 1900) and Welsh C Little Jim (f. 1906), imported in 1910 and 1909 respectively, were of particular importance. Dyoll Graylight was the son of Dyoll Starlight (f. 1894), who had Arabian blood and is listed as one of the foundation stallions for the Welsh Mountain Pony; he has also been called the most beautiful pony in the world. Graylight was imported to Australia by Anthony Hordern, a respected breeder of Welsh ponies who, along with other members of his family, was influential in the foundation of the APSB.

Other important early stallions were the imported Hungarian pony Bonnie Charlie (n/d), who is reputed to have come to Australia as part of a traveling circus, and the Australian-bred Tam O'Shanter (f. 1882), by the imported Exmoor stallion Sir Thomas, one of only two Exmoors to come to Australia (the other being Dennington Court). Additional stallions of significance to the Australian pony were Lowlynn Silver Chief (f. 1947), who had Welsh Mountain and Arabian bloodlines, and Barolin Feluka (f. 1957), also of Welsh Mountain and Arabian heritage.

The Australian Pony studbook was closed to outside blood in 1960 with the exception of crosses to APSB Welsh Mountain and Section B. The combination of Welsh Mountain Pony and Arabian is very evident in the Australian Pony, which is a pony of tremendous quality and beauty, and generally exhibits particularly good, free-flowing movement with great cadence. The very great qualities of the Australian Pony are promoted through the work of the Australian Pony Owners and Breeders Association, which was established in 1979.

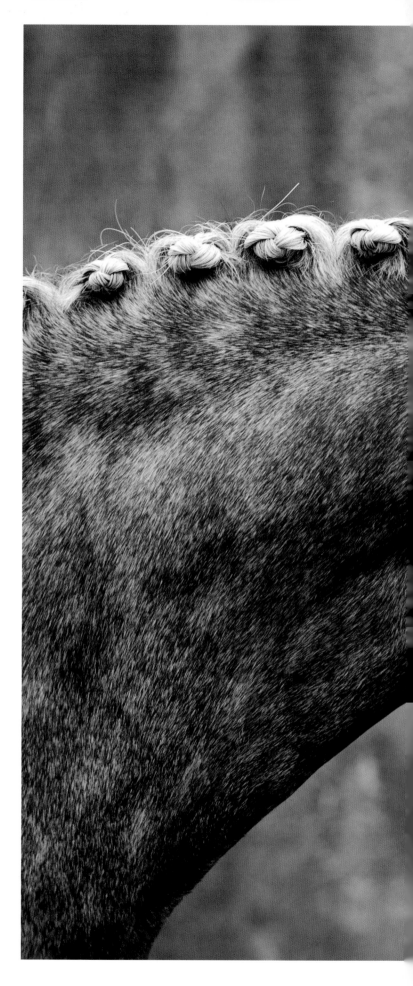

AUSTRALIAN STOCK HORSE
HISTORIC – AUSTRALIA – COMMON

HEIGHT	
14–16 h.h.	*Rib cage is well-sprung and hindquarters are powerful.*
APPEARANCE	COLOR
A finely modeled, attractive head, well-set neck, and sloped shoulders. Withers are defined, chest is deep but not too wide, and back is of medium length and strong.	*Any color.*
	APTITUDE
	Riding, working livestock, dressage, jumping, eventing, competitive and Western riding horse sports

THE AUSTRALIAN STOCK HORSE is often referred to as "the horse for every need," and there is perhaps no better description of this extraordinarily talented and versatile breed. These horses can excel in virtually every equestrian sphere, from show jumping to polo, campdrafting to dressage, and everything in between.

As with all Australian breeds, the roots of the Australian Stock Horse trace back to horses imported from the eighteenth century onward and brought to Australia by early colonists. These included Arabians and Barbs, British pony breeds, Thoroughbreds, Iberian horses, European breeds, Indonesian breeds, and some draft breeds, providing a diverse gene pool from which the Australian breeds later emerged. The Australian Stock Horse's history is inextricably linked to that of the Australian Waler, and both breeds could be considered one until the end of World War II. The first place horses arrived in Australia was New South Wales, and today this remains a center of Australian horse breeding. Horses from there became known as Walers and were the original Australian working horse; they were highly sought after by the army because of their incredible tenacity and versatility.

Among the horses to influence the Waler were early English Thoroughbreds, which were first introduced to Australia at the very end of the eighteenth century; by the 1830s, they were being imported in large numbers. Many of these imported Thoroughbreds were crossed to the existing mares, who had by this time developed into hardy, enduring creatures. These crosses began to produce a type of horse that was elegant, athletic, and extremely hardy. Often these horses were used extensively on Australia's giant cattle ranches or stations and were referred to as Stock horses or Station horses.

Through the twentieth century, the role of the horse began to change. The demand for working horses decreased and there was a move toward breeding a modern, competitive type suitable for horse sports. There was an increase in crossbreeding to Thoroughbreds and Arabians, with some crosses also made to the American Quarter Horse, which had arrived in Australia in the mid-1950s. This impressive horse developed into a distinct type—a high-quality, athletic, and elegant animal—and in 1971 it was finally given a proper name and a society to protect it. The Australian Stock Horse Society was formed in June of that year, and a studbook was established to try to preserve its important heritage. Today the society has numerous branches across Australia; it serves to protect the breeding records of the Stock Horse through registration and to promote the breed through competitions and exhibitions.

The Stock Horse is now widespread in Australia and has had far greater influence in its formation from other breeds than the older Waler. In particular, there has been Thoroughbred, Arabian, and some pony influence, as well as influence from Waler bloodlines. Although it is used throughout the equestrian leisure industry and competes in almost all disciplines, it is also still used as a working animal on many of Australia's cattle stations. The Stock Horse excels at working livestock and exhibits a natural affinity for cattle, able to track and follow them at great speed. It is from this that the Australian sport of campdrafting developed, and the Australian Stock Horse is the true champion in this field. Campdrafting tests the horse's intelligence, agility, obedience, speed, and ability to work cattle and involves a single mounted rider cutting a cow from a group and maneuvering it through a series of obstacles in an enclosed area according to a set pattern.

SELLE FRANÇAIS
MODERN – FRANCE – COMMON

HEIGHT	COLOR
15.1–17 h.h.	*Mostly chestnut or bay;*
APPEARANCE	*occasionally gray; rarely*
An extremely attractive,	*red roan.*
high-quality head with a	**APTITUDE**
straight or slightly convex	*Riding, racing, dressage,*
profile. Arched neck, defined	*show jumping, eventing,*
withers, sloping shoulder, and	*showing, competitive*
powerful hindquarters.	*horse sports*

NORMANDY, WHERE THE SELLE FRANÇAIS, or French Saddle Horse, developed, has a long tradition of breeding excellent horses to fulfill different requirements and is home to two of France's historic national studs. Since its development, the Selle Français has proved itself to be one of the leading competitive warmblood breeds, particularly in show jumping. Generally, they are intelligent, athletic, balanced, and muscular horses renowned for their kind dispositions.

In earlier times, the Norman horse was larger in height and frame than many of its ancient contemporaries and was long valued as a warhorse. Evidence of the size and quality of Norman horses can be seen in the Bayeux Tapestry, which records the Norman invasion of England in 1066. Large numbers of these superior horses were brought over to England, where they had an improving influence on the British horses of the time. Many hundreds of years later, from the end of the eighteenth century, the English Thoroughbred, half-bred, and Norfolk Trotter (Roadster) would in turn greatly improve the Norman horse, which was also influenced by Arabian blood.

Through systematic breeding of these English horses, and some Arabians, with local Norman mares, the Anglo-Norman horse was developed into two types. The first was a heavier cob and draft horse type influenced by crosses with Boulonnais and Percheron stallions. These were big, strong horses, notably agile for their size, and often exhibited an excellent trot. The second Anglo-Norman type was a classy riding horse suitable for use in the military and for horse sports; this type would become the Selle Français.

A subtype that developed from this riding horse was a sleek light-draft or harness horse. This type was greatly influenced by Norfolk Roadster blood and was renowned for its enormous trotting ability—it eventually developed into the French Trotter. These different types of horse developed along slightly different lines according to their geographic location. The region of La Hague, for example, which sits on the tip of the Cotentin Peninsula, produced saddle horses of Arabian influence during the nineteenth century when there were a number of Arabian stallions in the area, whereas much of the rest of Cotentin is associated with trotting horses. The area of Bessin has a long tradition of producing first-class saddle horses, and today many Selle Français trace their roots to this area.

France's horse stock was depleted after the two world wars. Anglo-Norman mares that had survived were bred to Thoroughbred stallions, many of which were standing at the national studs, and these stallions, including Orange Peel (f. 1919), Lord Frey (f. 1916), Ultimate (f. 1941), Furioso (f. 1939), and Rantzau (f. 1946), gave rise to some of the leading show-jumping horses of the twentieth and twenty-first centuries through their progeny. During the 1990s, twenty-six of the top hundred show jumpers were descendants of Orange Peel, and his grandson Ibrahim (f. 1952) gave rise to two of the great modern Selle Français bloodlines through his sons Quastor (f. 1960) and the outstanding Almé Z (f. 1966).

In December 1958, all the regional studbooks of Anglo-Norman riding horses were amalgamated into the studbook for the Cheval de Selle Français by ministerial decree, and the first volume of the studbook was published in 1965. The Selle Français, of which there are two recognized types—those that excel at show jumping, dressage, and eventing and a lighter-framed type used for non-Thoroughbred racing in France—is bred in the United States, Australia, and Europe, and across the rest of the world.

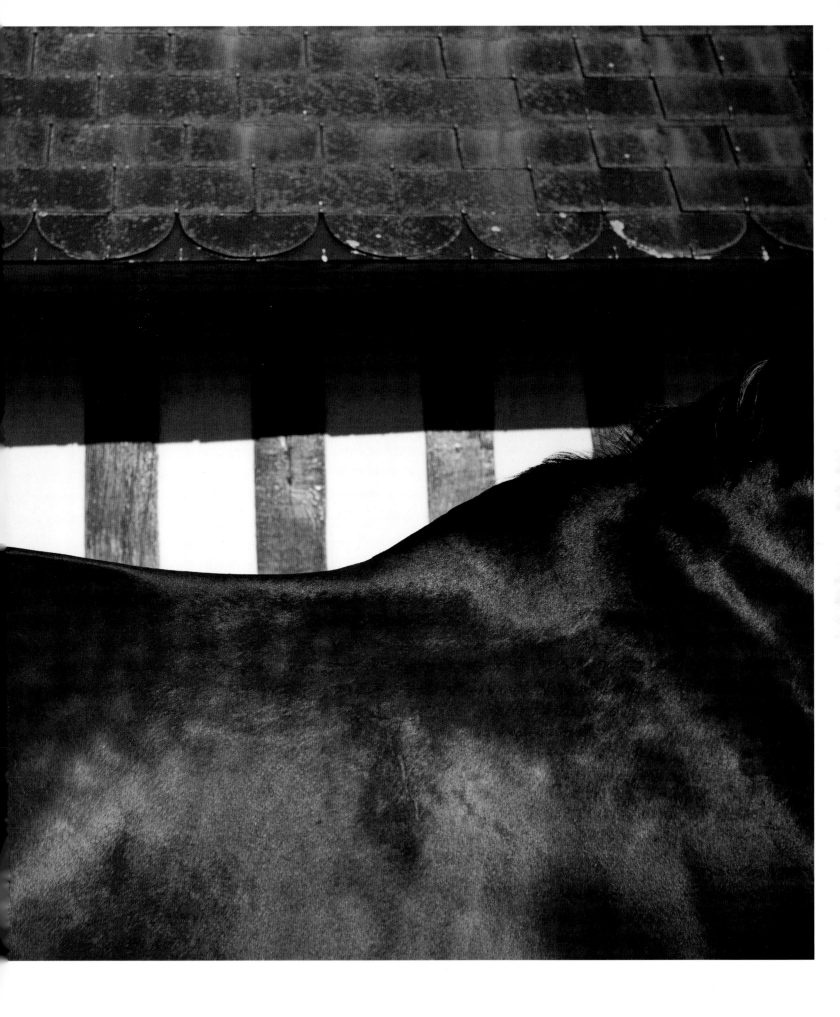

OUTSTANDING AGILITY

OLDENBURG

HISTORIC — GERMANY — COMMON

HEIGHT	*muscular shoulder.*
16–17.2 h.h.	*Reasonably flat, strong croup*
APPEARANCE	*with muscular hindquarters.*
A head with a straight or	**COLOR**
slightly ram-like profile	*Mostly bay, black, brown, or gray.*
well-set to a muscular,	**APTITUDE**
well-arched neck. Deep	*Riding, dressage, show jumping,*
through chest with defined	*eventing, carriage driving,*
withers and an excellent,	*competitive horse sports*

THE OLDENBURG HORSE was one of the most famous and respected horses in seventeenth-century Europe and so revered that the horses were often presented as gifts to visiting royalty and dignitaries. Today the modern Oldenburg is a perfect example of an old breed redefined to suit modern tastes; highly sought after as a competition horse, it particularly excels at dressage and show jumping.

The origins of the Oldenburg go back to Count Johann the Younger (1540–1603), a keen horseman who ruled Oldenburg from 1573 to 1603. He implemented a program of breeding that was heavily based on horses of Friesian origin bred primarily as warhorses. He was succeeded by his son Graf Anton Gunther von Oldenburg (1583–1667), also an enthusiastic horseman, who greatly expanded horse breeding in the area. He established a number of stud farms using the base stock of Friesian-influenced horses from his father's stables and sourced different horses— Spanish, Neapolitan, Polish, Turkish, Danish, English, and North African stock, including Barbs—in his travels across Europe and North Africa. When crossed with the Friesian-influenced horses and other local stock, a magnificent type was produced. Gunther's own bred stallion Kranich (f. c. 1640), on whom he performed classical dressage, was particularly admired, and paintings of Kranich reveal a beautiful gray horse of expressly Spanish looks with a majestic bearing and an abundant mane and tail.

Under Gunther's rule, the Oldenburg developed into a type not dissimilar in appearance to the Kladruby: a reasonably heavy framed horse of majestic appearance with obvious Spanish influence. The horses were used for classical dressage and as warhorses, and a heavier type was used as a carriage horse. On Gunther's death, Oldenburg came under Danish rule and the emphasis of horse breeding moved away from quality to quantity, primarily for use as warhorses or agricultural animals. The Oldenburg lost its elegance and developed a more rustic appearance.

Early in the nineteenth century there was a move to improve the Oldenburg's quality, aided by an 1820 law that required Oldenburg stallions to be judged and certified before they could be used for breeding. During this period, Spanish, Neapolitan, Barb, French, and English blood were used on Oldenburg mares, and a type known as the Oldenburg Karossier emerged. Up until World War I, breeding centered on the production of heavy cavalry and coach horses, which were also widely used in agriculture. The horses were prized during the war, but the breed suffered huge losses. After World War II, workhorses faced obsolescence, but canny Oldenburg breeders once again began producing a horse to meet contemporary requirements.

Breeding of the modern Oldenburg sports horse began during the late 1950s. German breeders again looked to the horses of France to upgrade the Oldenburg, using Norman and Anglo-Norman blood as well as some Thoroughbred blood. The Norman stallion Condor (f. 1946) and Anglo-Norman Furioso II (f. 1965), who also influenced the Hanoverian breed, were important, as well as the Thoroughbred stallions Adonis XX and Lupus (f. 1961). The modern Oldenburg is a horse par excellence, and Oldenburg-bred horses have achieved international acclaim in several equestrian disciplines. The high quality of the Oldenburg has been achieved through the enforcement of a strict registration process that involves rigorous inspections before horses may be entered into the studbook, and stallions have to undergo extensive performance testing before they can be fully approved for breeding.

HOLSTEIN

ANCIENT — GERMANY — COMMON

HEIGHT	COLOR
16–17 h.h.	*Mostly bay, black,*
APPEARANCE	*brown, or gray.*
A highly attractive, balanced	**APTITUDE**
horse whose frame and build	*Riding, dressage, show*
reflects the influence of	*jumping, eventing, showing,*
Thoroughbred blood but with	*carriage driving, competitive*
added solidity. A top athlete	*driving, competitive horse*
in all respects.	*sports, cavalry*

THE MAGNIFICENT HOLSTEIN HORSE (or Holsteiner) is Germany's oldest warmblood breed and originated in the state of Schleswig-Holstein, specifically the Elmshorn district of Holstein, around seven hundred years ago. Horses have lived on the marshy lands surrounding the Elbe River and its tributaries since very early times and probably originally came from western Asia brought by nomadic people. These horses would have had desert-bred characteristics similar to the ancient Turkmenian, but through the centuries evolved to adapt to the colder, damper climate of northern Germany.

The earliest considered horse breeding in this area is thought to have been undertaken by the monks of Uetersen Monastery on the fertile Haseldorf marshes in the thirteenth century. The area became a center of horse breeding, with local landowners and nobles leading the activities. After the Reformation (begun in 1517 in Saxony), the fine horses from the local monasteries were acquired by the landowners and were further improved by the use of stallions of Spanish, Eastern, and Neapolitan blood. The Dukes of Schleswig-Holstein greatly encouraged the breeding of horses to produce big, strong animals suitable for use on the land and in war. These horses rapidly gained a glowing reputation across Europe and from the sixteenth century were exported to Denmark, Spain, Italy, and France as warhorses and were used across Germany to improve regional stock such as the Westphalian horses, the Mecklenburgs, and the Hanoverians at the Celle and Dillenburg studs. The quality of the Holstein horses was cemented through very early breeding restrictions, and in 1713, the crown implemented a form of stallion inspection, based on conformation and health, to control the way in which the breed would develop.

During the eighteenth century the Holstein was used extensively throughout the different German states to improve their own horses. Perhaps most famous was the use of Holstein stallions at the Celle Stud in Lower Saxony, which eventually resulted in the development of the impressive Hanoverian horse through crossbreeding. In the early nineteenth century, English Thoroughbred blood was introduced to produce a slightly lighter-weight horse of great refinement, and from the 1830s, there were further crosses to Yorkshire Coach Horses and horses from Hanover and Oldenburg.

Despite the Holstein's tremendous qualities, the breed's numbers had declined drastically by the end of World War II. The state-owned stud of Traventhal, founded in 1874, was closed in 1960, and Holstein breeders had to reorganize their breeding strategy. The stallions from Traventhal were moved to Elmshom, which has since been able to restore the number and quality of breeding stock. A rigorous process of reestablishing the Holstein breed was done with heavy use of Anglo-Norman and Thoroughbred blood, including the stallions Cottage Son (f. 1944), Ladykiller (f. 1961), Anblick (f. 1938), Marlon (f. 1958), and the Selle Français Cor de la Bryère (f. 1968) and Almé Z (f. 1966).

Holstein breeding stock is closely monitored, and only licensed and approved stock may be used for breeding if they are to be entered into the studbook. Stallions are tested when they are two and a half years old and are judged on all aspects, including conformation, type, and movement. Only a small percentage of stallions put forward are granted a breeding license. At three, they undergo an additional hundred days of testing, and only if they are successful at this will they be entered into the studbook. Mares are also inspected and can be entered into various mare books.

OUTSTANDING AGILITY

HANOVERIAN
HISTORIC – GERMANY – COMMON

HEIGHT
Ideally 16.2 h.h.
APPEARANCE
An attractive head well-set to a long, muscular, well-arched neck. Extremely powerful shoulders and hindquarters. Well-defined withers, a well-sprung rib cage, good

depth through the chest, and strong limbs with hard feet.
COLOR
Mostly chestnut, bay, black, or gray.
APTITUDE
Riding, dressage, show jumping, eventing, carriage driving, competitive horse sports

THE HANOVERIAN HORSE was developed in Lower Saxony in northwest Germany, a place where the climate is moderate and the soils are largely fertile. This is a breed that has been specifically developed over a period of three centuries to meet the changing demands of the public, and such is its importance, the flag and coat of arms of the region bear a white Hanoverian on a red shield. The breed is a product of highly intelligent, systematic breeding and ranks as the most widespread and famous of the many European warmblood breeds; their extraordinary versatility has seen Hanoverians compete and win at the highest levels in dressage, show jumping, eventing, and competitive driving.

The breed traces its history to 1735, when George II (1683–1760), Elector of Hanover and King of England, established a state breeding stud at Celle, primarily using Holstein stallions and early English Thoroughbreds. The initial objective of the state-run stud was to provide local farmers with access to high-quality stallions at a substantially reduced price, with the eventual goal of improving and upgrading the horses in the area. From the very beginning, meticulous records were kept at the stud, which proved particularly useful when the official Hanoverian Studbook was implemented in 1888 by the Royal Agricultural Society.

In 1899, the chamber of agriculture took over the responsibility for the studbook, and in 1922 the Verband Hannoverscher Warmblutzüchter (Society of Hanoverian Warmblood Breeders) was formed and remains the

governing body today. The Verband keeps the studbook and operates to advise and monitor the breeding of the Hanoverian to maintain a system of continual improvement and breeding true to type.

From the foundation of Celle in 1735 and the recognition of the Hanoverian horse, the breeding objectives for the horses can be loosely considered in four periods. The early period was from 1735 to the end of Napoleonic domination in Hanover in 1813. The Napoleonic Wars (c. 1799–1815) had resulted in considerable depletion of stock at the stud, and by 1816 there were only thirty out of a previous hundred stallions still standing there. The second period, from 1815 to 1870, saw the reestablishment of the stallions through a large influence of privately owned English Thoroughbred and part-bred blood, as well as horses from Mecklenburg. These two periods were chiefly concerned with producing a large, muscular horse for use in the cavalry and one suitable for light agricultural work. Despite this goal, the extent of Thoroughbred blood resulted in an overall lightening of the frame, and at this time around a third of the stock at Celle was Thoroughbred.

Near the end of the third period, from roughly 1870 to 1945, there was a move toward producing a horse that was more suited to riding and less of an agricultural animal. The fourth period, which comes right up to the present, has seen a continued move away from agricultural and military requirements and toward producing top-class sports horses. To this end, Trakehner blood was introduced, as well as additional Thoroughbred blood and even some Anglo-Arabian.

The extraordinary success of the modern warmblood breeds, and especially the Hanoverian, is in large part a result of the rigorous systems of grading and selection that the various societies enforce. The Hanoverian Verband insists on an incredibly high standard for breeding mares and stallions, both of which must be graded before being entered into the breeding studbooks.

DANISH WARMBLOOD

MODERN – DENMARK – COMMON

HEIGHT	constitution and good
Average 16.2 h.h.	temperament.
APPEARANCE	**COLOR**
Elegant, beautiful, and	Mostly bay, black,
supremely athletic. They	or chestnut.
exhibit excellent balanced and	
proportionate conformation,	**APTITUDE**
and have been systematically	Riding, showing, dressage,
bred to be of sound	show jumping, competitive
	horse sports

DENMARK HAS HAD A LONG ASSOCIATION with horses, dating back to at least the Nordic Bronze Age (1800–600 B.C.E.) and probably much earlier. One of the most beautiful excavated finds from this period is the Sun Chariot of Trundholm (c. 1500–1400 B.C.E.), a bronze statue of a horse, probably a mare, pulling a four-wheeled chariot carrying the sun. This extraordinarily sophisticated sculpture depicts a particularly elegant, finely built horse with an athletic frame. This was almost certainly a horse of great quality, a trait the Danish have maintained in their horses to the present. The Danish Warmblood (Dansk Varmblod) is one of the youngest warmblood breeds, but it has centuries of excellent horse stock at its foundations.

The oldest of the Danish breeds is the Frederiksborg, which developed in the sixteenth century, primarily from Iberian stock. The breed evolved after the 1536 Count's War and the country's move from Roman Catholicism to Lutheranism when King Christian III (1503–59) confiscated quality breeding horses from the Catholic monasteries to supplement the royal horses. King Frederick II (1534–88) established the Royal Stud at Hillerødsholm, renamed Frederiksborg around 1562, which was later taken over by his son Christian IV (1577–1648). Christian was a keen horseman and imported large numbers of the finest horses that he could find, the majority of which were Iberian. Many of the horses in Denmark were also sourced from the neighboring German state of Schleswig-Holstein, which was a Danish duchy until 1864 and was itself home to highly respected warhorses. The relationship between Danish royalty and horses has been long and fruitful, and the monarchy has traditionally been involved with horse breeding; today, Princess Benedikte is the patroness of Dansk Varmblod (the Danish Warmblood Society). She has bred three Grand Prix dressage horses, and her daughter Nathalie rides and trains at the highest level. Appropriately, the brand for the Danish Warmblood features a crown over a wave and is used to identify progeny of breeding stock graded within Dansk Varmblod.

The Frederiksborg is at the foundation of the Danish Warmblood, but Thoroughbred blood was introduced in the twentieth century to lighten the heavier old Danish breed and to produce a more athletic horse suited to modern equestrian competitions. This half-bred combination was then further improved by the addition of Selle Français, Trakehner, Polish Wielkopolski, and additional Thoroughbred blood. The Danish Warmblood is now a horse of supreme athletic ability, calm temperament, and great competitive scope.

In 1962, the Danish Sport Horse Society and the Danish Light Horse Association were formally established, and by 1978 they had been amalgamated to form Dansk Varmblod. The society's objective is to produce top-level competition horses, and it has achieved this in a very short time. Danish Warmbloods are among the best competition horses, thanks to the strict grading and selection process of breeding stock, goal-oriented breeding, performance testing, and a willingness to use foreign stallions if they are of superlative quality. The extensive grading and selection process is applied to both mares and stallions and rigorously tests all aspects of the horses and their abilities. The horses are bred primarily to excel in dressage and show jumping, though these talented horses have also proved themselves at eventing. In 2004, the society established the Show Jumper Program specifically to build upon and develop bloodlines in this respect, and only mares and stallions that have proved their jumping ability are accepted into the program.

OUTSTANDING AGILITY

DUTCH WARMBLOOD

MODERN – NETHERLANDS – COMMON

HEIGHT
Average 16.2 h.h.
APPEARANCE
An attractive head with a well-arched, muscular neck. Powerful shoulders with a good slope, defined withers, a well-sprung rib cage, and a deep chest. Hindquarters are powerful, the tail is set and carried high, and the legs are strong.
COLOR
Bay, black, chestnut, or gray.
APTITUDE
Riding, showing, dressage, show jumping, eventing, competitive horse sports

DESPITE ITS SMALL SIZE, the Netherlands boasts one of the largest sport-horse breeding studbooks in existence. This is the Koninklijke Vereniging Warmbloed Paardenstamboek Nederland, or the Royal Warmblood Studbook of the Netherlands, commonly referred to as the KWPN, an abbreviation also used to describe the Dutch Warmblood or Royal Dutch Sport Horse. A national studbook was established in 1969 from an amalgamation of regional studbooks first instituted in 1887 by King William III (1817–90) and was given its "Royal" prefix by Queen Beatrix (b. 1938) in 1988. Today the KWPN horse is found across the world and ranks as one of the most successful and popular of the warmblood breeds, consistently competing at the highest levels in dressage, show jumping, competitive driving, and, more recently, eventing.

The KWPN organization also accounts for Dutch harness horses and Gelder horses, and it is these that are at the foundation of the modern Dutch Sport Horse. For centuries, Dutch farmers bred a consistently sound and strong agricultural horse, one that was suitable for all light farm work and was particularly good when used in harness. These horses were the mainstay of small farms right up until the twentieth century, when they were finally largely replaced by motorized vehicles. In the northern part of the country around the province of Groningen, the local farmers developed a heavy, muscular horse noted for the strength of its hindquarters. This area has heavy, marine clay soils, and horses needed to be sufficiently strong and robust to work in the fields throughout the day. These horses were developed from a base of Friesian stock and the old type of heavier Oldenburg horse.

In the central, eastern part of the country in the province of Gelderland, the soils were much lighter and sandier, and there farmers bred a much lighter-weight horse that excelled in carriage work. Local mares were crossed with imported English coaching stock such as the Yorkshire Coach Horse and the Norfolk Roadster (both now extinct), Cleveland Bay, and Hackney, as well as some Thoroughbred, Arabian, and Anglo-Norman blood. This resulted in an excellent, versatile, and elegant harness horse. After World War II, some breeders of the Gelderland horse chose to adapt their breeding to produce an even flashier harness horse that dominated in the show ring, and today this is recognized as the Dutch Harness Horse. Other breeders continued to breed the original Gelderland horse, which is impressive both under saddle and in harness.

Dutch horse breeders also recognized the shift in the horse market and requirements that occurred after World War II and set about the systematic production of a sports horse to fulfill modern requirements. Crossbreeding horses of the Groningen and Gelderland regions produced a robust, sound, and quiet saddle horse of admirable qualities. This was the foundation of the sports horse, which developed through crosses to Thoroughbred, Anglo-Norman, Holstein, and Hanoverian blood, among others. The rapid emergence and success of the Dutch Sport Horse is due entirely to the intelligent breeding strategy of the Dutch and their intense selection process for breeding stock, which focuses on breeding horses for jumping and dressage ability. Overall health, soundness, and an equable temperament are the top priorities for breeders, and Dutch horses have become particularly noted for these traits.

Before a stallion can be approved for breeding, he is rigorously tested in all aspects, including health, semen quality, temperament, conformation, movement, and rideability. The testing involves a series of selection processes culminating in the performance test, which lasts either fifty or seventy days. During this period, the stallions are trained and ridden by KWPN representatives (and invited guest riders) and are judged intensely on their performance and temperament. They undergo a veterinary evaluation and may be ejected from the testing at any point if they are thought unsuitable.

Stallions that pass this final testing are approved for breeding and can also be awarded predicates for passing on outstanding traits to their progeny. There are two types of predicate, the *keur* and the *preferent*. For a stallion to earn a keur, his progeny must be assessed when he is at least seven years of age. If he has passed his excellent conformation and sporting ability on to his offspring, he might be awarded the keur. The preferent is the highest award and can even be awarded posthumously. It is awarded only to horses that already have a keur and who have produced excellence in their offspring.

Similar emphasis on quality is placed on breeding mares, who are judged in regional shows and are eligible for judging from the age of three. The mares are assessed on conformation, movement, and jumping (if applicable); if deemed suitable, they are eligible for registration in the studbook and can even be branded with the noble lion KWPN brand. Mares can be awarded the following predicates in order of merit from lowest to highest: *ster*, keur, PROK, IBOP, EPTM, elite, sport, preferent, and *prestatie*. These appear on the horse's registration papers and are a mark of considerable respect. Mares awarded the ster at their first inspection go forward to the Central Inspection where they are judged again and may be awarded the keur. The top mares from these inspections are put forward for the National Mare Inspection, which is open only to the very best mares and is one of the most prestigious events for the breed. For mares to win a keur or higher, they must undergo performance testing, and their progeny must also prove their abilities. This selection process has ensured that the Dutch Sport Horse is always of the highest quality.

BELGIAN WARMBLOOD
MODERN – BELGIUM – COMMON

**HEIGHT**
Average 16.2 h.h.
APPEARANCE
A refined, elegant athlete with a predisposition for jumping. Balanced through the frame with powerful hindquarters and good sloping shoulders

that allow for its smooth paces.
COLOR
Any solid color.
APTITUDE
Riding, showing, dressage, show jumping, eventing, competitive horse sports

HISTORICALLY, BELGIUM HAS BEEN most associated with its tremendous draft horses, primarily the Belgian Brabant. These impressive horses were bred into slightly different types over time to fulfill different requirements, greatly respected as warhorses during the Middle Ages and yet equally at home working the land. The horses were so greatly prized that breeding specific saddle horses for leisure riding only was virtually unheard of. As a result, although Belgium was a great producer of horses, these horses were not suitable for the changing times of the twentieth century. As the role of the workhorse and cavalry animal steadily diminished and there was an international move toward competitive horse sports, the Belgian equine industry was forced to change to keep up with market demands, yet it managed this transition with superb efficiency.

Although there was no single recreational Belgian saddle-horse type, people still rode, and lighter-weight agricultural horses were often put under saddle. In 1937, Canon André De Mey founded the Rural Cavalry in Boezinge, West Flanders, to inspire people to ride in their free time. Members were enthusiastic and became known as the "Canon's horsemen"; they rode horses that served as working animals during the week and exhibited substantial variation in type. The following year, they organized a highly successful show that included jumping competitions, dressage displays, and other equestrian events. Of the horses entered, there were twenty-five heavy types and fourteen of lighter frame, possibly the result of Thoroughbred or trotting horse blood on draft mares. The

success of this first show underlined the need for a better type of saddle horse in line with Belgium's neighbors France, Germany, and the Netherlands.

The base stock used in the formation of Belgium's emerging sport horse were the lighter-weight native mares crossed with Dutch Gelderlanders to produce a heavyweight but high-quality riding horse. This cross was improved through sustained use of the finest horses from neighboring countries, namely the Holstein, Hanoverian, Selle Français, Anglo-Arabian, KWPN, and Thoroughbred. The first stallion inspection was organized in June 1953, and shortly afterward the minister of agriculture allowed the systematic breeding of the Belgian Warmblood. In 1955, a studbook was opened and the National Breeding Association of the Saddle Horse was formed. In 1970, this was changed to the National Breeding Association of Warmbloods, and today the Belgian Warmblood is known as the Belgische Warmbloed Paard, or BWP. It was also during the 1970s that the first BWPs were exported to the United States, now one of the largest breeding centers.

The outstanding merits of the BWP can be attributed to the use of superb stallions of foreign origin in establishing the breed. These include, but are not limited to, the Hanoverians Flugel van la Roche (f. 1956), Lugano van la Roche (f. 1963), and Bolero (f. 1975); the Holstein Codex (f. 1962); the Trakehner Abglanz (f. 1943); the Selle Français Cor de la Bryère (f. 1968); and the Thoroughbreds Cottage Son (f. 1944) and Ladykiller (f. 1961). As a result, the BWP carries some of the finest bloodlines in the world, reflected in its truly impressive talents. Like other warmbloods, Belgian breeding stock has to undergo intensive inspections before being eligible to breed.

Belgium is also home to the Belgian Sport Horse, which is essentially the same as the BWP but operates its own breed registry, the Royal Belgian Sport Horse Society, or Studbook sBs. This traces to 1920, with its foundation in the production of cavalry horses and now the modern sports horse.

OUTSTANDING AGILITY

IRISH SPORTS HORSE
MODERN — IRELAND — COMMON

HEIGHT	**COLOR**
15.2–16.3 h.h.	*Any solid color,*
APPEARANCE	*occasionally*
An athletic, elegant,	*parti-colored.*
high-quality horse,	
sound in wind and limb and	**APTITUDE**
possessed of a particularly	*Riding, showing, dressage,*
sensible and kind	*show jumping, eventing,*
temperament.	*hunting, competitive*
	horse sports

THE IRISH SPORTS HORSE (ISH, or Irish Hunter) is a top-class competition horse and ranks among the most talented of jumping horses. Irish Sports Horses regularly dominate the World Breeding Federation for Sports Horses stallion eventing rankings, a shining testament to the abilities of this breed.

The ISH developed through crosses between Irish Drafts and Thoroughbreds, and in recent years there has also been some influence from Continental warmblood breeds such as the Holstein, Selle Français, Hanoverian, and Dutch Warmblood. Although the Thoroughbred and warmblood influence on the ISH has contributed considerably toward the breed's tremendous athleticism and agility, it is the Irish Draft that has stamped the ISH with its admirable character and quintessential Irish sense.

By around the tenth century, the small, gallant, much respected Irish Hobby had developed. Though now extinct, the Hobby contributed greatly to the development of a number of breeds from the Irish Draft to the Connemara. During the Middle Ages, the Irish horse was influenced by larger, heavier breeds from France and Belgium and later by Iberian horses. Throughout its early development, the Irish horse was required to be extremely versatile, and with this foundation the Irish Draft developed certain characteristics that lie at the root of the modern ISH: an innate honesty, a sensible attitude, a huge heart, and courage. Irish Sport Horses are noted for their athletic, effortless, and brave jumping ability, and the importance of the Irish Draft's influence cannot be underestimated.

The ISH was developed and took shape during the twentieth century; it was first known as the Irish Hunter—a reflection of its chief function—or Irish part-bred before being recognized as a distinct breed. As breeding of the part-bred horse continued and breeding aims were consolidated, a distinctive type emerged, now called the ISH, with its own studbook. The ISH studbook and the Irish Draft studbook come under the Irish Horse Register, which has been maintained by Horse Sport Ireland since 2008. Before this, the studbooks had been maintained by the Irish Horse Board since 1993. In order for a horse to be registered, both parents must be registered with the Irish Horse Register. ISH stallions to be used for breeding undergo a rigorous inspection process that includes an assessment of their conformation, movement, athleticism, and jumping ability. Recently, mare inspections have also been implemented to help the continual improvement of the breed. After the inspection, mare owners are given an in-depth profile of their horse, outlining her strengths and weaknesses based on linear scoring to enable more informed breeding decisions. "Approved" stallions and "select" mares are now also eligible for a five-star grading system based on both their own and their progeny's performance in dressage, show jumping, and eventing.

Some of the finest ISH bloodlines trace to the Irish Draft stallion King of Diamonds (f. 1962), whose progeny included the show-jumping stars Special Envoy (f. 1980), ridden by Nelson and Rodrigo Pessoa, and international show-jumping legends Millstreet Ruby (f. 1984) and Mill Pearl (f. 1979). The Irish Draft Clover Hill (f. 1973) sired thirty-nine international show jumpers and has contributed significantly to the ISH, as has the Irish Draft Sea Crest (f. 1979) who produced the brilliant ISH Cruising (f. 1985). The Holstein Cavalier Royale (f. 1978) is another to contribute to the ISH. He was the son of the great Selle Français Cor de la Bryère (f. 1968), while his mother, the Holstein Ligustra (f. 1974), traces her lineage to the omnipotent Thoroughbred Ladykiller (f. 1961).

INDEX

Abdullah (stallion) 226
Abeyan (stallion) 53
Abglanz (stallion) 100
Adaev 36
agriculture 116, 119
airs above the ground 75, 82, 87, 88
Ajax (stallion) 129
Akbar, Emperor 112, 247
Akhal Teke 18, **30–3**, 100, 174, 213
Alexander the Great 30
Alfenas, Gabriel Baron of 170
Allandorf (stallion) 187
Allan F-1 187
Alsup, Moses Locke 188
Alter Real **92–3**, 170
American Bashkir Curly **198–201**
American Belgian 134
American Curly Horse see American Bashkir Curly
American Eclipse (stallion) 219, 221
American Horse 190
American Indians 72, 155–6, 159, 179, 181
American Bashkir Curly 199
Appaloosa 172, 174
Banker Horse 193
American Paint **178–9**
American Quarter Horse 156, 157, 177, 179, **180–3**, 200, 263
American Saddlebred 157, 187, 188, **190–1**, 200
American Standardbred 57, 187, 205, 219, **222–7**, 233
American Thoroughbred **218–19**
Andalusian 73, **80–3**, 154, 210
Alter Real's origins 93
Barb's origins 78
Boulonnais' origins 132
Cleveland Bay's origins 238
Friesian's origins 57
Lusitano similarities 91
Paso Fino's origins 166
Andrade, Ruy d' 35, 85, 93
Anglo-Norman 213, 229, 264
Antonius, Helmut Otto 27
Appaloosa **172–5**, 177
Arabian 18, **206–9**, 210
Alter Real's origins 93
American Bashkir Curly's origins 200
Andalusian's origins 82, 91

Ariègeois' origins 61
Assateague and Chincoteague 195
Australian Pony's origins 260
Barb's origins 77
Boulonnais' origins 132
Breton's origins 131
Dartmoor's origins 127
Dutch Warmblood's origins 275
Finnish Universal's origins 245
Friesian's origins 57
Godolphin 78, 96, 181, 213
Hackney's origins 237
Haflinger's origins 125
Highland's origins 152
Lusitano's origins 91
Manipuri's origins 251–2
New Forest Pony's origins 53
Norman Cob's origins 229
origins 30, 33, 35
Percheron's origins 96
Polo Pony's origins 255
Pony of the Americas' origins 177
Thoroughbred's origins 213, 216–17
Trakehner's origins 100
Welsh Pony's origins 49
Ardennais 131, 134, 141
Argentinean Criollo **168–9**, 256
Argentinean Polo Pony 255–6
Ariègeois **60–1**
Arnarson, Ingólfur 40
Artois, Robert Comte d' 132
Asiatic Wild Horse 18, 20, **22–5**, 27
Fjord's origins 121
Highland's origins 152
Sorraia's origins 84
Assateague **194–5**
Assyrians 19
Astley, Philip 69
Asturian 42, 81, 84, 146, 154, 166, 193
Australian Polo Pony 255–6
Australian Pony **258–61**
Australian Stock Horse 106, **262–3**
Australian Thoroughbred **216–17**
Australian Waler 75, **104–9**, 256, 263
Austria
Haflinger 125
Lipizzaner 87–8

Noriker 71
Spotted Pinzgauer 71
Avelignese 125
Avilés, Pedro Menéndez de 180
Ayllón, Lucas Vázquez de 193

Babieca 73, 82
Bactrian horsemen 30
Bains Horse 152
Bakewell, Robert 141
Bakewell Black 141
Balder (stallion) 243
Baldishol Church tapestry 67
Banker Horse **192–3**
Barb see North African Barb
Barnum, P. T. 199
Barolin Feluka (stallion) 260
Bashkir 36, 199
Basuto 75, 106
Batchler, Jack 183
Baume, Antoine de Pluvinel de 78
Bayard (stallion) 134
Bedouins 207–8
Belgian Brabant 117, **134–5**, 141, 279
Belgian Draft 137
Belgian Heavy Draft see Belgian Brabant
Belgian Warmblood **278–9**
Belgische Warmbloed Paard (BWP) 279
Bell, John 24
Bellfounder (stallion) 226
Bennett, James Gordon 256
Berik 36
Betty Leedes (mare) 213
Biddell, Herman 144
Bidet Breton 131
bidets 229
Bilek, Professor Prantisek 241
Blackfoot 156
Black Hand (stallion) 177
Blakes Farmer (stallion) 143
Blaze (stallion) 137–8, 213, 223, 237
blood sweating 30, 33
Boer horse 75, 106
Boer War 75, 106
Bonnie Charlie (stallion) 260
Boomhower, Leslie L. 177
Booth, Mordecai 181, 219
Borda, Gustavo de la 164
Boston (stallion) 221
Boulogne, Eustache Comte de 132
Boulonnais 96, 117, 119, 131, **132–3**

Bovenlanders 58
Brabant see Belgian Brabant
Braganza family 93
Brazil, Mangalarga Marchador 170
Breton 61, 117, 119, **130–1**
Brilliant (stallion) 134
Brimmer horse 188
Broomfield's Champion (stallion) 138
Bruce, Sanders 221
Brutus (stallion) 219
Budyonny horse 98
buffalo horses 156
Bulle Rock (stallion) 219
bullfighting 64, 75, 91
bull running 64
buzkashi 246
Byerley Turk (stallion) 33, 213

Caesar, Julius 49, 55, 63, 77, 132, 134, 136
Camargue horse 61, **62–5**, 78, 82
Camden, William 143
campdrafting 249, 263
Canadian Horse 159, 184, 223
Canadian Pacer 187, 190, 223
canals 119
Cannon Ball (stallion) 46
Canute's Forest Law 53
Caprilli, Federico 248
capriole 75, 88
Carpathian Pony see Hucul
Carthusian 82
Caspian 18, 20, 27, **34–5**, 77, 207
Castillo, Diaz del 179
Cavendish, William 58, 78
Cayuse Indian pony 156
Celtic Pony 18, 49
Celtic tribes 46, 81, 146
Cerbat Mustangs 159
Chancellor (stallion) 217
Chapman Horse 238
chariot racing 20, 35, 202, 223
Charlemagne 73
Charles II, Archduke 87
Charles II, King 203
Chauvet Cave 23
Chetak 110, 112
Chetak Trust 112
Cheval de Corlay 131
Chickasaw Indians 156, 181
Chickasaw pony 156

China 21, 72, 116
Asiatic Wild Horse 24
polo 246
Chincoteague **194–5**
Christian III, King 95, 272
Christian IV, King 95, 272
chromosomes, Asiatic Wild Horse 23
circus 69
Cleveland Bay 202, **238–9**, 275
Clover Hill (stallion) 281
Clyde (stallion) 138
Clydesdale 117, 119, 123, **136–9**, 146, 152
coaching 205
Colombia, Paso Fino 166
Colombian Criollo see Paso Fino
Colosses de la Mehaique 134
Columbus, Christopher 154, 163, 166
Comanche 179
Comet (stallion) 123
Connemara **46–7**, 78, 181, 255
Conquerant (stallion) 231
Copperbottom (stallion) 187
Copper D (stallion) 200
Cortés, Hernán 154
Cossacks 98
Cotham Dare (stallion) 188
courbette 75, 88
coursers 73
Criban Victor (stallion) 51
Crin Blanc 64
Criollo **168–9**, 256
Crisp's Horse (stallion) 143
Crusades 73
Cuba, Paso Fino 166
Cuchulainn Saga 146
cuirassiers 75
Curlies see American Bashkir Curly
curly-coated horses 198–201
Czech Republic
Hucul 29
Kladruby 241

Dacians 29
Dales 55, 57, 117–18, **122–3**
Damele, John 199–200
Danish Warmblood **272–3**
Darley Arabian (stallion) 49, 213, 219, 237
Dartmoor 117–18, **126–7**, 255
De La Warr, Anne 150

Denmark
  Danish Warmblood 272
  Frederiksborg 95
  Knabstrup 67–9
Denmark (stallion) 190
destrier 73
Diamond Denmark (stallion) 190
Diomed (stallion) 183, 219, 221
Dølahest *see* Døle Gudbrandsdal
Døle Gudbrandsdal 57, 118, **242–3**
Døle Horse *see* Døle Gudbrandsdal
Døle Trotter 243
Dominican Republic, Paso Fino 166
Dom Pedro I 170
Don 75, **98–9**
Donna (mare) 100
dressage 249
  see also airs above the ground
  Akhal Teke 33
  Andalusian 82
  Danish Warmblood 272
  Frederiksborg 95
  Friesian 57–8
  Lipizzaner 87, 88
  Lusitano 91
  Oldenburg 267
  Trakehner 100
Driver (stallion) 237
driving trials 205
Dutch Draft 58
Dutch Harness Horse 275
Dutch Warmblood **274–7**
Dwarka (stallion) 127
Dyoll Graylight (stallion) 260
Dyoll Starlight (stallion) 49, 51, 53, 260

ears, Marwari 110
Ebhart, F. 35
El Badavi XXII (stallion) 125
El Cid 73, 82
El Morzillo (stallion) 154
England
  Cleveland Bay 238
  Dales 122–3
  Dartmoor 127
  Exmoor 38
  Fell 55
  Hackney 237
  New Forest Pony 53
  Shire 141
  Suffolk Punch 143–4
  Thoroughbred 210–13

English Thoroughbred *see* Thoroughbred
eventing 248–9
Exmoor 18, 19, **38–9**, 260

Farmer's Fancy (stallion) 138
Fashion (stallion) 221
Fearnought (stallion) 219
Fell **54–5**, 57
Fenwick, Edward 219
Ferghana 21, 30, 67
Fête des Gardiens 64
fighting horses 42
Finnhorse *see* Finnish Universal
Finnish Universal 57, **244–5**
Firouz, Louise 30, 35
Fitzstephen, William 202
Fjord 18, 117, 118, **120–1**
Flaebehoppen (mare) 67, 69
Flaebestallion (stallion) 69
Flanders Horse 134, 141
Flemish horse 137, 141
Florida Cracker 156
Folie, Josef 125
Folie (stallion) 125
Forest Horse 18, 71, 117, 132, 134, 136, 141
forestry 118
Foundation for the Preservation and Protection of the Przewalski Horse (FPPPH) 24
fox trot 188
France
  Ariègeois 61
  Boulonnais 132
  Breton 131
  Camargue horse 62–4
  French Trotter 231
  Norman Cob 229
  Percheron 96–7
  Selle Français 264
Francisco, Joào 170
Frederik II, King of Denmark 67
Frederiksborg 67, **94–5**, 272
French Thoroughbred 221
French Trotter 229, **230–1**, 264
Friedrich Wilhelm I of Prussia, King 100
Friesian 20, **56–9**, 61, 117
  Clydesdale's origins 137
  Dales' origins 122
  Døle Gudbrandsdal's origins 43
  Dutch Warmblood's origins 275
  Fell's origins 55

Finnish Universal's origins 245
Mustang's origins 159
Selle Français' origins 267
Shire's origins 141
Furioso (stallion) 213
Furioso breed 75, 213

Gaines Denmark (stallion) 190
gait
  see also trotting races
  American Saddlebred 190
  American Standardbred 223
  Banker Horse 193
  Camargue horse 64
  Connemara 46
  Finnish Universal 245
  Friesian 57
  Hackney 237
  Icelandic Horse 42
  Mangalarga Marchador 170
  Missouri Fox Trotter 188
  pacing 73, 205, 223
  Paso Fino 166
  Peruvian Paso 163
  Rocky Mountain Horse 196
  Tennessee Walking Horse 187
  Welsh Cob 51
Galician 81
Gallipoly (stallion) 96
Galloway 55, 122, 181, 190, 210
Garrano 81, 84–5, 154, 163, 166
Gelder horses 275
Gelderlanders 279
Genghis Khan 20, 73–4, 246
George II, King 271
Germany
  Hanoverian 271
  Holstein 268
  Oldenburg 267
  Trakehner 100–2
Giovanni (stallion) 187
Glancer (stallion) 138
Gmelin, Samuel Gottlieb 27
Godolphin Arab (stallion) 78, 96, 181, 213
Golden Gleam (stallion) 46
Great Horse 134, 141, 146
Greeks 20, 71, 202
Gris du Hainaut 134
Grisone, Federico 74
Gros de la Dendre 134

Hackney 57, 119, 202, 213, 226, **236–7**
  Dutch Warmblood's origins 275
  Welsh Pony's origins 49, 51

Hadrian's Wall 20, 55, 57, 122, 137
Haflinger 117, **124–5**
Haines, Francis 174
Hannibal 91
Hanoverian 100, 213, 268, **270–1**
harness development 21, 116
harness racing 202, 205
  see also trotting races
  American Standardbred 223, 226
  Finnish Universal 245
  Orlov Trotter 233
Harrison Chief (stallion) 190
Hatley, George 174
"Heavenly Horses" of Ferghana 21, 30, 67
Heavy Breton 131
Heck horses 27
Heck, Lutz and Heinz 27
Hector (stallion) 217
Hedgeford (stallion) 190
Hegardt, Harry 27
Hegardt horse 27
Heir of Linne (stallion) 231
Hendricks, Bonnie 184
Henry, Marguerite 195
Henry VIII 117, 210, 213
Herod (stallion) 213
Highland 18, 117–18, **152–3**
Hittites 19
Holland
  see also Friesian
  Dutch Warmblood **274–7**
Holstein 213, **268–9**
Homer 91
Hope sisters 150
Hordern, Anthony 260
Hucul 18, 19, 27, **28–9**, 100
Hungarian Hussars 75
Hungarian pony 260
hunting 203–4, 248
Hurlingham Club 255, 256
Hussars 75
Hyksos 81

Iberian horses 20, 27, 46, 74–5, 78, 281
  see also Alter Real; Andalusian; Lipizzaner; Lusitano; Spanish horses
  Camargue's origins 63
Icelandic Horse 18, **40–5**, 117
Idaho (stallion) 200

India
  Manipuri 251–2
  Marwari 110–12
  polo 246, 247
Indian Country Bred pony 105
Indian Half Bred 105
Ingólfur Arnarson 40
Ingres (stallion) 129
Iomud 33
Iran
  see also Persia
  Caspian 35
Ireland, Connemara 46
Irish Draft 117, 119, **146–7**, 281
Irish Hobby 46, 146, 181, 190, 210, 281
Irish Hunter *see* Irish Sports Horse
Irish Sports Horse **280–1**
Italy
  Maremmana 129
  racing 203

Jabe 36
Jack (stallion) 150
James I 203
Janus (stallion) 181, 219
jawbone, Exmoor 38
Jean I (stallion) 134
Jean Le Blanc (stallion) 96
Jerez de la Frontera 67, 73, 82, 93, 180
Jersey Act 221
Jigg (stallion) 213
Johann the Younger, Count 267
Johnston, Velma B. "Wild Horse Annie" 160
jousting 74
Jude (stallion) 127
Justin Morgan (stallion) 184
Jutland 143, 144

Kangba, King 251
Kassette (mare) 100
Kathiawari 110
Kazakh **36–7**
Kazakhstan, Kazakh 36
Kelly, Francesca 112
Kentucky Saddler *see* American Saddlebred
keur 277
Kiger Mustangs 159
Kikkuli 19
King of Diamonds (stallion) 281
Kisber Felver 75

Kladruby **240–1**
Knabstrup **66–9**
Konik 18, 27, 100
Koninklijke Vereniging
    Warmbloed
    Paardenstamboek
    Nederland (KWPN) 275,
    277
koumiss 36
Kranich (stallion) 267

Lamorisse, Albert 64
Lampit's Mare 138
Landnámabók 40
Lascaux cave paintings 27, 63
Lavater (stallion) 231
Leat, The (stallion) 127
Lecompte (stallion) 221
Leili (mare) 112
levade 75, 88
Lewis, Meriwether 172
Lexington (stallion) 221
Limenito (stallion) 164
Limousin 78
Lincolnshire Black 57, 141
Lipizzaner 75, **86–9**, 95, 241
Lithuania, Trakehner 100–2
Little Jim (stallion) 260
Lokai 199
Londonderry, Lord 150
Louis XIV 78
Lowlynn Silver Chief (stallion) 260
Lucas, Lord 53
Lunn, Judge 67, 69
Lusitano **90–1**, 154

Maggie Marshall (mare) 187
mail system 116
Mancinelli, Graziano 129
Mangalarga Marchador **170–1**
Manipuri **250–3**, 256
marcha batida 170
marcha picada 170
Maremmana **128–9**
Mareyeuses 132
Marialva, Marquis of 93
Marshland (stallion) 237
Marske (stallion) 53
Martel, Charles 72, 96
Marwari 75, **110–15**
Matchem (stallion) 219
Maximilian II 87, 241
Mecklenburg horses 132, 271
Mendoza, Pedro de 169
Mérens 57
Merlin (stallion) 49, 51
Messenger (stallion) 190, 205,
    213, 219, 223, 226

Mey, Canon André De 279
Middle East, Arabian 207–8
Mikkel (stallion) 69
Miller's Damsel (mare) 219
Mill Pearl 281
Millstreet Ruby 281
mining 118, 127, 149–50
Missouri Fox Trotter 157,
    188–9
Mohammed, Prophet 72
Mongolia, Asiatic Wild Horse
    23–4
Mongolian horse 23, 24, 73–4,
    245, 246
    Barb's origins 77
    Camargue's origins 63
    Manipuri's origins 251, 252
Monkey (stallion) 219
Moors 72–3, 81, 82, 96
Morgan 57, 157, **184–5**, 190,
    200
Moroccan Barb *see* North
    African Barb
Mulgrave Supreme (stallion)
    238
Muniqi Arabian 33, 213
Mustang 27, 157, **158–61**,
    199–200

Narragansett Pacer 187, 190,
    196, 223
Neapolitan 129
Netherlands
    see also Friesian
    Dutch Warmblood 275–7
Nevada King (stallion) 200
New Forest Pony **52–3**, 255
Nez Percé Indians 156, 172, 174
Niaux Cave paintings 61, 63
Nisean horse 20, 77, 246
Nogai 98
Nonius 75
Norfolk Phenomenon (stallion)
    231, 237
Norfolk Roadster 51, 119, 129,
    213, 223, 264
    Breton's origins 131
    Dales' origins 122–3
    Dutch Warmblood's origins
    275
    French Trotter's origins 231
    Hackney's origins 237
    Highland's origins 152
    Norman Cob's origins 229
Norfolk Trotter *see* Norfolk
    Roadster
Noriker 18, 20, **70–1**, 117
Norman Cob **228–9**

Norman horse 264
North African Barb 33, **76–9**,
    210
    Americas 154
    Andalusian's origins 82
    Assateague and
        Chincoteague 195
    Boulonnais' origins 132
    Camargue's origins 63
    Cleveland Bay's origins 238
    Connemara's origins 46
    Mangalarga Marchador's
        origins 170
    Maremmana's origins 129
    New Forest Pony's origins
        53
    Norman Cob's origins 229
    Paso Fino's origins 166
    Peruvian Paso's origins 163
    Polo Pony's origins 255
    Thoroughbred's origins 213
    Waler's origins 105
    Welsh Pony's origins 51
North Star (stallion) 213
North Swedish horse 57, 118
Northumberland (stallion) 216
Norway
    Døle Gudbrandsdal 243
    Fjord 18, 121
Numidians 77

Odin (stallion) 243
Oldenburg 57, 213, **266–7**, 275
Oldenburg, Graf Anton
    Gunther von 267
Oldenburg Karossier 267
Old English Black 57, 141
Old Skip horses 188
Old Tobe (stallion) 196
Oppenheimer LXII (stallion)
    144
Orange I (stallion) 134
Original Shales (stallion) 123,
    213, 223, 237
Orlov, Count Alexius
    Girgorievich 233
Orlov Trotter 57, **232–5**
Othello (stallion) 129
Oxus Treasure 35

pacing 73, 205, 223
Packington Blind Horse 141
Pakistan, polo 246–7
palfreys 73
Parthians 20, 30
Paso Fino **166–7**
Paterson, John 137
Patton, General George 88

Patton, James 219
Pazyryk caves 19
Pêche Merle caves 67
penning 195
Percheron 61, **96–7**, 117, 119,
    131
Persia 20, 30, 116
    see also Iran
    polo 246
    Seal of Darius 35
Peru, Paso Fino 166
Peruvian Paso **162–5**, 166
Peter McCue (stallion) 183
Petite Boulonnais 132
Phillip II of Macedon 30
Picts 136
pig sticking 247–8
Pinto 179, 195
Pinzgauer-Noriker *see* Spotted
    Pinzgauer
pit ponies 118, 127, 149–50
Pizzaro, Francisco 154, 163
Pliny the Elder 91
Pluto (stallion) 95
Podhajsky, Colonel Alois
    88
Poland
    Hucul 29
    Tarpan 27
    Wielkopolski 272
Poliakov, J. S. 24
Polish Wielkopolski 272
polo 21, 246–7
    Dartmoor 127
    Manipuri 251–2
    Polo Pony 254–7
Polo Pony **254–7**
Ponce de León, Juan 154
Pony of the Americas **176–7**
Portugal
    Alter Real 93
    Lusitano 91
    Sorraia 84–5
Posidonius 81
Postier 131
Pottok pony 81
Pratap, Maharana 110, 112
preferent 277
Przewalski, Nikolai 24
Przewalski's Horse *see* Asiatic
    Wild Horse
Puerto Rico, Paso Fino 166
Pura Raza Española *see*
    Andalusian

Qin Shi Huang tomb 21
Quarter Horse 177, **180–3**,
    200, 263

racing 19, 202–5
    see also chariot racing;
        harness racing; trotting
        races
    American Thoroughbred
        219, 221
    Australian Thoroughbred 216
    Quarter Horse 181, 183
    Thoroughbred 210, 213
    Trakehner 100
railways 119
Rajtilak (stallion) 112
Raleigh, Sir Walter 193
Ramsdales, Robert and Philip 237
Rare Breeds Survival Trust,
    Exmoor 38
Rathores 110
Rebel (stallion) 46
re-creation, Tarpan 27
Red Ruby King (stallion) 200
Reed, Colonel Charles 88
reintroductions, Asiatic Wild
    Horse 24
Reve d'Or (stallion) 134
Richard II, King 210
Rockingham (stallion) 216
Rocky Mountain Horse **196–7**
Rocky Mountain Stud Colt
    (stallion) 196
Romania, Hucul 29
Romans 20, 61, 116, 136
    Andalusian 82
    bidets 229
    chariot racing 202
    Dales 122
    Fell 55
    Noriker 71
    Welsh Pony 49, 51
Rossier 131
Rotrou, Robert Count of 96
rounceys 73
Roxana (mare) 213
Royal Belgian Sport Horse
    Society 279
Royal College of Veterinary
    Surgeons 119
Royal Dutch Sport Horse *see*
    Dutch Warmblood
Rudolf II, Emperor 241
Russia 199
    Don 98
    Orlov Trotter 233
    Tarpan 27
Russian Bashkir 199
Russian Trakehner 102
Rysdyk, Bill 226
Rysdyk's Hambletonian
    (stallion) 219, 226

Sacramoso Solo XXXI (stallion) 241
Saddlebred 157, 187, 188, **190–1**, 200
saddle development 72
Sandalwood 259
Schiltberger, Johann 23–4
Schweiken pony 100
Scotland
  Clydesdale 136–8
  Highland 152
  Shetland 149–50
Scot Shales (stallion) 237
Scythians 19, 20, 30, 72, 100
Sea Crest (stallion) 281
Seal of Darius 35
Selle Français 229, **264–5**, 272
Shagya Arabian 75
Shales horse 119
Shamadom Ayangba 251
Shan 251
Shark (stallion) 217
Sherer, Lieutenant Joseph 247, 252
Shetland 117–18, 127, **148–51**, 177, 195
Shiloh (stallion) 183
Shire 57, 117, 119, **140–1**, 146
Shishkin, Vasily 233
Shoshone tribe 172
show jumping 248
  Danish Warmblood 272
  Irish Sports Horse 281
  Maremmana 129
  Trakehner 100
Siberian Yakut 149
Silos Apocalypse manuscript 67
Singh, Bhagwat 112
Singh, Maharaja Churachand 252
Singh, Raja Bhupat 112
Singh, Ranjit 112
Singhji, Umaid 112
Sir Archy (stallion) 183, 221
Sir George (stallion) 237
Sir Henry (stallion) 221
Sir Quid Pigtail (stallion) 231
Sir Thomas (stallion) 260
Skibby Church fresco 67
Skorkowski, E. 35
Sleipnir 42
Slovak Republic, Hucul 29
Sol de Oro (stallion) 164
Solutré 62–3
Solway Master Bronze (stallion) 51
Sommier 131
Sorraia 27, 77, **84–5**, 154, 163, 166, 169
Southern Plantation Horse see Tennessee Walking Horse
Spahi 78

Spain
  Andalusian 81–2
  Ariègeois 61
  Sorraia 84–5
Spanish horses 20, 46, 72, 73, 75
  see also Andalusian; Iberian horses; Lipizzaner
  American history 154–7
  Argentinean Criollo's origins 169
  Banker Horse's origins 193
  Highland's origins 152
  Knabstrup's origins 67
  Mustang's origins 159
  Noriker 71
  Peruvian Paso's origins 163
  Quarterhorse's origins 180–1
  Rocky Mountain Horse's origins 196
Spanish Jennet 42, 154, 163, 166, 170, 190, 193, 226
Spanish Riding School 67, 74–5, 87–8
Special Envoy 281
Speed, J. G. 18, 35
spotted horses/ponies
  American Paint 178–9
  Appaloosa 172–5, 177
  Knabstrup 66–9
  Pony of the Americas 176–7
  Spotted Pinzgauer 70–1
Spotted Pinzgauer **70–1**
Standardbred 57, 187, 205, 219, **222–7**, 233
Star Denmark (stallion) 190
Steel Dust (stallion) 183
Steeltrap (stallion) 217
steeplechases 204
Stewart, Captain Robert 252
stirrups 21, 72
Strabo 91
Stroebel, Gordon 27
Sublime (stallion) 170
Suffolk Punch 117, 119, **142–5**
Sumerians 19
Sumpter Denmark (stallion) 190
Sun Chariot of Trundholm 272
Superbe (stallion) 67, 69
Syrian 152

Tacitus 82
Taki see Asiatic Wild Horse
Tam O'Shanter (stallion) 260
Tan-y-Bwlch Berwyn (stallion) 51
Tarpan 18, 20, **26–7**
  Barb's origins 77
  Finnish Universal's origins 245
  Fjord's origins 121
  Hucul's origins 29
  Sorraia's origins 84

Tennessee Pacer see Tennessee Walking Horse
Tennessee Walking Horse 157, **186–7**
Tetrarch (stallion) 213
Thompson, Claude 174
Thoroughbred 205, **210–15**
  see also American Thoroughbred; Australian Thoroughbred
  American Saddlebred's origins 190
  American Standardbred's origins 223
  Argentinean Criollo's origins 169
  Australian Stock Horse's origins 263
  Barb's origins 78
  Breton's origins 131
  Cleveland Bay's origins 238
  Danish Warmblood's origins 272
  Døle Gudbrandsdal's origins 243
  Dutch Warmblood's origins 275
  French Trotter's origins 231
  Hackney's origins 237
  Hanoverian's origins 271
  Holstein's origins 268
  Irish Sports Horse's origins 281
  Maremmana's origins 129
  Missouri Fox Trotter's origins 188
  New Forest Pony's origins 53
  Norman Cob's origins 229
  origins 30, 33
  Polo Pony's origins 255, 256
  Quarter Horse's origins 181, 183
  Selle Français' origins 264
  Trakehner's origins 100
  Welsh Pony's origins 49, 51
Thunderclap XX (stallion) 100
Timor 259
Tiuti, Juan Jeronimo 82
Tobe (stallion) 196
tölt 42
Tom Hal (stallion) 190
training, first manual 19
Trakehner **100–3**, 213, 271, 272
trotting races 205
  American Standardbred 223, 226
  Døle Gudbrandsal 243
  French Trotter 231
  Orlov Trotter 233
True Briton (stallion) 184
Tschiffely, A. F. 169

Tundra Horse 18, 149
Turkmenian 18, 21, 100, 210
  Akhal Teke's origins 30, 33
  Barb's origins 77
Turkmenistan, Akhal Teke 30–3
Turkoman 33
Turn Row Horse see Tennessee Walking Horse
Tuttle, Sam 196

Ugarte, Federico de la Torre 164
United Kingdom 117–18
  Cleveland Bay 238
  Clydesdale 136–8
  Dales 122–3
  Dartmoor 127
  Exmoor 38
  Fell 55
  Hackney 237
  Highland 152
  New Forest Pony 53
  Polo Pony 255–6
  racing 202
  Shetland 149–50
  Shire 141
  Suffolk Punch 143–4
  Thoroughbred 210–13
  Welsh Pony 49–51
United States 154–7
  American Bashkir Curly 199–200
  American Paint 179
  American Quarter Horse 180–3
  American Saddlebred 190
  American Standardbred 223–6
  American Thoroughbred 219
  Appaloosa 172–4
  Assateague 195
  Banker Horse 193
  Chincoteague 195
  Missouri Fox Trotter 188
  Morgan 184
  Mustang 159–60
  Polo Pony 255–6
  Pony of the Americas 177
  racing 203
  Rocky Mountain Horse 196
  Tennessee Walking Horse 187
Ursus del Lasco 129

Veneti 131
Vetulani, Tadeusz 27
Victoria, Queen 53
Vikings 121, 143
Visigoths 81
Vladimir Heavy Draft 144

Waler 75, **104–9**, 256, 263
Wales 49–51
warfare 19–20, 72–5
  Akhal Teke 30
  Andalusian 82
  Barb 78
  Dales 122–3
  Don 98
  Finnish Universal 245
  Friesian 57
  Haflinger 125
  Lusitano 91
  Manipuri 251
  Marwari 110, 112
  Percheron 96, 97
  Shire 141
  Suffolk Punch 144
  Waler 105, 106
Washington (stallion) 216
Washington Denmark (stallion) 190
Welara 49
Welsh Cob 20, 49, 51, 119
Welsh Mountain Pony 49, 259, 260
Welsh Pony 20, 46, **48–51**, 123
  New Forest Pony's origins 53
  Polo Pony's origins 255
  Section A see Welsh Mountain Pony
  Section B 49
  Section C 49, 51, 259, 260
  Section D see Welsh Cob
Westchester Polo Club 256
Wild Free-Roaming Horse and Burro Act 160
William I of England 53, 82
Wilson, Christopher 237
World-Fengur 42
Wroot's Pretender (stallion) 237
Wu Ti, Emperor 21

Yakut 199
Yirrassan (stallion) 53
Yorkshire Coach Horse 213, 237
  Dutch Warmblood's origins 275
  Holstein's origins 268
Yorkshire Roadster 119, 123, 202, 237
  see also Norfolk Roadster
  Cleveland Bay's origins 238
Young Rattler (stallion) 231

Zapata, Don Andre 164
Zapata, Don Pedro Jose 82
Zapata, La (mare) 164
Zhuirik 36
Zhurdak 36
Zorah (stallion) 53

CREDITS

2 *Rustico* (Lusitano)
Moravita
Ton & Aletta Duivenvoorden
info@moravita.com
www.moravita.com

5 *Sunheri* and *Rani* (Marwari)
Dharumpara Stud
Satish Seemar
www.satishseemar.com

6–7 Camargue
Association des Éleveurs de Chevaux
de Race Camargue
www.aecrc.com

8–9 Banker Horse
Corolla Wild Horse Fund
Karen McCalpin
director@corollawildhorses.org
www.corollawildhorses.org

10–11 *Sena* (Lusitano)
Morgado Lusitano
António Maria Carneiro Pacheco
info@morgadolusitano.pt
www.morgadolusitano.pt

12–13 Icelandic
Þingeyrar
Gunnar Ríkharðsson & Helga Thoroddsen
thingeyrar@thingeyrar.is
www.thingeyrar.is

14–15 Mustang
Return to Freedom Wild Horse Sanctuary
Neda de Mayo
info@returntofreedom.org
www.returntofreedom.org

19 *Tyllagush* (Akhal Teke)
Studfarm Gurtbil
Maria Motsak
begoniya97@mail.ru
www.gurtbil.ru

20–21 Icelandic
Þingeyrar
Gunnar Ríkharðsson & Helga Thoroddsen
thingeyrar@thingeyrar.is
www.thingeyrar.is

22, 25 Asiatic Wild Horse
Hustai National Park
Professor N. Bandi
takhi@hustai.mn
www.hustai.mn

26 Tarpan foal
RSPB Minsmere Nature Reserve
Andy Needle
andy.needle@rspb.org.uk
www.rspb.org.uk

28 *Attila Goral von Birkenhain* (Hucul)
Silke & Thomas Falschlunger
silke.falschlunger@gmx.at
www.huzule.at

31 *Altyn-Pasha* (Akhal Teke)
Studfarm Gurtbil
Maria Motsak
begoniya97@mail.ru
www.gurtbil.ru

32 *Tyllagush* (Akhal Teke)
Studfarm Gurtbil
Maria Motsak
begoniya97@mail.ru
www.gurtbil.ru

34 *Casbrook Kozzarr Zeven* (Caspian)
Miran & Xerxes Caspians & Best Carriages
Pandora and Eric Best
Pandora.Rene@environment-agency.gov.uk
www.bestcarriages.co.uk

37 Kazakh Eagle Hunter Bakayak Batan
Bayan-Ölgii Province, Mongolia

39 Exmoor foal
The Marlborough Downs Riding Centre
Jilly Carter
mail@mantongrange.com

41, 43, 44–45 Icelandic
Þingeyrar
Gunnar Ríkharðsson & Helga Thoroddsen
thingeyrar@thingeyrar.is
www.thingeyrar.is

47 *Atlantic Royal Star* (Connemara)
Sophie Ellis

48, 51 *Oldforge the Gladiator* (Welsh Section D)
Catchpool Shetlands
Lara Stevens
info@kingsheadgower.co.uk
www.catchpoolshetlands.co.uk

50 *Kirred Benjamin* (Welsh Section A)
Longlands Farm
Julia Evans
epevans@btconnect.com
www.longlandscarefarm.co.uk

52 New Forest Pony
New Forest National Park, UK
www.new-forest-national-park.com

54 *Charlie* (Fell)
Parklands Farm
Helen L. Plank
helenparklands@aol.com

56 *Quintus Van't Geerland* (Friesian)
Moravita
Marjolein Drenth
info@moravita.com
www.moravita.com

59 *Poet of Meadowcove* (Friesian)
Fryslan Valley Sport Horses
Arnold & Lisa Warmels
www.fryslanvalley.com

60 *Jaffa* (Ariègeois)
Centre d'élevage du Cheval de Mérens
Simone & Xavier Paquin
siemerens@orange.fr
http://sie-merens.com

62–63, 65 Camargue
Association des Éleveurs de Chevaux
de Race Camargue
www.aecrc.com

66, 68 *Lori's Flashpoint AF Lyn* (Knabstrup)
Cayuse Sportaloosas
Vince & Samantha McAuliffe
sportaloosa@bigpond.com
www.cayuseappaloosas.com

70 *Linda* (behind) & *Leila* (in front) (Noriker
& Spotted Pinzgauer)
Enrico Nagler
press@altabadia.org
www.altabadia.org

70 *Rebell* (Noriker & Spotted Pinzgauer)
Andrea Comploi
press@altabadia.org
www.altabadia.org

73 *Gajraj* (Marwari)
Marwari Bloodlines
Francesca Kelly & Raghuvendra Singh Dundlod
fkelly8254@aol.com
http://horsemarwari.com

74 *Sena* (Lusitano)
Morgado Lusitano
António Maria Carneiro Pacheco
info@morgadolusitano.pt
www.morgadolusitano.pt

76 *Lasnami* (Barb)
Élevage de chevaux Barbes et Arabe-Barbes
Claire Martin
harasdufreysse@gmail.com
http://harasdufreysse.com

79 *Jaouad* (Barb)
Élevage de chevaux Barbes et Arabe-Barbes
Claire Martin
harasdufreysse@gmail.com
http://harasdufreysse.com

80 *Narcissus* (Andalusian)
Martin Robles Rodriguez
martinypaquita@gmail.com

83 Andalusian
Sierra Trails
Dallas Love
info@spain-horse-riding.com
www.spain-horse-riding.com

84–85 Sorraia
Coudelaria Alter Real
Francisco Beja
far@alterreal.pt
http://far.alterreal.pt

86, 88 *Smokey* (Lipizzaner)
Moravita
Ton & Aletta Duivenvoorden
info@moravita.com
www.moravita.com

89 *Favori XXVII* (Lipizzaner)
Haras du Pin
Muriel Meneux
harasdupintourisme@orange.fr
www.haras-national-du-pin.com

90 *Rustico* (Lusitano)
Moravita
Ton & Aletta Duivenvoorden
info@moravita.com
www.moravita.com

90 *Sena* (Lusitano)
Morgado Lusitano
António Maria Carneiro Pacheco
info@morgadolusitano.pt
www.morgadolusitano.pt

92 *Coronel* (Alter Real)
Coudelaria Alter Real
Francisco Beja
far@alterreal.pt
http://far.alterreal.pt

94 *Hojbaks Paztinak* (Frederiksborg)
Moravita
Ton & Aletta Duivenvoorden
info@moravita.com
www.moravita.com

97 *Comberton William* (Percheron)
Joli Farm
Jo Wallis
joollett@yahoo.co.uk

99 *Traverz* (Don)
Paul Olegovich Moschalkova
argamak@inbox.ru
www.horses.ru/museum.htm

101, 103 *Hinnerk TSF* (Trakehner)
La Berangerie
Christian Pellerin
juliepellerin@me.com

104 *Newhaven Snap* (Waler)
Wiradjuri Walers
Brad Cook & Deborah Kelly
wiradjuri.walers@gmail.com
http://wiradjuriwalers.webs.com

107 *Wiradjuri CJ Murphy* (Waler)
Wiradjuri Walers
Brad Cook & Deborah Kelly
wiradjuri.walers@gmail.com
http://wiradjuriwalers.webs.com

108–9 Australian Brumby
Kosciuszko National Park
info@australianbrumbyalliance.org.au
www.australianbrumbyalliance.org.au

111 *Gajraj* (Marwari)
Marwari Bloodlines
Francesca Kelly & Raghuvendra Singh Dundlod
fkelly8254@aol.com
http://horsemarwari.com

113 Marwari
Marwari Bloodlines
Francesca Kelly & Raghuvendra Singh Dundlod
fkelly8254@aol.com
http://horsemarwari.com

114, 115 *Rani, Sunheri, Kala Kanta* (Marwari)
Dharumpara Stud
Satish Seemar
www.satishseemar.com

117 Shetland
Catchpool Shetlands
Lara Stevens
www.catchpoolshetlands.co.uk

118, 120 *Morkel* (Fjord)
Norsk Hestesenter (Norwegian Equine Center)
Marie Thorson Kolstad
kari.hustad@nhest.no
www.nhest.no

122–23 *Copley Lane Master John* (Dales)
Carmilo Stud
Sandra George
carmilo@hotmail.co.uk

124 *Carina* (Haflinger)
Maneggio Teresa
Evelyn Adang
evelyn@maneggioteresa.it
www.maneggioteresa.it

126 *Foxleat Victory* (Dartmoor)
Dixieland Dartmoors
Jamie Sheehy
dixieland@hotmail.co.uk
www.dixielanddartmoors.co.uk

128 *Indomito del Belagaio* (Maremmana)
Dott. A. Andrighetti
a.andrighetti@corpoforestale.it

130 *Kaline de Rivière* (Breton)
Pierre Bailleyeax

133 *Unic* and *Ulhan de Colincthun*
(Boulonnais)
Ferme de Colincthun
Philippe Peuvion

135 *Thunder* (Belgian Brabant)
Parelli Natural Horsemanship, Parelli Center
www.parelli.com

136–37, 139 *Bluffview's Shelly Ann*
(Clydesdale)
Jack & Carol Angelbeck
friesian1040@aol.com
www.friesianusa.com

140 *Monty* and *Prince* (Shire)
Wadworth Breweries
Charles Bartholomew
triciahurle@wadworth.co.uk
www.wadworth.co.uk

142 *Donhead Hall Alexandra* (Suffolk Punch)
Randolph Hiscock
randyhiscock@talk21.com

144 *Tulip* (Suffolk Punch)
Mrs. Buckles

145 *Tollemache Dorothy* (Suffolk Punch)
Lord & Lady Tollemache

147 *Bobby, Lord of the Manor* (Irish Draft)
Lucinda Freedman
Cliveden Stud
lucindaburrell@aol.com

148 *Madame Charmain of Catchpool* and
Collette of Catchpuddle (Shetland)
Catchpool Shetlands
Lara Stevens
www.catchpoolshetlands.co.uk

148 *Camelot of Catchpool* and *Farah of
Catchpool* (Shetland)
Catchpool Shetlands
Lara Stevens
www.catchpoolshetlands.co.uk

150 *Diamante of Catchpool, Amber of Catchpuddle
& Kransit of Gott* (Shetland)
Catchpool Shetlands
Lara Stevens
www.catchpoolshetlands.co.uk

153 *Lucy First Class of Dinefwr* (Highland)
Lucinda Dargavel

155 *Foxlynch Tiglath* (Appaloosa)
Jackie Lund

156 Argentinean Criollo
Estancia Los Potreros
The Beggs
bookings@ride-americas.com
www.estancialospotreros.com

158, 160–61 Mustang
Return to Freedom Wild Horse Sanctuary
Neda de Mayo
info@returntofreedom.org
www.returntofreedom.org

162 *LEA Poema* (Peruvian Paso)
La Estancia Alegre, Inc.
Barbara Windom
barbara@leaperuvianhorses.com
www.laestanciaalegre.com

165 *LEA Sacajawea* (Peruvian Paso)
La Estancia Alegre, Inc.
Barbara Windom
barbara@leaperuvianhorses.com
www.laestanciaalegre.com

167 *Profeta de Besilu* (Paso Fino)
Besilu
The Besilu Collection
ctobon@besilucollection.com
www.besilu.com

168 Argentinean Criollo
Estancia Los Potreros
The Beggs
bookings@ride-americas.com
www.estancialospotreros.com

171 *Apolo do Salto, Norte do Conforto, Ourofino El Far,
Urano* and *Patek de Maripá* (Mangalarga Marchador)
Mangalarga Marchador stallions of the vitrine horse project
Astrid Oberniedermayr & Dieter Mader
www.abccmm.com.br, www.klassisch-iberisch.de

173 *Chameleon* (Appaloosa)
Finca La Guabina, Cuba

175 *DZ Weedo* (Appaloosa)
Char O Lot Ranch
Sue Schembri
info@charolotranch.com
www.charolotranch.com

176 *Ali* (Pony of the Americas)
KS's Pony Farm
Kenneth & Pat Steele
KSsPOAs@aol.com
www.ksponyfarm.com

178 *Sonnys Amigo Bar* (American Paint)
Eagle Point Ranch
Terry & Marsha Dixon
eaglepoint@ripnet.com
www.eaglepointranch.ca

180–82 American Quarter Horse
San Cristobal Ranch
Grant & Connie Mitchell
singletonhorses@mac.com
www.singletonranches.com

185 *Shanghai* (Morgan)
Widenhill
Tami Johnson
morgans@windenhill.com
http://windenhill.com

186 *Purple Sonny Delight* (Tennessee Walking Horse)
Double Springs Farm LLC
Pam Rooks
tracecoll@aol.com
www.doublespringsfarmllc.com

189 *Niangua's Carousel Dancer* (Missouri Fox Trotter)
Sandy Brown
ssb9840@embarqmail.com

191 *CH Titelist Symbol* (American Saddlebred)
Stephens College
ebeard@stephens.edu
www.stephens.edu

192 Banker Horse
Corolla Wild Horse Fund
Karen McCalpin
director@corollawildhorses.org
www.corollawildhorses.org

194 Chincoteague Pony
Chincoteague Island
Assateague Island National Seashore National
Park Service
www.nps.gov/asis/naturescience/horses.htm
Chincoteague National Wildlife Refuge
Chincoteague Volunteer Fire Company
FW5RW_CNWR@fws.gov
www.fws.gov/northeast/chinco

197 *G.S. Autumn* (Rocky Mountain Horse)
Dream Gait Stables
Christy DeWeese
dreamgaitstables@insightbb.com
www.dreamgaitstables.com

198, 201 *TFN Warrior's Apo Hopa* and *TFN Woyawaste
Cikala* (American Bashkir Curly)
Three Feathers Native Curly Horses
Shawn Tucker
threefeathers@earthlink.net
www.three-feathers.com

203 Dole Gudbrandsdal
Norsk Hestesenter (Norwegian Equine Center)
kari.hustad@nhest.no
www.nhest.no

204–5 *Stainmore Wolfhound* (Cleveland Bay)
Ridgemor Farm, Inc.
Natalia Mock tratraver@aol.com
www.ridgemor.net

206 *Simeon Shifran* (Arabian)
Simeon Stud
Marion Richmond
simeonst@bigpond.net.au
www.simeonstud.com

209 *R.S. Almontasir* (Arabian)
Al Shahama Equestrian Club
Rashed Musabah Salem Rashed Al Shamsi
saeed@sheq-club.com
www.sheq-club.com

211 *On Borrowed Wings, Starluck, Preuty Boy*
(English Thoroughbred)
Mr. A. T. A. Wates

211 *Alberta's Run* (English Thoroughbred)
Gleadhill House Stud Limited
kathrynrevitt@hemway.co.uk
www.hemway.co.uk

212 *Guaranda (GB)* (English Thoroughbred)
Plantation Stud
adrian@plantationstud.com
www.plantationstud.com

214–15 English Thoroughbred
McPherson Racing
Graeme & Seanin McPherson
info@mcphersonracing.co.uk
www.mcphersonracing.co.uk

216–17 Australian Thoroughbred
Royal Randwick Australian Jockey Club
www.ajc.org.au

218 *Mr. Besilu* (American Thoroughbred)
Besilu
The Besilu Collection
ctobon@besilucollection.com
www.besilu.com

220 *Loves Illusion* (American Thoroughbred)
Ridgemor Farm, Inc.
Natalia Mock
tratraver@aol.com
www.ridgemor.net

222, 224–25 American Standardbred
Pompano Racetrack
John Yinger
http://pompano-park.isleofcapricasinos.com

227 *Sea the Gray* (American Standardbred)
Olympus Sport Horses
Andrew & Heather Caudill
oshcaudill@aol.com
http://oshorses.com/

228 Norman Cob
Haras du Pin
Muriel Meneux
harasdupintourisme@orange.fr
www.haras-national-du-pin.com

230 *Uvularia* (French Trotter)
Ecurie Cheffreville
Bertrand de Folleville
bertranddefolleville@orange.fr

232 *President* (Orlov Trotter)
Central Moscow Hippodrome
V. Kazakov
www.cmh.ru

234–35 *Optik* (Orlov Trotter)
Central Moscow Hippodrome
LLC "SFAT"
www.cmh.ru

236 *Perry Bridge Romany Prince* (Hackney)
Sharon & Rubin Carter
rsgc1@btinternet.com

239 *Stainmore Wolfhound* (Cleveland Bay)
Ridgemor Farm, Inc.

Natalia Mock tratraver@aol.com
www.ridgemor.net

240 *Siglavy Pakra Mantova* (Kladruby)
Moravita
Ton & Aletta Duivenvoorden
info@moravita.com
www.moravita.com

242 *Høiby Kabben* (Døle Gudbrandsdal)
Norsk Hestesenter (Norwegian Equine Center)
Stian Ellefsen
kari.hustad@nhest.no
www.nhest.no

244 *Violento* (Finnish Universal)
Mari Niittumaa
anne.laitinen@hippolis.fi

247 Polo Pony
Watership Down Polo Club
Madeleine Lloyd Webber

249 Polo Pony
Watership Down Polo Club
Madeleine Lloyd Webber

250 *Manipuri King* (Manipuri)
Whispering Bamboo River Lodge,
Assam, India
Annegret & Doljit Pangging
doljit@gmail.com

252 *Manipuri Great* (Manipuri)
Whispering Bamboo River Lodge,
Assam, India
Annegret & Doljit Pangging
doljit@gmail.com

253 *Manipuri Tawango* and *Chingkey* (Manipuri)
Whispering Bamboo River Lodge, Assam, India
Annegret & Doljit Pangging
doljit@gmail.com

254 *La Nueva T* (Polo Pony)
Nico Talamoni
ntalamoni@gmail.com

257 *Chico, Texas,* and *Negro* (Polo Pony)
South West Polo
Mrs. Jemima Brockett
southwestpolo@hotmail.com
www.poloonthebeach.com

258 *Koora-Lyn Cosack* (Australian Pony)
Koora-Lyn Australian Pony Stud
Lynette Hohlweck
info@kooralyn.com
www.kooralyn.com

261 *Koora-Lyn Enchanted* (Australian Pony)
Koora-Lyn Australian Pony Stud
Lynette Hohlweck
info@kooralyn.com
www.kooralyn.com

262 *Shining Buddy* (Australian Stock Horse)
Shining Stock Horses
Nicholas Horn
nic-nic13@hotmail.com

265 *Diamant de Semilly* (Selle Français)
Haras du Beaufour
The Levallois Family

266 *Alfie* (Oldenburg)
Lovehill Farm
Nikki Webster
nikki.webster@btinternet.com

269 *Isle of Athens* (Holstein)
Isle of Wight Farm
Gary Edmonds & Julie Biliston
islewight@bigpond.com
www.islewight.com

270 *West Point* (Hanoverian)
Parelli Natural Horsemanship, Parelli Center
www.parelli.com

273 *Come to Me* (Danish Warmblood)
Hill Cottage Dressage Centre
Charlotte Pedersen
charlottestibbard@hotmail.com
www.hillcottagedressage.com

274 *AEA Tuschinski* (Dutch Warmblood)
AEA Burong
Dirk Dijkstra & Alisha Griffiths
info@aeaburong.com
www.aeaburong.com

276 *AEA Metallic* (Dutch Warmblood)
AEA Burong
Dirk Dijkstra & Alisha Griffiths
info@aeaburong.com
www.aeaburong.com

278 *Extreme of Cavallini* (Belgian Warmblood)
Paddock Woods Stallions
Max Routledge
stud@pwstallions.co.uk
www.pwstallions.co.uk

280 *TSH Highland McGuire* (Irish Sports Horse)
How High
Bec & James Lindwall
info@howhigh.com.au
www.howhigh.com.au

ACKNOWLEDGMENTS

This book could not have been achieved without the extraordinary help and kindness willingly offered by a large number of people. We would like to extend our most sincere thanks to all those who have contributed their time, advice, and beautiful horses; to those who have provided information, to the editors, the publishers, and to those people who gave their unstinting support. Finally, apologies to anyone who might have been forgotten:

Adilkhan Saburov
Adrian & Jan Quinn
Alison Collins
Anne Barnard
Ben & Ogi Moyle
Minotti Sha
Christopher Adams
Dolores Bigot
Grant & Connie Mitchell
Greg Quinn
Heather Studdy
Jeremy Seel
Jimmy Martin
Johnny Roberts
Julia Kuznetsova
Julie Pellerin
Kari Hustad
Lea Stacey
Leila Kinnari
Lucy Monteprado
Manfred & Sybille Canins
Mark Wordsworth
Marion Richmond
Matti Lakkisto
Michael Gruber
Michael Harrisson
Naomi Williams
Robert Clark
Robin Sarmento
Sandra Moog
Sanjar Alin
Sarah Botham
Satish Seemar
Stephen Rew
Tito & Natasha Pontecorvo
Tom Pond
Tony Stromberg
Trevor Davis
Violet Bruce
Will & Zoe Stamper
Youdhvir Seemar
Zhanna Adilbekova

And lastly we would like to thank the following for believing in this book and for all of their work to make it happen:
Tristan de Lancey
Jane Laing
Philip Contos

For further information and to purchase limited edition prints, please visit **www.astridharrisson.com**.